Verse by Verse Commentary on the Gospel of

MARK

Enduring Word Commentary Series
By David Guzik

The grass withers, the flower fades,
but the word of our God stands forever.
Isaiah 40:8

Contents

For Tim and Martina Patrick
With warm appreciation and thanks

Mark 1 - The Beginning of the Gospel

A. Introduction: The unique character of the Gospel of Mark.

1. Revelation 4:7 describes the cherubim around God's throne as beings with four faces: a *lion*, a *calf*, a *man*, and an *eagle*. By long tradition, the church has attributed one of these "faces" to each of the Gospels, according to the character and message of the particular Gospel. In the cathedrals of Europe this motif is repeated again and again by carvings or paintings of each one of these creatures, typically with a book. By tradition, the creature that represents the Gospel of Mark is the *calf* or the *ox* - a creature of *work* and *service*. The Gospel of Mark shows Jesus as the *Servant* of God, as a *Workman* of God.

a. For this reason, the Gospel of Mark is a "busy" book. In this Gospel, Jesus seems the busiest, quickly moving from one event to another. One of the key words in the Gospel is *immediately*, occurring more than 40 times in Mark. We see Jesus as a *servant* - busy meeting needs and busy being God's Messiah.

b. In the Gospel of Mark, the emphasis is on the *deeds* of Jesus more than on the *words* of Jesus. "The Gospel of Mark pictures Christ in action. There is a minimum of discourse and a maximum of deed." (Robertson)

2. Strong church tradition says that the Apostle Peter is the main source of Mark's gospel. Some think of Mark as "The Gospel According to Peter."

a. One indication of Peter's influence is that Peter speaks very affectionately of Mark, referring to him as *Mark my son* in 1 Peter 5:13. He also wrote that Mark was with him in 1 Peter 5:13.

i. Mark (who is also called John-Mark in passages like Acts 12:25) was a failure in ministry as pictured in the book of Acts with Paul (Acts 15:36-41). His relationship with Paul was restored in the end (2 Timothy 4:11).

ii. Like Mark, Peter also knew what it was like to be a failure in following Jesus after having denied Him three times. He too was restored in the end.

b. Another indication of Peter's influence is the vivid, eyewitness detail of this Gospel. It is "fullest of striking details that apparently came from Peter's discourses which Mark heard, such as green grass (6:39), two thousand hogs (5:13), looking round about (3:5,34)." (Robertson)

i. "Mark's Gospel throbs with life and bristles with vivid details. We see with Peter's eyes and catch almost the very look and gesture of Jesus as he moved among men in his work of healing men's bodies and saving men's souls." (Robertson)

c. A third indication of Peter's influence is that "Peter usually spoke in Aramaic and Mark has more Aramaic phrases than the other, like *Boanerges* (3:17), *Talitha cumi* (5:41), *Korban* (7:11), *Ephphatha* (7:34), *Abba* (14:36)." (Roberston)

3. Many believe Mark to be the first of the four Gospels written, and that it was written in Rome.

a. Most scholars agree that the Gospel of Mark was the first of the four written, though some believe that Matthew was perhaps first.

i. "One of the clearest results of modern criticsl study of the Gospels is the early date of Mark's Gospel. Precisely how early is not definitely known, but there are leading scholars who hold that A.D. 50 is quite probable." (Robertson)

b. Mark was not one of the 12 disciples. Perhaps the only mention of him in the Gospel is a shadowy reference in Mark 14:51-52. As a youth, he perhaps was part of the larger group that followed Jesus.

c. The early church met at the home of Mark's mother, Mary, in Jerusalem (Acts 12:12).

d. To the hard-working and accomplishment-oriented Romans, Mark wrote a gospel that emphasized *Jesus as God's Servant*. Because no one cares about the pedigree of a servant, the Gospel of Mark has no genealogy of Jesus.

i. Another indication that Mark wrote his Gospel for the Roman mind is that he uses more Latin words than any of the other Gospels. "There are also more Latin phrases and idioms like *centurio* (15:39), *quadrans* (12:42), *flagellare* (15:15), *speculator* (6:27), *census* (12:14), *sextarius* (7:4), *praetorium* (15:6), than in the other Gospels." (Robertson)

ii. When Bible translators go to a people who have never had the Scriptures in their own language, they usually begin by translating the Gospel of Mark. Mark is the most translated book in the entire world. One reason is that it is the shortest Gospel, but the other reason is that this Gospel was written for people unfamiliar with first century Judaism. Mark wrote it for the Romans.

B. John the Baptist and preparation for the coming of Jesus, the Messiah.

1. (1-5) The place and ministry of John the Baptist.

The beginning of the gospel of Jesus Christ, the Son of God. As it is written in the Prophets:

"Behold, I send My messenger before Your face,
Who will prepare Your way before You.
The voice of one crying in the wilderness:
'Prepare the way of the LORD; make His paths straight.'"

John came baptizing in the wilderness and preaching a baptism of repentance for the remission of sins. Then all the land of Judea, and those from Jerusalem, went out to him and were all baptized by him in the Jordan River, confessing their sins.

a. **The beginning of the gospel of Jesus Christ, the Son of God**: Every great story has a **beginning**, and Mark takes us to his **beginning of the gospel**. The ancient Greek word for **gospel** means "good news," so this book is *the good news of* **Jesus Christ, the Son of God**. It is the *good news* concerning Jesus.

i. Every word in Mark's description of Jesus is important. First, this is the *good news* of **Jesus**, a genuine, historical person who walked this earth like other men. It is the *good news* of the **Christ** (which simply means "Messiah"), the promised, anointed Savior of men. And it is the *good news* of **the Son of God**, and a **Son** in more than a sense that we think of all men coming from God. Jesus is the unique **Son of God**, who is also **God the Son**.

ii. Lane on the word **gospel**: "Among the Romans it meant 'joyful tidings' and was associated with the cult of the emperor, whose birthday, attainment to majority and accession to power were celebrated as festival occasions for the whole world. The reports of such festivals were called 'evangels' in the inscriptions and papyri of the Imperial Age. A calendar inscription from about 9 B.C., found in Priene in Asia Minor, says of the emperor Octavian (Augustus): 'the birthday of the god was for the world *the beginning of joyful tidings* which have been proclaimed on this account.' This inscription is remarkably similar to

Mark's initial line and it clarifies the essential content of an evangel in the ancient world: *an historical event which introduces a new situation for the world.*"

b. **As it is written in the Old Testament**: The first thing Mark says about the ministry of John the Baptist is that it was prophesied in the Old Testament (Malachi 3:1 and Isaiah 40:3). Those passages predicted this forerunner who would **prepare the way of the LORD**, this forerunner whom God would call **My messenger**.

i. **My messenger** is important because this is the first authentically prophetic voice to Israel (with the slight exceptions of Anna and Simeon in Luke 2) for 300 years. Some thought that God stopped sending prophets because He had nothing more to say, but John shows this wasn't the case at all.

ii. If we wondered what Mark meant when he called Jesus the **Son of God**, here he clarified it. Mark says the ministry of John the Baptist was to **prepare the way of the LORD**, and he prepared the way of *Jesus*. In Mark's mind, Jesus is **LORD**.

c. **Prepare the way of the LORD; make His paths straight**: The passage Mark quoted from (Isaiah 40:3) had in mind the building up of a great road for the arrival of a majestic king. The idea was to fill in the holes and to knock down the hills that are in the way.

i. The idea of preparing the way of the LORD is a word picture because the real preparation must take place in our hearts. Building a road is very much like the preparation God must do in our hearts. They are both expensive, they both must deal with many different problems and environments, and they both take an expert engineer.

ii. Jesus was the coming Messiah and King, and John the Baptist was the one **crying in the wilderness**. Through his message of repentance, he worked to **prepare the way of the LORD**. We often fail to appreciate how important the *preparatory* work of the LORD is. Any great work of God begins with great *preparation*. John wonderfully fulfilled this important ministry. "John was God's bulldozer to build that highway." (Steadman)

d. **John came baptizing in the wilderness and preaching a baptism of repentance for the remission of sins**: This describes *how* John prepared the way. He **came baptizing**, offering a ceremonial washing that confessed sin and *did something* to demonstrate repentance.

i. **Baptism** simply means to "immerse or overwhelm." John didn't sprinkle when he **came baptizing**. As was the custom in some other

Jewish ceremonial washings, John completely immersed those he baptized. "Naturally, therefore, the baptism was not a mere sprinkling with water, but a bath in which his whole body was bathed." (Barclay)

ii. Baptism was already practiced in the Jewish community in the form of ceremonial immersions but typically it was only among Gentiles who wished to become Jews. For a Jew in John's day to submit to baptism was essentially to say, "I confess that I am as far away from God as a Gentile and I need to get right with Him." This was a real work of the Holy Spirit.

iii. John's baptism might have been related to the Jewish practice of baptizing Gentile converts or to some of the ceremonial washings practiced by the Jews of that day. Though it may have some links, at the same time is was *unique* - so unique that John simply became known as "the Baptizer." If a lot of people had been doing what John did, it wouldn't be a unique title.

iv. Christian baptism is like John's in the sense that it demonstrates repentance, but it is also more. It is being *baptized into Christ*, that is, into His death and resurrection (Romans 6:3).

e. **Then all the land of Judea, and those from Jerusalem**: John's ministry met with wonderful response. There were many people who recognized their sinfulness and their need to get ready for the Messiah. They were also willing to *do* something about it.

i. John's main message wasn't, "You're a sinner, you need to repent." John's main message was "*The Messiah is coming.*" The call to repentance was the *response* to the news that the Messiah was coming.

2. (6-8) John the Baptist: the man and his message.

Now John was clothed with camel's hair and with a leather belt around his waist, and he ate locusts and wild honey. And he preached, saying, "There comes One after me who is mightier than I, whose sandal strap I am not worthy to stoop down and loose. I indeed baptized you with water, but He will baptize you with the Holy Spirit."

a. **Clothed with camel's hair and with a leather belt**: In his personality and ministry, John the Baptist was patterned after the bold Elijah (2 Kings 1:8), who fearlessly called Israel to repentance.

b. **There comes One after me who is mightier than I**: The message of John the Baptist was simple. John preached Jesus, not himself. John pointed to Jesus, not to himself.

c. **Whose sandal strap I am not worthy to stoop down and loose**: This might sound like spiritual exaggeration on John's part. But John said this because in his day, the rabbis taught that a teacher might require just about anything of his followers, *except* to make them take off their sandals. That was considered to be too much. But John said that he was not even worthy to do this for Jesus.

> i. Babylonian Talmud, *Ketuboth* 96a: "All services which a slave does for his master a pupil should do for his teacher, with the exception of undoing his shoes." (Cited in Lane)

d. **He will baptize you with the Holy Spirit**: John recognized that his baptism was only a *prelude* to what Jesus would bring. The Messiah would bring an immersion in the Holy Spirit that was greater than the immersion in water as a demonstration of repentance.

> i. John's baptism could demonstrate repentance, but it could not truly cleanse one from sin, nor could it impart the Holy Spirit in the way Jesus would after His work on the cross was completed.

3. (9-11) The baptism of Jesus.

It came to pass in those days *that* Jesus came from Nazareth of Galilee, and was baptized by John in the Jordan. And immediately, coming up from the water, He saw the heavens parting and the Spirit descending upon Him like a dove. Then a voice came from heaven, "You are My beloved Son, in whom I am well pleased."

a. **Jesus came from Nazareth of Galilee, and was baptized by John in the Jordan**: Jesus was not baptized because He needed cleansing from sin; He was sinless, as John himself understood (Matthew 3:14). Instead, Jesus was baptized in keeping with His entire mission on earth: to do the will of the Father and to identify with sinful man.

> i. Jesus didn't *have* to be baptized. He also didn't *have* to die on a cross in our place. He did both things to express His solidarity with fallen man.

b. **Immediately**: The ancient Greek word is *euthus*, and this is the first of more than 40 times this word is used in the Gospel of Mark.

c. **You are My beloved Son, in whom I am well pleased**: When this voice of God the Father spoke from heaven, everyone knew that Jesus was not just another man being baptized. They knew Jesus was the perfect (**in whom I am well pleased**) Son of God, identifying with sinful man. By this, everyone knew that Jesus was different. Jesus was baptized to be identified *with* sinful man, but He was also baptized to be identified *to* sinful man.

i. This strange scene displayed a humble beginning:

- **Jesus**: A common, unremarkable name.

- **From Nazareth**: An unremarkable, despised village.

- **Of Galilee**: The unspiritual region, not the "Bible belt" of the area at that time.

- **Was baptized**: Identified with sinful man.

- **In the Jordan**: An unremarkable - often even unpleasant - river. "Early rabbinic tradition explicitly disqualifies the River Jordan for purification, [according to] The Mishnah, *Parah* VIII. 10." (Lane)

ii. The scene also displayed great glory:

- **The heavens parting**: Heaven opened wide for this. The ancient Greek for this phrase is strong. It has the idea that sky was torn in two, "being rent asunder, a sudden event." (Bruce)

- **The Spirit descending**: The Spirit of God was present, and in some way His presence was discernable.

- **Like a dove**: Luke 3:22 puts it like this: *And the Holy Spirit descended in bodily form like a dove upon Him.* In some way the Spirit was present and "flew down" on Jesus **like a dove**.

- **A voice came from heaven**: It's rare in the Bible when we read that God speaks audibly from heaven, but this is one of those glorious occasions.

- **You are My beloved Son, in Whom I am well pleased**: What could be more glorious than to have God the Father praise and affirm you publicly?

d. **And the Spirit descending upon Him like a dove**: This wasn't just a fluttering cloud hovering above Jesus; it had the actual appearance of **a dove**. Luke 3:22 says, *the Holy Spirit descended in bodily form like a dove upon Him*. It doesn't mean that the Holy Spirit *was* a dove, but appeared **like a dove**. We also know that John the Baptist saw the Holy Spirit coming down on Jesus (John 1:32).

i. The Holy Spirit is associated with a **dove** because of Genesis 1:2, where the brooding of the Spirit over the waters at creation suggested to some ancient rabbis the action of a dove. Also, doves are gentle, non-threatening birds, they do not resist, and they do not fight back. It represents the gentle, faithful work of the Holy Spirit.

ii. This is one of the familiar passages of the New Testament that shows us the entire Trinity in action. God the Son is baptized, God the Father speaks from heaven, and God the Holy Spirit descends like a dove.

iii. So far in the Gospel of Mark we see four witnesses, each testifying to the identity of Jesus. What more evidence do we need?

- Mark said Jesus is the *Son of God* (Mark 1:1).
- The prophets said Jesus is LORD (Mark 1:2-3).
- John the Baptist said Jesus was the *One after me who is mightier than I* (Mark 1:7-8).
- God the Father said Jesus is the *Beloved Son* of God (Mark 1:10-11).

4. (12-13) Jesus' temptation in the wilderness, among the wild beasts.

Immediately the Spirit drove Him into the wilderness. And He was there in the wilderness forty days, tempted by Satan, and was with the wild beasts; and the angels ministered to Him.

a. **Immediately the Spirit drove Him into the wilderness**: After the dramatic appearance of the Holy Spirit at His baptism, the *work* of the Spirit in Jesus was to *lead* Him - rather, to *drive* Him **into the wilderness**.

i. "Mark has used a strange word. 'The Spirit driveth Him forth'; quite literally, 'the Spirit casteth Him forth.' It is the very work afterward employed of the casting out of demons by Christ." (Morgan)

b. **And He was there in the wilderness forty days, tempted by Satan**: Jesus was identified with sinners in His baptism. Here He was also identified with sinners in their *temptations*. Hebrews 4:15 reminds us, *For we do not have a High Priest who cannot sympathize with our weaknesses, but was in all points tempted as we are, yet without sin.*

i. **Forty** - as in the **forty days** of Jesus in the wilderness - is a number that often shows a time of *testing* or *judgment*. In Noah's flood, it rained for 40 days and 40 nights. Israel was in the wilderness 40 years. Moses kept sheep in the wilderness for 40 years. This is Jesus' time of *testing*.

c. **Forty days, tempted by Satan**: Matthew and Luke detail three specific temptations Jesus suffered in these days and how Jesus resisted Satan each time by standing on the Word of God. Mark tells us that Jesus faced more than the three dramatic temptations described by Matthew and Luke. This entire period was a time of testing.

d. **Was with the wild beasts**: Matthew and Luke make no mention of this, but it is significant. In the ancient Greek grammar, the emphasis is on

with. In other words, Jesus was at peace **with the wild beasts**. This shows two things:

- Jesus is the Second Adam, and like unfallen Adam, He enjoys a peaceful relationship with all the animals.

- Jesus remains the unfallen, sinless one despite all the temptation, with authority over **the wild beasts**.

    i. "These fell creatures saw in Christ the perfect image of God; and therefore reverenced his as their Lord, as they did Adam before his fall." (Trapp)

e. **And the angels ministered to Him**: The sense in Mark is that the **angels ministered to Him** at *the end* of this time of intense temptation. This shows Jesus' authority, not only over **the wild beasts**, but also over **the angels**. They are His servants.

    i. "Morally victorious, He was Master of the creation beneath Him, and the angels ran upon His errands, for such is the real suggestiveness of the word. Thus He is seen as God's Man, perfect in spite of the temptation!" (Morgan)

C. Four disciples are called.

1. (14a) The Galilean ministry of Jesus begins.

Now after John was put in prison, Jesus came to Galilee,

a. **After John was put in prison**: There is a detailed description of John's fate in prison in Mark 6:17-28.

b. **Jesus came to Galilee**: Jesus spent most of His time in the region of **Galilee**, usually only going up to Jerusalem for the appointed feasts. Galilee was a large, populated area north of Judea and Jerusalem, where Jews and Gentiles lived together, though usually in their own distinct cities.

    i. Galilee was not a small backwater region. According to the ancient Jewish historian Josephus, Galilee was an area of about 60 by 30 miles and had 204 villages, with none less than 15,000 people. This means there were more than 3 million people in the extended region.

2. (14b-15) What Jesus did in His ministry.

Preaching the gospel of the kingdom of God, and saying, "The time is fulfilled, and the kingdom of God is at hand. Repent, and believe in the gospel."

a. **Preaching the gospel of the kingdom of God**: Jesus was a *preacher* and He brought the message of God's rule on earth, though not in the manner that was popularly expected or desired. Most people wanted a political kingdom that would replace the oppressive occupation of the Romans.

i. Contrary to the expectations of most people in His day, Jesus brought a kingdom of love, not subjugation; of grace, not law; of humility, not pride; for all men, not only the Jews; to be received voluntarily by man, not imposed by force.

ii. The Gospel of Mark - and the rest of this chapter - will stress the *work* of Jesus and His wonderful miracles. But with this opening statement, Mark reminds us that the focus of Jesus' ministry was **preaching the gospel of the kingdom of God**. Jesus was a preacher who did wonderful miracles, not a miracle worker who sometimes preached.

b. **Saying, "The time is fulfilled, and the kingdom of God is at hand"**: When Jesus preached the **gospel of the kingdom of God**, He wanted people to know that it was *near* - as close as your **hand**. It wasn't as distant or as dreamy as they had imagined. Now was the time for them to encounter **the kingdom of God**.

i. **The time is fulfilled**: There are two ancient Greek words that can be translated *time*. One is *chronos*, meaning simple chronological time. The other is *kairos*, meaning "the strategic opportunity, the decisive time." Jesus used this second word when He said, "**the time is fulfilled**." His idea was, "The strategic time for the kingdom of God is now. Now is your time of opportunity. Don't let it pass you by."

c. **Saying... "Repent"**: When Jesus preached the **gospel of the kingdom of God**, He wanted people to know what entering that kingdom was like. They could not enter the kingdom going the same way they had been going. They had to *change their direction* to experience **the kingdom of God**.

i. Some people think that repentance is mostly about *feelings*, especially feeling sorry for your sin. It is wonderful to feel sorry about your sin, but **repent** isn't a "feelings" word. It is an *action* word. Jesus told us to make a change of the mind, not merely to feel sorry for what we have done. Repentance speaks of a change of direction, not a sorrow in the heart.

ii. Repentance does not describe something we must do *before* we come to God; it describes what coming to God is like. If you are in New York, and I tell you to come to Los Angeles, I don't really need to say "Leave New York and come to Los Angeles." To come to Los Angeles *is* to leave New York, and if I haven't left New York, I certainly can't come to Los Angeles. We can't come to the **kingdom of God** unless we leave our sin and the self-life.

d. **Saying... "Believe"**: When Jesus preached the **gospel of the kingdom of God**, He wanted people to know what it was like to live in the kingdom. The kingdom Jesus preached was not just about a moral renewal. It was about trusting God, taking Him at His word, and living a relationship of dependence on Him.

i. The ancient Greek word Jesus used for **believe** (*pisteuo*) means much more than knowledge or agreement in the mind. It speaks of a relationship of trust and dependence.

ii. "There are many people who believe the Gospel, but they do not believe *in* it. It was an appeal not only to accept it as an intellectually accurate statement; but to rest in it, to repose in it. It was a call to let the heart find ease in it." (Morgan)

3. (16-20) Four disciples are called.

And as He walked by the Sea of Galilee, He saw Simon and Andrew his brother casting a net into the sea; for they were fishermen. Then Jesus said to them, "Follow Me, and I will make you become fishers of men." They immediately left their nets and followed Him. When He had gone a little farther from there, He saw James the *son* of Zebedee, and John his brother, who also *were* in the boat mending their nets. And immediately He called them, and they left their father Zebedee in the boat with the hired servants, and went after Him.

a. **He saw Simon and Andrew**: This was not the first time Jesus had met this group of men. John 1:35-4:54 describes their previous meeting.

b. **For they were fishermen**: These were common men, without theological credentials or status in the world. Jesus met them as they labored as common men. Jesus chose these disciples not for who they were, but for what Jesus could do *through* them.

i. "Surely the good qualities of successful fishermen would make for success in the difficult ministry of winning lost souls: courage, the ability to work together, patience, energy, stamina, faith, and tenacity. Professional fishermen simply could not afford to be quitters or complainers!" (Wiersbe)

c. **Follow Me**: With this invitation, Jesus shows what Christianity is all about: following *Jesus*. At its root, Christianity is not about theological systems, rules, or even helping people - it is about following Jesus.

i. "Nevertheless it is true, by New Testament times, the phrase 'to follow' had added to itself an ethical aspect, for it is always the superior who walks ahead, and the inferior who follows: therefore, at the least, a rabbi-disciple relationship was implied." (Cole)

d. **I will make you become fishers of men**: Jesus said He would **make** them fishers of men. If these men received something wonderful in following Jesus, it was only right for them to give it to others, and to "catch" men into the same kingdom of God.

i. When Jesus called them to be fishers of men, He called them to do what He did. He was the greatest fisher of men ever. But He wanted *others* to do the work He did; first these four, then twelve, then hundreds, then thousands and thousands upon thousands through the centuries.

ii. **I will make you become**: "Implying a gradual process of training." (Bruce)

e. **Mending their nets**: "Mark's term means properly to put in order, or to make ready, and so includes cleansing, mending and folding the nets in preparation for the next evening's fishing." (Lane) Significantly, a derivative of this same word is used in Ephesians 4:12 where Paul describes the work of *equipping the saints*. As Strong's definition relates, to *equip* therefore means to complete thoroughly, to repair or adjust, to fit, frame, mend, to make perfect, to perfectly join together, to prepare, or restore.

D. A busy day in Galilee.

1. (21-22) Jesus teaches in the synagogue.

Then they went into Capernaum, and immediately on the Sabbath He entered the synagogue and taught. And they were astonished at His teaching, for He taught them as one having authority, and not as the scribes.

a. **They went into Capernaum**: One can go to **Capernaum** today and see the remains of an ancient Jewish synagogue, which still has the foundation of this same building Jesus **taught** in.

b. **Immediately on the Sabbath He entered the synagogue and taught**: Typically, the *synagogue* had no set teachers. Instead they had the custom of "the freedom of the synagogue," where learned guests were invited to speak on the Scripture reading for that day. This custom gave Jesus the opportunity to preach.

c. **They were astonished at his teaching**: We are not told what Jesus taught, but we are told of the effect the teaching had on His audience. They had never heard anyone teach quite like this before.

d. **For He taught them as one having authority, and not as the scribes**: The **scribes** of Jesus' day rarely taught boldly. They would often simply quote a variety of Rabbis as interpreters. Jesus taught with boldness.

i. Jesus taught with **authority** because He *had authority*. He brought a divine message and was confident that it was from God. He wasn't quoting from man, but from God.

ii. Jesus taught with **authority** because He *knew what He was talking about*. You can't teach with **authority** if you aren't familiar with your material.

iii. Jesus taught with **authority** because He *believed what He taught*. When you believe what you teach, it comes through to your audience with **authority**.

iv. We first saw the *submitted* Jesus - submitted to His Father in baptism, submitted to the Holy Spirit in going out to the wilderness. Now we see the *authority* of Jesus. Authority flows from submission. We aren't safe with real *authority* from God unless we are also submitted to God.

- Jesus showed authority when He was with the wild beasts.
- Jesus showed authority when the angels served Him.
- Jesus showed authority announcing the presence of the kingdom of God and commanding men to repent and believe.
- Jesus showed authority calling disciples after Himself.
- Jesus will show many more striking displays of authority.

2. (23-24) An outburst from an unclean spirit.

Now there was a man in their synagogue with an unclean spirit. And he cried out, saying, "Let *us* alone! What have we to do with You, Jesus of Nazareth? Did You come to destroy us? I know who You are; the Holy One of God!"

a. **A man... with an unclean spirit**: In describing the man who was demon possessed, Mark used the same grammar Paul used to describe the Christian's being "in Christ" (1 Corinthians 1:30). This **unclean spirit** was the evil lord of this poor man's life.

i. The similarity in the wording between the Christian having Jesus and this man having a demon demonstrates that He is in us, and we are in Him. We are "Jesus possessed" in the right sense, because His filling and influence is only for good.

ii. Even as Jesus can live in us, so one uninhabited by Jesus can be inhabited by a demon if the invitation is extended, either consciously or unconsciously. Exposure to things such as spiritism, astrology, occult practices and drugs are dangerous. They open doors to the demonic world that are better left closed.

b. **I know who You are; the Holy One of God!** The demon himself testified that Jesus was holy and pure. The demons admitted that their wilderness temptations failed to corrupt Jesus.

3. (25-28) Jesus rebukes the spirit and gains great acclaim.

But Jesus rebuked him, saying, "Be quiet, and come out of him!" And when the unclean spirit had convulsed him and cried out with a loud voice, he came out of him. Then they were all amazed, so that they questioned among themselves, saying, "What is this? What new doctrine *is* this? For with authority He commands even the unclean spirits, and they obey Him." And immediately His fame spread throughout all the region around Galilee.

a. **Jesus rebuked him**: Jesus didn't need to rely on hocus-pocus or ceremonies. He simply demonstrated the authority of God.

b. **Be quiet**: Jesus often told demons to shut up. Today, many self-styled deliverers from demon possession encourage the demons to speak, or even *believe* what the demons say. Jesus avoided such theatrics and merely delivered the afflicted man.

c. **Be quiet, and come out of him!** There were other exorcists in Jesus' day. He was not the only one who tried to cast out demons. But there was a huge difference between Jesus and other exorcists. They used long, fancy, elaborate, superstitious ceremonies and they often failed. Jesus never failed to cast out a demon, and He never used an elaborate ceremony.

i. Lane describes an ancient account from Josephus about the work of an ancient exorcist named Eleazar, around the time of Jesus: "He put to the nose of the possessed man a ring which had under its seal one of the roots prescribed by Solomon, and then, as the man smelled it, drew out the demon through his nostrils, and, when the man at once fell down, adjured the demon never to come back into him, speaking Solomon's name and reciting the incantations which he had composed. Then, wishing to convince the bystanders and prove to them that he had this power, Eleazar placed a cup or foot-basin full of water a little way off and commanded the demon, as it went out of the man, to overturn it and make known to the spectators that he had left the man."

ii. "The people were accustomed to the use of magical formulae by the Jewish exorcists (Matthew 12:27; Acts 19:13), but here was something utterly different." (Robertson)

4. (29-31) Peter's mother-in-law is healed.

Now as soon as they had come out of the synagogue, they entered the house of Simon and Andrew, with James and John. But Simon's wife's mother lay sick with a fever, and they told Him about her at once. So He came and took her by the hand and lifted her up, and immediately the fever left her. And she served them.

a. **They entered the house of Simon and Andrew**: Jesus came into this humble house in Capernaum and met a sick woman. Jesus didn't only "perform for the crowds." Here, He ministered to one person in a private home. Jesus' interest was in meeting the needs of individuals and not in promoting Himself. He didn't need the power of crowd dynamics to help His ministry.

b. **So He came and took her by the hand and lifted her up, and immediately the fever left her**: In this healing of Peter's mother-in-law, Jesus showed both *simplicity* and *power*. Jesus healed with the same authority that He used to cast out demons.

i. "Peter's mother-in-law was suffering from what the Talmud called 'a burning fever.' It was, and still is, very prevalent in that particular part of Galilee. The Talmud actually lays down the methods of dealing with it. A knife made wholly of iron was tied by a braid of hair to a thorn bush. On successive days there was repeated, first, *Exodus* 3:2, 3; second *Exodus* 3:4; and finally *Exodus* 3:5. Then a certain magical formula was pronounced, and thus the cure was supposed to be achieved. Jesus completely disregarded all the paraphernalia of popular magic, and with a gesture and a word of unique authority and power, he healed the woman." (Barclay)

c. **And she served them**: Peter's mother-in-law responded the way we should when Jesus blesses us. She immediately served Jesus out of gratitude.

5. (32-34) Healing among a multitude.

At evening, when the sun had set, they brought to Him all who were sick and those who were demon-possessed. And the whole city was gathered together at the door. Then He healed many who were sick with various diseases, and cast out many demons; and He did not allow the demons to speak, because they knew Him.

a. **When the sun had set**: Jesus was ministering after sundown, ending the Sabbath day (Mark 1:21). Free from the Sabbath restrictions on travel and activity, the people came to Jesus to be healed.

b. **Then He healed many**: It was a busy day, and then Jesus ministered after nightfall to **the whole city** that had **gathered together at the door**. Jesus worked very hard to serve the needs of others and always put their needs before His.

E. Preaching and healing in Galilee.

1. (35) Jesus prays in a solitary place.

Now in the morning, having risen a long while before daylight, He went out and departed to a solitary place; and there He prayed.

a. **Now in the morning**: After a long day, we would certainly excuse Jesus for sleeping in. Yet He, **having risen a long while before daylight**, made *less* time for sleep and *more* time for prayer.

i. "Look no man in the face till thou hast seen the face of God. Speak thou with none till thou hast had speech with the Most High." (Spurgeon)

b. **He prayed**: Jesus did not need to pray because He was weak but because He was strong, and the source of His strength was His relationship with God His Father. Jesus knew that pressure and busyness should drive us *towards* prayer, not *from* prayer.

i. We don't know exactly what Jesus prayed for, but as much as anything, Jesus used this time of prayer for that close, intimate communion with God the Father that He longed for, which nourished and strengthened His soul. We can also surmise that Jesus prayed for Himself. He prayed for His disciples. He prayed for those He met and ministered to the previous night. He prayed for those He would meet and minister to that coming day.

c. **A solitary place**: Jesus knew the importance of **solitary** time with God. While it is good and important for us to join with others in the presence of God, there is much in our Christian life that can only be learned and experienced in **a solitary place** with God.

i. "Woe unto that man whose devotion is observed by everybody, and who never offers a secret supplication. Secret prayer is the secret of prayer, the soul of prayer, the seal of prayer, the strength of prayer. If you do not pray alone, you do not pray at all. I care not whether you pray in the street, or in the church, or in the barrack-room, or in the cathedral; but your heart must speak with God in secret, or you have not prayed." (Spurgeon)

ii. "There is in public and private prayer a more united strength and interest, but in secret prayer an advantage for more free and full communication of our souls unto God. Christ for this chooseth the morning, as the time freest from distractions and company; and a solitary place, as fittest for a secret duty." (Poole)

iii. This passage shows us many things about the prayer life of Jesus.

- For Jesus, fellowship with God was something for more than just the Sabbath.

- Jesus wanted to be alone to pray.

- Jesus wanted to be alone, so He could pour out His heart to His Father.

2. (36-39) The tour through the Galilee region.

And Simon and those *who were* with Him searched for Him. When they found Him, they said to Him, "Everyone is looking for You." But He said to them, "Let us go into the next towns, that I may preach there also, because for this purpose I have come forth." And He was preaching in their synagogues throughout all Galilee, and casting out demons.

a. **Searched for Him**: This was early in Jesus' relationship with His disciples. As they got to know Him, they learned that whenever they could not find Him, He was probably off in solitary prayer.

b. **Everyone is looking for You**: The disciples probably thought Jesus would be pleased at His popularity and would want to spend more time with the crowd He gathered and impressed the day before.

c. **Let us go into the next towns**: Jesus did not stay in that town and "ride" the crest of His popularity there. He knew His ministry was to **preach** all across Galilee. His ministry was not being famous or enjoying the fame.

i. The clear emphasis on Jesus' ministry is preaching: **for this purpose I have come forth**. The healing and miraculous ministry of Jesus was impressive and glorious, but it was never His emphasis.

3. (40) A leper comes to Jesus.

Now a leper came to Him, imploring Him, kneeling down to Him and saying to Him, "If You are willing, You can make me clean."

a. **A leper came to Him**: Leprosy was one of the horrific diseases of the ancient world. Today, leprosy afflicts 15 million across the world, mostly in third world nations.

i. Leprosy begins as small red spots on the skin. Before too long the spots get bigger and start to turn white, with a shiny or scaly appearance. The spots soon spread over the body and hair begins to fall out - first from the head, then even from the eyebrows. As things get worse, fingernails and toenails become loose; they start to rot and eventually fall off. Then the joints of fingers and toes begin to rot and fall off, piece by piece. Gums begin to shrink, and they can't hold the teeth anymore, so each tooth is lost. Leprosy keeps eating away at the face until the nose, the palate, and even the eyes rot - and the leper wastes away until he or she dies.

ii. As horrible as the physical suffering was, the worst part of having leprosy might have been the way people treated the leper. In the Old Testament, God said that when there were lepers among the people of Israel, they should be carefully quarantined and examined (Leviticus 13-14). Lepers had to dress like people who were in mourning for the dead, because they were considered to be the living dead. They had to warn the people around them by crying out, "Unclean! Unclean!" whenever people were near them. This was not because leprosy was highly contagious. It was because God used this disease as a striking example of sin and its effect on us.

iii. The people of Jesus' day went further than the Old Testament told them to. Back then, they thought two things about a leper: *you are the walking dead* and *you deserve this because this is the punishment of God against you*. Jewish custom said that you should not even greet a leper. Custom said you had to stay six feet (two meters) from a leper. One Rabbi bragged that he would not even buy an egg on a street where he saw a leper, and another boasted that he threw rocks at lepers to keep them far from him. One other Rabbi didn't even allow a leper to wash his face.

b. **Imploring Him, kneeling down to Him**: Knowing how terrible the disease was, it does not surprise us that the leper was so desperate in his approach to Jesus.

c. **You can make me clean**: The leper really believed in the power of Jesus, and had confidence that Jesus *could* heal him. This shows that the leper had great faith because as far as we know, Jesus had not yet healed a leper in His ministry.

i. In that day, everyone knew *only* God could heal a leper. There was no cure, and no one just got better. A leper could never get better without a direct healing from God.

d. **Make me clean**: The leper knew what he needed from Jesus. He didn't ask to be healed, but *cleansed*. The leper needed much more than healing.

　　i. Whatever you *think* you need from God, what you most need from Jesus is cleansing - to be cleansed from sin and a life lived for self.

4. (41-45) Jesus cleanses the leper.

Then Jesus, moved with compassion, stretched out *His* hand and touched him, and said to him, "I am willing; be cleansed." As soon as He had spoken, immediately the leprosy left him, and he was cleansed. And He strictly warned him and sent him away at once, and said to him, "See that you say nothing to anyone; but go your way, show yourself to the priest, and offer for your cleansing those things which Moses commanded, as a testimony to them." However, he went out and began to proclaim *it* freely, and to spread the matter, so that Jesus could no longer openly enter the city, but was outside in deserted places; and they came to Him from every direction.

a. **Jesus, moved with compassion**: We are often moved with compassion when we meet sick people, but lepers usually did not arouse compassion. Their whole appearance was too repulsive, and they usually made people feel *disgust* instead of compassion.

　　i. Luke says this man was *full of leprosy* (Luke 5:12), meaning that the disease was in the advanced stages. This man's whole body and life was rotting.

b. **Put out His hand and touched him**: Jesus healed many people many different ways, but here He chose to heal this man with a touch. He could have spoken a word or even just thought a thought and the man would have been healed, but Jesus used a touch.

　　i. This was important because people were forbidden to touch this man on account of his leprosy. Since his disease was in the advanced stages, he was a leper a long time. It was a long time since he had felt a loving touch.

　　ii. It was against Jewish ceremonial law to touch a leper. Yet Jesus did not break that law, because as soon as He touched the man, he was no longer a leper.

c. **Show yourself to the priest**: Jesus told the former leper to go to the priests to carry out the ceremony the law required when a leper was cleansed. Jesus did this first to honor the law of God, but also **as a testimony** to the priests that an incurable disease had been cured.

i. The elements used in the Levitical ceremony for the cleansing of a leper (cedar wood, hyssop, and scarlet) are the same elements used in cleansing someone who was defiled by a dead body (Numbers 19:6, 19:13, 19:18 and Leviticus 14:4-7).

ii. Since lepers were never healed, these priests had never conducted this ceremony. When they had to look up the procedure for this ceremony and had to carry it out for the first time, it would be a strong witness that the Messiah was among them.

d. **Say nothing to anyone... But he went out and began to proclaim it freely**: The man may have meant well and might have thought he was helping Jesus, but his disobedience hindered the ministry of Jesus. **Jesus could no longer openly enter the city**. It's best to always obey Jesus, and we should never think that we have a better plan than He does.

Mark 2 - Controversy with Religious Leaders

A. The power of Jesus to forgive and to heal.

1. (1-4) Jesus teaches and is interrupted.

And again He entered Capernaum after *some* days, and it was heard that He was in the house. Immediately many gathered together, so that there was no longer room to receive *them*, not even near the door. And He preached the word to them. Then they came to Him, bringing a paralytic who was carried by four *men*. And when they could not come near Him because of the crowd, they uncovered the roof where He was. So when they had broken through, they let down the bed on which the paralytic was lying.

a. **There was no longer room to receive them, not even near the door**: Mark 1:28 says that after a dramatic rescue of a demon-possessed man, *immediately His fame spread throughout all the region around Galilee.* At this point in His ministry, Jesus attracted crowds wherever He went.

b. **And He preached the word to them**: Mark doesn't tell us what Jesus **preached**, yet he still emphasized the preaching ministry of Jesus as he did in Mark 1:28 and Mark 1:38-39.

i. "It is clear that he was avoiding the streets because they had been turned into a healing campaign. Everywhere he went people besieged him with requests for healing and the casting out of demons, so that he was unable to do what he had come to do primarily, which was to preach the Word." (Steadman)

c. **When they could not come near Him because of the crowd, they uncovered the roof where He was**: Because of the crowded room, the friends of the paralyzed man had to lower him down through the roof. This was an unusual way to interrupt a sermon.

i. **Uncovered the roof:** The roof was usually accessible by means of an outside stairway and was made of thatch, dirt or tile laid over beams. It could be taken apart, and the friends of the paralyzed man lowered their friend down to Jesus.

ii. Morgan on **they uncovered the roof:** "Such a rendering is entirely misleading. The force of the word is that they broke up the roof of the house, tearing up the fabric, in order to lower the man down on his pallet into the presence of Jesus."

d. **So when they had broken through, they let down the bed on which the paralytic was lying:** This proved the determination and faith of the friends of the paralytic man. They counted on Jesus healing their friend, because it would be a lot harder to bring him back up through the roof than lowering him down. They counted on him *walking* out of the room.

2. (5-7) Jesus forgives the sins of the paralyzed man.

When Jesus saw their faith, He said to the paralytic, "Son, your sins are forgiven you." And some of the scribes were sitting there and reasoning in their hearts, "Why does this *Man* speak blasphemies like this? Who can forgive sins but God alone?"

a. **When Jesus saw their faith:** Jesus looked up at the four men struggling with crude ropes tied to each corner of the stretcher with a paralytic on it. He looked at them and **saw their faith.** Their faith could be *seen.* Their bold, determined action to bring their friend to Jesus proved they had real faith.

b. **Son, your sins are forgiven you:** We can imagine how the friends on the roof felt. They went to a lot of trouble to see their friend healed of his paralysis, and now the teacher only wants to *forgive his sins.* We might imagine them shouting, "No, he's paralyzed! We wanted him to walk, not to be forgiven!"

i. Yet, Jesus knew what the man's *real* need was and what his *greatest* need was. What good was it if the man had two whole legs and walked right into hell with them. Whenever there is a problem, almost always, *sin* is the real problem. Jesus got right to the problem.

ii. Jesus did not mean that the paralyzed man was especially sinful or that his paralysis was directly caused by sin. Instead, He addressed the man's greatest need and the common root of all pain and suffering - man's sinful condition.

iii. "Forgiveness is the greatest miracle that Jesus ever performs. It meets the greatest need; it costs the greatest price; and it brings the greatest blessing and the most lasting results." (Wiersbe)

c. **Who can forgive sins but God alone?** The scribes used the right kind of logic. They correctly believed that only God could forgive sins, and they are even correct for examining this new teacher. Their error was in refusing to see who Jesus is: God the Son, who has the authority to forgive sins.

> i. "The words suggest a gradual intensification of the fault-finding mood: first a general sense of surprise, then a feeling of impropriety, then a final advance to the thought: why, this is blasphemy!" (Bruce)

> ii. "Again and again during the life of Christ the same dilemma was to re-appear. If he were not divine, then he was indeed a blasphemer; there could be no third way out." (Cole)

3. (8-12) Jesus demonstrates His authority to forgive sins and His power to heal disease.

But immediately, when Jesus perceived in His spirit that they reasoned thus within themselves, He said to them, "Why do you reason about these things in your hearts? Which is easier, to say to the paralytic, '*Your* sins are forgiven you,' or to say, 'Arise, take up your bed and walk'? But that you may know that the Son of Man has power on earth to forgive sins"; He said to the paralytic, I say to you, arise, take up your bed, and go to your house." Immediately he arose, took up the bed, and went out in the presence of them all, so that all were amazed and glorified God, saying, "We never saw *anything* like this!"

a. **Jesus perceived in His spirit that they reasoned thus**: In a stunning moment, these scribes knew Jesus could read their evil hearts. This should have helped persuade them that Jesus really was God, having power to forgive sins.

> i. It is hard to know if Jesus **perceived** this by His divine nature or by His human nature with the spiritual gift of discernment or a word of wisdom. Trapp finds Scriptural basis for either approach: "That is, by his Deity, as 1 Timothy 3:16; Hebrews 9:14. Or by his own spirit, as 1 Peter 3:8, not by inspiration, as 2 Peter 1:21."

b. **Which is easier**: For men, both real forgiveness and the power to heal are impossible, but for God, both are easy. It is a logical assumption that if Jesus has the power to heal the man's disease, He also has the authority to forgive his sins.

> i. In a way, it was "harder" to heal the man than to forgive his sins, because forgiveness is invisible - no one could verify at that moment the man was forgiven before God. Yet it could be instantly verified whether or not the man could walk. Jesus is willing to put Himself to the test.

ii. Jesus also met the scribes on their own scholarly ground. "The Rabbis had a saying, 'There is no sick man healed of his sickness until all his sins have been forgiven him'... to the Jews a sick man was a man with whom God was angry." (Barclay)

c. **The Son of Man**: Jesus often referred to Himself with this title. The idea is not of "perfect man" or "ideal man" or "common man," but a reference to Daniel 7:13-14, where the coming King of Glory, coming to judge the world, has the title *Son of Man*.

i. Jesus used this title often because in His day, it was a Messianic title free from political and nationalistic sentiment. Jesus could have more commonly referred to Himself as "King" or "Christ," but those titles, in the ears of His audience, sounded like "the One Who Will Defeat the Romans." **Son of Man** was "Christ's favourite designation of himself, a claim to be the Messiah in terms that could not easily be attacked." (Robertson)

d. **Immediately he arose**: Imagine the tension in this scene. The scribes were tense because Jesus challenged them and said He would demonstrate He was the Son of God. The paralyzed man was tense because he wondered if Jesus really would heal him. The crowd was tense because they sensed the tension of everyone else. The owner of the house was tense because he wondered how much it would cost to repair his roof. And the four friends were tense because they were getting tired by now. The only one *not* tense was Jesus because He had perfect peace when He said, "**arise, take up your bed, and go to your house.**" The man was **immediately** healed. The *power* of Jesus to heal and the *authority* to forgive sins were **immediately** vindicated.

i. Imagine if Jesus *had failed*. His ministry would be shattered. The crowd would slowly leave the house. The scribes would smile and say, "He can't heal *or* forgive." The four men would struggle to pull up the paralyzed man who looked more dejected and embarrassed than ever. The homeowner would look at his roof and think it was all for nothing.

ii. But Jesus did not and could not fail because all He needed to heal this man was *His word*. There is wonderful healing power in the word of Jesus, in the promises of Jesus, for those who *come to Him in faith*. This man came to Jesus in faith, even if it was the borrowed faith of his friends.

e. **All were amazed and glorified God, saying, "We never saw anything like this!"** Jesus carried the day, and the people were **amazed** to see the power of God in action.

i. "The experts in the law were hoist with their own petard. On their own stated beliefs the man could not be cured, unless he was forgiven. He *was* cured, therefore he *was* forgiven. Therefore Jesus' claim to forgive sin *must* be true." (Barclay)

B. Jesus eats with sinners.

1. (13-14) Levi is called to be a disciple.

Then He went out again by the sea; and all the multitude came to Him, and He taught them. As He passed by, He saw Levi the *son* of Alphaeus sitting at the tax office. And He said to him, "Follow Me." So he arose and followed Him.

a. **He taught them**: Jesus fulfilled the focus of His ministry as described in Mark 1:38: *Let us go into the next towns, that I may preach there also, because for this purpose I have come forth.* Jesus knew how to stay on focus.

b. **He saw Levi... sitting at the tax office**: Levi (also known as Matthew in Matthew 9:9) was a tax collector. In that day, tax collectors were despised as traitors and extortioners.

i. The Jewish people rightly considered them *traitors* because they worked for the Roman government and had the force of Roman soldiers behind them to make people pay taxes. They were the most visible Jewish collaborators with Rome.

ii. The Jewish people rightly considered them *extortioners* because they could keep whatever they over-collected. A tax collector bid among others for the tax collecting "contract." For example, many tax collectors might want to have the "tax contract" for a city like Capernaum. The Romans awarded the contract to the highest bidder. The man collected the taxes, paid the Romans what he promised, and kept the remainder. Therefore, there was a lot of incentive for tax collectors to over-charge and cheat any way they could. It was pure profit for them.

iii. "When a Jew entered the customs service he was regarded as an outcast from society: he was disqualified as a judge or a witness in a court session, was excommunicated from the synagogue, and in the eyes of the community his disgrace extended to his family." (Lane)

c. **And He said to him, "Follow Me"**: Understanding how almost everyone hated tax collectors, it is remarkable to see how Jesus loved and called Levi. It was a well-placed love because Levi responded to Jesus' invitation by leaving his tax collecting business and following Jesus.

i. In one way, this was more than a sacrifice than some of the other disciples made. Peter, James, and John could more easily go back to their fishing business, but it would be hard for Levi to go back to tax collecting. "Tax collector jobs were greatly sought after as a sure way to get rich quickly." (Wessel)

2. (15-17) Jesus is accused of fraternizing with sinners.

Now it happened, as He was dining in *Levi's* house, that many tax collectors and sinners also sat together with Jesus and His disciples; for there were many, and they followed Him. And when the scribes and Pharisees saw Him eating with the tax collectors and sinners, they said to His disciples, "How *is it* that He eats and drinks with tax collectors and sinners?" When Jesus heard *it*, He said to them, "Those who are well have no need of a physician, but those who are sick. I did not come to call *the* righteous, but sinners, to repentance."

a. **As He was dining in Levi's house, that many tax collectors and sinners also sat together with Jesus and His disciples**: Most people consider this a "going-away" party Levi threw for his friends upon leaving the tax collecting business. Jesus sat and ate with **tax collectors and sinners** and eating at the same table with people was a sign of friendship and relationship.

i. Here lies the scandal - *Jesus was the friend of sinners*. Of course, the sinners knew this and responded to Jesus' love and friendship: **for there were many, and they followed Him.**

b. **When the scribes and Pharisees saw Him eating with the tax collectors and sinners**: The **Pharisees** objected to Jesus keeping company with sinners. The Pharisees were a respected conservative religious group but were often at odds with Jesus.

i. The name *Pharisee* meant "separated ones." They separated themselves from everything they thought was unholy, and they thought everyone except themselves was separated from the love of God.

c. **Those who are well have no need of a physician**: Jesus' answer was both simple and profound. Jesus was the **physician** of the soul, and it made sense for Him to be with those who were sick with sin.

i. Jesus is the perfect doctor to heal us of our sin.

- He is always available.
- He always makes a perfect diagnosis.
- He provides a complete cure.
- He even pays the doctor's fee.

C. Controversies about fasting and the Sabbath.

1. (18-20) Why don't Jesus and His disciples fast?

The disciples of John and of the Pharisees were fasting. Then they came and said to Him, "Why do the disciples of John and of the Pharisees fast, but Your disciples do not fast?" And Jesus said to them, "Can the friends of the bridegroom fast while the bridegroom is with them? As long as they have the bridegroom with them they cannot fast. But the days will come when the bridegroom will be taken away from them, and then they will fast in those days."

a. **Why do the disciples of John and of the Pharisees fast, but Your disciples do not fast?** The Pharisees were well known for fasting twice a week (Luke 18:12). It made sense for the disciples of John to fast because his ministry stressed repentance. Yet Jesus and His disciples did not have the same emphasis on fasting as these other spiritual men.

i. God is not against fasting; He is *for* fasting. But fasting has its time and place in the Christian life. Most of us have *no time* or *no place* for fasting, and so we are out of balance. These questioners came from the other side.

b. **Can the friends of the bridegroom fast while the bridegroom is with them?** By using the illustration of a wedding (**the bridegroom**), Jesus drew on a powerful picture among the Jews. During the weeklong wedding celebration, rabbis declared that *joy* was more important than observing *religious rituals.*

i. In the days of Jesus some Rabbis declared that if the observance of any law came in the way of having a good time during a wedding, you didn't have to keep the law. You could just go and have a good time. "Marriage feasts were times of extraordinary festivity, and even of *riot*, among several people of the east." (Clarke)

ii. Jesus' message was bold and clear: "I'm not like the Pharisees or John the Baptist. I am the Messiah, the bridegroom to the people of God. Wherever I am, it is appropriate to have the joy we associate with weddings."

c. **The days will come... they will fast in those days**: Jesus knew His physical, immediate presence would not always be with the disciples. When He was physically gone, it would be more appropriate to fast.

2. (21-22) The illustrations of garments and wineskins and their relation to the new work of Jesus.

No one sews a piece of unshrunk cloth on an old garment; or else the new piece pulls away from the old, and the tear is made worse. And no one puts new wine into old wineskins; or else the new wine bursts the wineskins, the wine is spilled, and the wineskins are ruined. But new wine must be put into new wineskins.

a. **No one sews a piece of unshrunk cloth on an old garment**: The danger of trying to put something new on something old is clear in the illustration of a garment and its patch. But the same principle was true for wineskins. A wineskin expanded under the pressure of fermentation. So if new and unfermented wine was put in an old and brittle wineskin, it was sure to burst.

b. **New wine must be put into new wineskins**: Jesus' point was made clear by these examples. You can't fit His new life into the old forms. Jesus traded fasting for feasting; sackcloth and ashes for a robe of righteousness; a spirit of heaviness for a garment of praise; mourning for joy; and law for grace.

i. Through the centuries, old rigid forms could rarely contain the work of the Holy Spirit. Through the generations, God often looks for new wineskins because the old ones won't stretch any further.

ii. Jesus came to introduce something new, not to patch up something old. This is what salvation is all about. In doing this, Jesus doesn't destroy the old (the law), but He fulfills it, just as an acorn is fulfilled when it grows into an oak tree. There is a sense in which the acorn is gone, but its purpose is fulfilled in greatness.

3. (23-24) Jesus and His disciples are accused of breaking the Sabbath.

Now it happened that He went through the grainfields on the Sabbath; and as they went His disciples began to pluck the heads of grain. And the Pharisees said to Him, "Look, why do they do what is not lawful on the Sabbath?"

a. **His disciples began to pluck the heads of grain**: There was nothing wrong with *what they did*, because their gleaning was not considered stealing according to Deuteronomy 23:25. The issue was only *the day* on which they did it. The Rabbis made an elaborate list of "dos" and "don'ts" relevant to the Sabbath, and this violated one of the items on this list.

i. When the **disciples began to pluck the heads of grain** on the Sabbaths, in the eyes of the religious leaders they were guilty of four violations of the Sabbath. They violated traditions against *reaping*, *threshing*, *winnowing*, and *preparing* food.

ii. At this time, Rabbis filled Judaism with elaborate rituals related to the Sabbath and the observance of other laws. Ancient Rabbis taught that on the Sabbath, a man could not carry something in his right hand or in his left hand, across his chest or on his shoulder. But you could carry something with the back of your hand, with your foot, with your elbow, or in your ear, your hair, or the hem of your shirt, or your shoe or your sandal. Or on the Sabbath, you were forbidden to tie a knot - except a woman could tie a knot in her girdle. So, if a bucket of water had to be raised from a well, you could not tie a rope to the bucket, but a woman could tie her girdle to the bucket.

b. **Look, why do they do what is not lawful on the Sabbath?** Jesus never violated God's command to observe the Sabbath or approved of His disciples violating God's command to observe the Sabbath. But He often broke man's legalistic additions to that law, and He sometimes *seemed* to deliberately break them.

4. (25-28) Jesus responds with two principles.

But He said to them, "Have you never read what David did when he was in need and hungry, he and those with him: how he went into the house of God *in the days* of Abiathar the high priest, and ate the showbread, which is not lawful to eat, except for the priests, and also gave some to those who were with him?" And He said to them, "The Sabbath was made for man, and not man for the Sabbath. Therefore the Son of Man is also Lord of the Sabbath."

a. **Have you never read what David did**: In referring to David's use of the "holy bread" in 1 Samuel 21:1-6, Jesus showed an important principle - *human need is more important than religious ritual.* The Sabbath was meant to serve man (**the Sabbath was made for man, and not man for the Sabbath**).

i. This is exactly what many people, steeped in tradition, simply cannot accept: that what God really wants is mercy before sacrifice (Hosea 6:6); that love to others is more important than religious rituals (Isaiah 58:1-9); that *the sacrifices of God are a broken spirit, a broken and a contrite heart; these, O God, You will not despise* (Psalm 51:17).

ii. "Any application of the Sabbath Law which operates to the detriment of man is out of harmony with God's purpose." (Morgan)

b. **In the days of Abiathar the high priest**: Some find a problem here because according to 1 Samuel 21:1, it says that *Ahimelech* was the high priest at that time, and that his son **Abiathar** served as high priest after him (1 Samuel 22:20 and 1 Chronicles 18:16). Most people reconcile 1 Samuel 21:1 with Jesus' statement here by saying that both father and son *together* served as co-high priests at that time, or by saying that Jesus simply said this happened **in the days of Abiathar**, that is *while he was alive*, not while he held the office of high priest.

    i. Wiersbe has a different solution: "Also it is likely that our Lord used 'Abiathar' to refer to the Old Testament *passage* about Abiathar rather than to the man. This is the way the Jews identified sections of the Word since their manuscripts did not have chapters and verses such as we have today in our Bibles."

c. **Therefore the Son of Man is also Lord of the Sabbath**: The second principle was even more dramatic. Jesus declared that He was the **Lord of the Sabbath**. If He, the very **Lord of the Sabbath**, was not offended by His disciple's actions, then these sideline critics should not have been offended either.

Mark 3 - Twelve Chosen to Follow Jesus

A. Jesus: hated, adored, and followed.

1. (1-6) The Lord of the Sabbath heals on the Sabbath.

And He entered the synagogue again, and a man was there who had a withered hand. So they watched Him closely, whether He would heal him on the Sabbath, so that they might accuse Him. And He said to the man who had the withered hand, "Step forward." Then He said to them, "Is it lawful on the Sabbath to do good or to do evil, to save life or to kill?" But they kept silent. And when He had looked around at them with anger, being grieved by the hardness of their hearts, He said to the man, "Stretch out your hand." And he stretched *it* out, and his hand was restored as whole as the other. Then the Pharisees went out and immediately plotted with the Herodians against Him, how they might destroy Him.

a. **A man was there who had a withered hand**: "The man's hand was withered, but God's mercy had still preserved to him the use of his feet: he uses them to bring him to the public worship of God, and Jesus meets and heals him there. How true is the proverb - *It is never so all with us, but it might be much worse!*" (Clarke)

b. **They watched Him closely, whether He would heal him on the Sabbath**: The critics of Jesus *expected* Him to heal this man with the withered hand. By their expectation, they admitted that Jesus had the power of God to work miracles. Knowing this, they **watched Him closely... so that they might accuse Him**. They knew what Jesus could do, yet their knowledge didn't draw them *to* Jesus. It was as if a man could fly, but the authorities wanted to know if he had a pilot's license.

i. The religious leaders **watched** Jesus **closely** but with no heart of love for Him. They knew *about* Jesus, but they did not know Him.

ii. They also *knew* Jesus would do something when He saw this man in need. In this sense, these critics had more faith than many of us because we sometimes doubt that Jesus wants to meet the needs of others.

c. **Is it lawful on the Sabbath to do good or to do evil, to save life or to kill?** In His question to the religious leaders, Jesus emphasized the truth about the Sabbath: there is never a *wrong* day to do something *truly good*.

i. According to their Sabbath traditions, if you cut your finger, you could stop the bleeding - but you could not put ointment on the cut. You could stop it from getting worse, but you weren't allowed to make it better.

d. **He had looked around them with anger, being grieved by the hardness of their hearts**: This is one of the few places where Jesus is described as having **anger**, and He was angry at the **hardness** of men's hearts.

i. Jesus was angry because this was a perfect opportunity for these critics of His to change their minds about Him and their traditions. But they refused to change their minds and rejected Jesus instead. In this we can see that Jesus deliberately used this occasion to provoke a response. Jesus *could* have done this the next day. Jesus *could* have done it privately. But He chose to do it at this time and place.

e. **Stretch out your hand**: In this, Jesus commanded the man with the withered hand to do something impossible - to move his paralyzed hand. But as the man put forth effort, God did the rest. God never commands us without enabling us.

i. "This man might have reasoned thus: 'Lord, my hand is *withered*; how then can I stretch it out? Make it whole first, and afterwards I will do as thou commandest.' This may appear *reasonable*, but in his case it would have been *foolishness*. At the command of the Lord he made the effort, and in making it the cure was effected!" (Clarke)

f. **The Pharisees went out and immediately plotted with the Herodians against Him, how they might destroy Him**: Jesus did nothing but a wonderful miracle. In response, two parties of former enemies (the **Pharisees** and the **Herodians**) agreed together in one cause: to **destroy** Jesus.

i. Luke 6:11 says that the critics of Jesus were *filled with rage* when Jesus healed this man. Which was more of sin against God and a violation of the Sabbath: When Jesus healed a man, or when these hate-filled men **plotted** the murder of a man who never sinned against anybody?

ii. A stanza from *My Song is Love Unknown* by Samuel Crossman catches the irony of this:

Why, what has my Lord done,
To cause this rage and spite?
He made the lame to run
And gave the blind their sight.
What injuries! Yet these are why
What injuries, yet these are why
The Lord Most High so cruelly dies.

iii. "The Herodians were not a religious party; they were a group of Jews who were sympathetic to King Herod and supported his rule." (Wiersbe)

2. (7-12) Multitudes come to Jesus.

But Jesus withdrew with His disciples to the sea. And a great multitude from Galilee followed Him, and from Judea and Jerusalem and Idumea and beyond the Jordan; and those from Tyre and Sidon, a great multitude, when they heard how many things He was doing, came to Him. So He told His disciples that a small boat should be kept ready for Him because of the multitude, lest they should crush Him. For He healed many, so that as many as had afflictions pressed about Him to touch Him. And the unclean spirits, whenever they saw Him, fell down before Him and cried out, saying, "You are the Son of God." But He sternly warned them that they should not make Him known.

a. **Jerusalem... Idumea... beyond the Jordan... Tyre and Sidon**: The crowds came to Jesus near the Sea of Galilee from distant places. Yet it seems that this crowd was attracted to Jesus more because of His miraculous works than because of His message (**when they heard how many things He was doing**).

i. It is wonderful for people to be attracted to Jesus. But if their focus is on *what He can do for them* instead of *Who He is*, they will not follow Him for long.

b. **Fell down before Him and cried out, saying, "You are the Son of God"**: "The demons addressed Jesus as the divine Son of God in a futile attempt to render him harmless. These cries of recognition were designed to control him and strip him of his power, in accordance with the conception that knowledge of the precise name or quality of a person confers mastery over him." (Lane)

3. (13-15) Jesus chooses the twelve.

And He went up on the mountain and called to *Him* those He Himself wanted. And they came to Him. Then He appointed twelve, that they might be with Him and that He might send them out to preach, and to have power to heal sicknesses and to cast out demons:

a. **And He went up on the mountain**: At this time Jesus was at a critical point in His ministry. Responding to the opposition, He spent a whole night in prayer (Luke 6:12) and chose 12 disciples.

- He had offended the traditions of the religious leadership, and they plotted His destruction.

- Great crowds followed Him, but they were not interested in spiritual things and could be quickly turned against Jesus.

- His response to all of this was to pray and choose leaders to train.

b. **Then He appointed twelve**: In one sense, there was nothing in Jesus' three years of ministry before the cross more important than this. These were the men who would carry on what He started; without them the work of Jesus would never extend throughout the whole world. Therefore, He made the choice with God's wisdom: He **called to Him those He Himself wanted**.

c. **He called to Him**: A disciple was a student, but not in a classroom and lecture sense. A disciple learned by being with and hearing from his master. A disciple was an *apprentice* and learned from the master firsthand.

d. **Then He appointed twelve, that they might be with Him**: He appointed these from among His larger circle of followers, and He appointed them **that they might be with Him**. The first job of the disciples was simply to **be with** Jesus, to learn from being around Him. Then, in a secondary sense He chose them **that He might send them out to preach**.

i. A preacher will only be as useful to Jesus to the extent that He has "been with" Jesus. There is little done for eternal good by those who preach without having a real, personal relationship with Jesus Christ.

ii. "A disciple was a learner, a student, but in the first century a student did not simply study a subject; he followed a teacher. There is an element of personal attachment in 'disciple' that is lacking in 'student.'" (Morris)

e. **He might send them out to preach, and to have power to heal sicknesses and to cast out demons**: When someone has *been with* Jesus, and is *sent out* to serve Him, they can expect that Jesus will give them the **power** to serve Him, including the power to see miraculous works (**heal sicknesses and to cast our demons**) done in their midst.

i. "The business of a ministers of Christ is, 1st. To *preach* the *Gospel*. 2nd. To be the *physician* of souls. And 3rd. To *wage* war with the *devil*, and destroy his kingdom." (Clarke)

4. (16-19) The twelve disciples listed.

Simon, to whom He gave the name Peter; James the *son* of Zebedee and John the brother of James, to whom He gave the name Boanerges, that is, "Sons of Thunder"; Andrew, Philip, Bartholomew, Matthew, Thomas, James the *son* of Alphaeus, Thaddaeus, Simon the Cananite; and Judas Iscariot, who also betrayed Him. And they went into a house.

a. **Peter; James... John**: We do not know very much about these 12 men. Of **Peter**, **James**, **John**, and **Judas** we know something about. But of the other eight, we know only their names. Their fame is reserved for heaven, where their names are on the 12 foundations of God's heavenly city (Revelation 21:14).

i. The Bible values fame, but fame in heaven. For the most part, this group was not "famous" in the sense that we think of fame in the Twentieth Century. We must learn to value and respect *heaven's* fame, not modern fame.

b. There are many interesting connections with this group. There are brothers (**James** and **John**, **Peter** and **Andrew**); business associates (**Peter**, **James**, and **John** were all fishermen); political opponents (**Matthew**, the Roman-collaborating tax collector, and **Simon**, the Roman-hating zealot); and one who would betray Jesus (**Judas Iscariot**).

i. Mark gives a "note for the Gentiles" by translating **Boanerges** - which means **Sons of Thunder** and is perhaps a reference to the fiery disposition of James and John (as they are displayed in Luke 9:54).

ii. **Canaanite** has nothing to do with geography. It is the Hebrew word for "zealous," identifying Simon as a member of the radical Zealot party.

iii. "Judas's surname of Iscariot probably indicates that he was a man from Kerioth: he thus seems to have been the only Judean among the twelve." (Geldenhuys)

iv. It seems that the names of the 12 disciples are usually arranged in pairs. "Since Jesus sent His Apostles out two by two, this was a logical way to list them." (Wiersbe)

• Peter and Andrew.

• James and John.

• Philip and Bartholomew (also called Nathanael in John 1:45).

- Thomas (his name means "twin") and Matthew (Levi).
- James, son of Alphaeus, and Thaddaeus (also called Judas, son of James in John 14:22).
- Simon the Zealot and Judas Iscariot.

c. **And Judas Iscariot, who also betrayed Him:** The choice of Judas was just as important as the choice of any of the other disciples, but many people wonder why Jesus choose Judas.

- It wasn't because Jesus didn't know how he would turn out. Jesus told His disciples that He chose them and knew one of them was a devil.
- It wasn't because He had no others to choose. He could raise up followers from stones, so He could easily have found someone else.
- It wasn't because He wanted a scandalous person, or a "bad boy" - we read of no scandal surrounding Judas during Jesus' ministry. The other disciples did far more stupid things during their three years with Jesus.

  i. A man once asked a theologian, "Why did Jesus choose Judas Iscariot to be his disciple?" The teacher replied, "I don't know, but I have an even harder question: Why did Jesus choose me?"

B. Jesus answers accusations.

1. (20-21) An accusation from His own family.

Then the multitude came together again, so that they could not so much as eat bread. But when His own people heard *about this,* they went out to lay hold of Him, for they said, "He is out of His mind."

a. **So that they could not so much as eat bread:** The idea is that the huge crowds so pressed upon Jesus and the disciples that they did not have the time or the space to eat.

b. **His own people:** This refers to Jesus' family and close friends. Since Jesus grew up in Galilee and practiced His ministry there, many knew Him before this time of wide popularity.

c. **He is out of His mind:** There was at least some reason why some from **His own people** thought that Jesus was **out of His mind**.

- He left a prosperous business to become an itinerant preacher.
- The religious and political leaders plotted to murder Him, but He did not back down (Mark 3:6). They were afraid for Jesus' sake.
- Huge crowds began to follow Jesus, and they knew how such fame and attention and celebrity could go to someone's head (Mark 3:7-8).

- He showed spiritual power and ministry He had never really shown earlier in His life (Mark 3:9-11). Was something very wrong?
- He picked such an unlikely group of disciples that His judgment could fairly be questioned (Mark 3:13-19).
- But there was one last straw: the pressures of this incredible ministry made Him miss regular mealtimes (**they could not so much as eat bread**).

i. Jesus constantly faced the rejection of the religious and political leaders of the day, and in a way their hatred of Jesus made sense - He actually threatened their status quo. Undoubtedly, it was far more painful and challenging for Jesus to deal with the way **His own people** rejected Him. It isn't easy to be profoundly *misunderstood* as you try to walk with God. "When the Lord said 'a man's enemies will be those in his own home' (see Matthew 10:36), He may well have been speaking from bitter experience." (Cole)

ii. The brothers of Jesus didn't believe in Him until after His resurrection, and during His earthly ministry they prodded Him to prove Himself (John 7:3-5).

2. (22) An accusation from the religious leaders.

And the scribes who came down from Jerusalem said, "He has Beelzebub," and, "By the ruler of the demons He casts out demons."

a. **The scribes who came down from Jerusalem**: This was an official delegation of experts **from Jerusalem** coming to Galilee to observe and assess the ministry of Jesus. The opinion of these **scribes** carried a lot of weight with many people.

i. "It is possible that they were official emissaries from the Great Sanhedrin who came to examine Jesus' miracles and to determine whether Capernaum should be declared a 'seduced city,' the prey of an apostate preacher." (Lane)

b. **He has Beelzebub**: Actually, they accused Jesus of being possessed by Satan. "He *hath* Beelzebub, implying that Beelzebub hath Him, using Him as his agent. The expression points to something more than an alliance [but] to possession, and than on a grand scale." (Expositor's)

i. They wouldn't say that Jesus was possessed by just *any* demon, but by Satan himself. This was "an involuntary compliment to the exceptional power and greatness of Jesus." (Expositor's)

ii. This wasn't the only time Jesus was insulted like this.

- "He has a demon and is mad. Why do you listen to Him?" (John 10:20)

- "Do we not say rightly that You are a Samaritan and have a demon?" (John 8:48)

- "We were not born of fornication." (John 8:41)

- "A glutton and a winebibber, a friend of tax collectors and sinners!' (Luke 7:34)

- "You have a demon." (John 7:20)

c. **By the ruler of demons He casts out demons**: Luke 11:14 tells us this accusation came in response to a dramatic demonic deliverance. The religious leaders attributed this working of Jesus to Satan (**Beelzebub**).

i. His own people *misunderstood* Jesus, but **the scribes who came down from Jerusalem** viciously and cynically attacked Jesus. Because of their official position, this was the first step in the plot to destroy Jesus referred to in Mark 3:6. Before they could destroy Him, they had to first discredit Jesus in the eyes of the multitude.

d. **Beelzebub**: This name clearly refers to Satan, but it is a difficult name to analyze. It may have been coined because it sounds similar to the Hebrew phrase for "Lord of the Flies."

i. "It is supposed that this idol was the same with *Baalzebub*, the *god fly*, worshipped at Ekron... who had his name changed afterwards by the Jews to *Baal zebul*, the *dung god*, a title of utmost *contempt*." (Clarke)

3. (23-27) Jesus answers those who attributed His work to Satan.

So He called them to *Himself* and said to them in parables: "How can Satan cast out Satan? If a kingdom is divided against itself, that kingdom cannot stand. And if a house is divided against itself, that house cannot stand. And if Satan has risen up against himself, and is divided, he cannot stand, but has an end. No one can enter a strong man's house and plunder his goods, unless he first binds the strong man. And then he will plunder his house."

a. **How can Satan cast out Satan?** Jesus showed that if He were an agent of Satan and was working against Satan, then surely Satan's kingdom was in a civil war and would not stand. Jesus said this to show that Satan would not work *against* himself.

b. **No one can enter a strong man's house and plunder his goods**: With this Jesus answered the charge that He was in league with the Devil. He said, "I'm not under Satan. Instead, I am proving that I am stronger than he is."

c. **Unless he first binds the strong man**: In this parable Satan is the **strong man** who guards what belongs to him. Jesus' ministry was defeating this **strong man**, both in the case of casting the demon out of the man who was mute and in the broader sense.

d. **Then he will plunder his house**: Jesus looked at every life delivered from Satan's domination and said, "I'm plundering the kingdom of Satan one life at a time." There is *nothing* in our life that *must* stay under Satan's domination. The **one who binds the strong man** and **will plunder his house** is our risen Lord.

4. (28-30) Jesus warns the religious leaders about the unforgivable sin.

"Assuredly, I say to you, all sins will be forgiven the sons of men, and whatever blasphemies they may utter; but he who blasphemes against the Holy Spirit never has forgiveness, but is subject to eternal condemnation"; because they said, "He has an unclean spirit."

a. **He who blasphemes against the Holy Spirit never has forgiveness**: This blasphemy against the Holy Spirit is serious indeed. The person guilty of this sin is **subject to eternal condemnation**. In other Gospels (such as in Luke 12:10), this sin is described as "unforgivable."

b. **Because they said, He has an unclean spirit**: These religious leaders were in danger of blasphemy of the Holy Spirit because they looked at the perfectly good and wonderful work of God in Jesus and officially pronounced it the evil of Satan. This pointed to a settled rejection of heart against Jesus - possible evidence of the blasphemy of the Holy Spirit.

i. "Notice that these men had not yet committed the unpardonable sin... Otherwise Jesus would never have warned them. By his own words, there is no use warning a man who has committed the unpardonable sin; he is beyond help." (Steadman)

c. **He who blasphemes against the Holy Spirit never has forgiveness**: Many people wonder what the blasphemy of the Holy Spirit is, and some wonder if they have committed this sin. The warning of Jesus makes us recognize the terrible danger of the blasphemy of the Holy Spirit and our need to avoid this sin at all cost. At the same time, we guard our hearts against the unwarranted accusation of this sin.

i. We understand what the blasphemy of the Holy Spirit is by first understanding what the ministry of the Holy Spirit is all about. Regarding the ministry of the Holy Spirit, Jesus said, *when He has come, He will convict the world of sin, and of righteousness, and of judgment* (John 16:8), and that *He will testify of Me* (John 15:26).

ii. Therefore, when we persistently reject the work the Holy Spirit wants to do in us and when we have a continued, settled rejection of what He wants to tell us about Jesus, then we blaspheme the Holy Spirit.

iii. The blasphemy of the Holy Spirit will never be forgiven - not because it is a sin "too big" for God to forgive, but because it is an attitude of heart that cares nothing for God's forgiveness. It never has forgiveness because it never *wants* forgiveness God's way.

iv. "These words were never intended to torment anxious souls honestly desiring to know Christ, but they stand out as a blazing beacon warning of the danger of persisting in the rejection of the Spirit's testimony of Christ, until the seared conscience no longer responds to the gospel message." (Ironside)

5. (31-35) Jesus describes His true family relationships.

Then His brothers and His mother came, and standing outside they sent to Him, calling Him. And a multitude was sitting around Him; and they said to Him, "Look, Your mother and Your brothers are outside seeking You." But He answered them, saying, "Who is My mother, or My brothers?" And He looked around in a circle at those who sat about Him, and said, "Here are My mother and My brothers! For whoever does the will of God is My brother and My sister and mother."

a. **His brothers and His mother**: Perhaps these relatives of Jesus **sent to Him** to carry out the plan described in Mark 3:21, to *lay hold of Him*, thinking that Jesus was *out of His mind*.

b. **Who is My mother, or My brothers?** We might have expected that Jesus' family would have special privileges before Him. It almost surprises us that they do not. Yet the brothers of Jesus never seemed to be supportive of His ministry before His death and resurrection (John 7:5).

i. **Brothers**: Jesus plainly had brothers. The Roman Catholic idea of the perpetual virginity of Mary is in contradiction to the plain meaning of the Bible. In fact, many reliable manuscripts add *and Your sisters* to **Your mothers and Your brothers**. "According to a reading in several MSS., these included *sisters* among those present." (Expositor's)

c. **Whoever does the will of God is My brother and My sister and mother**: Mark 3 ends with a huge contrast. There are religious leaders in danger of damnation and an invitation to *be part of Jesus' family*.

Mark 4 - Kingdom Parables and Kingdom Power

A. The parable of the soils and the purpose of parables.

1. (1-9) Presentation of the parable of the soils.

And again He began to teach by the sea. And a great multitude was gathered to Him, so that He got into a boat and sat *in it* on the sea; and the whole multitude was on the land facing the sea. Then He taught them many things by parables, and said to them in His teaching: "Listen! Behold, a sower went out to sow. And it happened, as he sowed, *that* some *seed* fell by the wayside; and the birds of the air came and devoured it. Some fell on stony ground, where it did not have much earth; and immediately it sprang up because it had no depth of earth. But when the sun was up it was scorched, and because it had no root it withered away. And some *seed* fell among thorns; and the thorns grew up and choked it, and it yielded no crop. But other *seed* fell on good ground and yielded a crop that sprang up, increased and produced: some thirtyfold, some sixty, and some a hundred." And He said to them, "He who has ears to hear, let him hear!"

a. **He got into a boat and sat in it on the sea**: Jesus often used a boat as His "pulpit" (Mark 3:9). It gave Him a place to speak away from the press of the crowds, it provided good acoustics, and it was probably a nice backdrop.

i. When Jesus taught from **a boat**, surely it was a new thing. We can imagine some critic saying, "You can't do that! Teaching belongs in the synagogue or in some other appropriate place." It would be easy to come up with objections: "The damp air might make people sick" or "There are a lot of mosquitoes down at the shore" or "Someone might drown." But Jesus knew that teaching from a boat suited His purposes well enough.

b. **Then He taught them many things by parables**: The word **parable** comes from the idea of "to set along side." As Jesus used parables, the idea was to set a spiritual truth along side a daily truth of living.

c. **A sower went out to sow**: In this parable, Jesus described something they were all familiar with - a farmer casting seed on the ground and the seed falling on different types of soil.

d. **And it happened, as he sowed**: The seed fell on three areas without lasting success: on the pathway (**the wayside**), on the rocky ground (**on rock**), and on the thorny ground (**among thorns**). But some of the seed fell on **good ground**.

> i. It wasn't that the farmer stupidly or carelessly sowed the seeds. Some seed fell on the pathway by accident (**some fell by the wayside**), but most of the seed was sown on ground that was plowed *after* the seed was cast. Therefore, you didn't know where rocks were or where thorns might grow.

> ii. Though this is commonly called *the parable of the sower*, it should really be called *the parable of the soils*. The difference is never the *seed*, but on the kind of *soil* it falls on.

e. **Some thirtyfold, some sixty, and some a hundred**: Of the seed that fell on the good ground, all of it produced - but not all produced to the same degree.

2. (10-12) The purpose of parables.

But when He was alone, those around Him with the twelve asked Him about the parable. And He said to them, "To you it has been given to know the mystery of the kingdom of God; but to those who are outside, all things come in parables, so that

'Seeing they may see and not perceive,
And hearing they may hear and not understand;
Lest they should turn,
And *their* sins be forgiven them.'"

a. **The twelve asked Him about the parable**: The spiritual meaning of the parable was not immediately apparent. The disciples of Jesus, including the twelve, didn't know what Jesus meant and they **asked Him about the parable**.

b. **To you it has been given to know the mystery of the kingdom of God**: Jesus would answer the disciples' question about the parable, but first He would teach them why He used parables.

i. The disciples, who wanted the things of God, were **given to know the mystery of the kingdom** - they could be spoken to plainly. But others were often taught with parables.

ii. In the Bible, a mystery isn't something you can't figure out. It is something that you would not know unless God revealed it to you. In the Biblical sense of the idea, you may know exactly what a mystery is, yet it is still a mystery because you would not have known unless God revealed it.

iii. Notice that even with this "simple" parable, the disciples themselves do not understand (Mark 4:10, 4:13, 4:33, 4:34).

c. **To those who are outside, all things come in parables, so that 'Seeing they may see and not perceive':** Parables, in their spiritual function, are more like riddles or puzzles than easy illustrations. They can be understood by those who have the right "key."

i. A parable isn't exactly an *illustration*. A good teacher can illustrate by stating a truth and then *illustrating* the truth through a story or an analogy. But when Jesus used parables, He didn't start by stating a truth. Instead, the parable was like a doorway. Jesus' listeners stood at the doorway and heard Him. If they were not interested, they stayed on the outside. But if they were interested, they could walk through the doorway and think about the truth behind the parable and what it meant to their lives.

ii. If you don't understand the key to the parable, you don't understand it at all. We can imagine what different people in Jesus' audience might have thought when He taught this parable with no explanation.

- The farmer thought, "He's telling me that I have to be more careful in the way I cast my seed. I guess I have been wasting an awful lot."

- The politician thought, "He's telling me that I need to begin a farm education program to help farmers more efficiently cast their seed. This will be a big boost in my reelection campaign."

- The newspaper reporter thought, "He's telling me that there is a big story here about the bird problem and how it affects the farming community. That's a great idea for a series in the paper."

- The salesman thought, "He's encouraging me in my fertilizer sales. Why, I could help that farmer more than he knows if he only used my product."

iii. But none of them could understand the *spiritual* meaning until Jesus explained the key to them: *The sower sows the word* (Mark 4:14). If you miss the key, you miss the whole parable. If you think the seed represents money, you miss the parable. If you think the seed represents love, you miss the parable. If you think the seed represents hard work, you miss the parable. You can only understand it by understanding the key: *The sower sows the word.*

iv. "Without the key the parables are hard to understand, for parables veil the truth of the kingdom being stated in terms of another realm. Without a spiritual truth and insight they are unintelligible." (Robertson)

d. **Lest they should turn, and their sins be forgiven them**: By quoting this passage from Isaiah 6:9, Jesus explained why He used parables. In teaching by parables, Jesus offered His hearers the opportunity to dig deep and find the truth, or to turn a blind eye to an interesting story. They might therefore avoid a greater condemnation for having rejected a clearly understood truth.

i. Jesus didn't use parables *to* blind people, but *because they were* blind. "Therefore Jesus used the parabolic method, not in order to blind them, but in order to make them look again; not in order to prevent them from coming to forgiveness, but in order to lure them toward a new attention." (Morgan)

ii. "So, that their guilt may not accumulate, the Lord no longer addresses them directly in explicit teachings during the period immediately preceding His crucifixion, but in parables." (Geldenhuys)

iii. In light of this, how blessed are those who *do* understand the parables of Jesus. Not only do they gain the benefit of the spiritual truth illustrated; they also display some measure of responsiveness to the Spirit.

3. (13-20) Parable of the sower explained.

And He said to them, "Do you not understand this parable? How then will you understand all the parables? The sower sows the word. And these are the ones by the wayside where the word is sown. When they hear, Satan comes immediately and takes away the word that was sown in their hearts. These likewise are the ones sown on stony ground who, when they hear the word, immediately receive it with gladness; and they have no root in themselves, and so endure only for a time. Afterward, when tribulation or persecution arises for the word's sake, immediately they stumble. Now these are the ones sown among thorns; *they are* the

ones who hear the word, and the cares of this world, the deceitfulness of riches, and the desires for other things entering in choke the word, and it becomes unfruitful. But these are the ones sown on good ground, those who hear the word, accept *it*, and bear fruit: some thirtyfold, some sixty, and some a hundred."

a. **Do you not understand this parable? How then will you understand all the parables?** Jesus considered this parable as essential to understanding His other parables.

b. **The sower sows the word**: Jesus said that the word of God is like a seed. It gets planted in our hearts and then has the potential to bear fruit. But not every seed grows into a plant and bears fruit. The kind of soil it lands on makes all the difference.

> i. The natural tendency is for the audience to critique the preacher. But here, Jesus the preacher critiques His audience. The issue is how well they will hear, not how well He will preach.

> ii. We learn something else here: It is by *preaching* that the seed is sown. You can study the seed, categorize the seed, analyze the seed, know the seed, or even love the seed. But if you don't sow it, nothing will grow.

> iii. But if the seed is **the word**, then every preacher must make sure he uses good seed. "It is a high offence against God to *change* the *Master's seed*, to *mix it*, or to sow *bad seed* in the *place* of it." (Clarke)

c. **These are the ones by the wayside where the word is sown**: Some people are like the ground on the pathway. This was hard ground because people walked on it all the time and beat it down into a path or a road. People like **the wayside** are hard to the word of God, and they allow no room for the seed of the word in their lives - it never enters.

> i. "There are some that hear the word, but never meditate upon it, never lay it to their hearts, never cover it with second thoughts." (Poole)

> ii. **Satan comes immediately and takes away the word that was sown in their hearts**: It is important to see that **Satan** doesn't want the word of God to take root in a person's heart. Like a bird swooping down and snatching a seed, he wants to "remove" the seed of the word from the "soil" of a person's heart. This is Satan's preferred result. He wants to keep the word from ever having a place in a person's life so that they will never be fruitful to God.

> iii. "Hard hearts must be 'plowed up' before they can receive the seed, and this can be a painful experience (Jeremiah 4:3; Hosea 10:12)." (Wiersbe)

d. **The ones sown on stony ground who, when they hear the word, immediately receive it with gladness; and they have no root in themselves, and so endure only for a time**: Some people are like the ground that is rocky but covered with a thin layer of topsoil. They receive the seed of the word with a flash of enthusiasm that quickly burns out.

i. **When tribulation or persecution arises for the word's sake, immediately they stumble**: The **stony ground** hearer isn't attacked directly by Satan, but by **tribulation or persecution**. Jesus knew that many have an immediately favorable reaction to the word of God, but they give it up quickly when it becomes difficult to follow Jesus.

ii. **No root in themselves**: Some professing Christians have no root in themselves. Their root is in their parents, or in their Christian friends, or in their pastor, or in enthusiastic surroundings. "Then there are many more, *whose religion must be sustained by enthusiastic surroundings. They* seem to have been baptized in boiling water; and unless the temperature around them is kept up to that point, they wither away... the religion that is born of mere excitement will die when the excitement is over." (Spurgeon)

e. **The ones sown among thorns; they are the ones who hear the word, and the cares of this world, the deceitfulness of riches, and the desires for other things entering in choke the word, and it becomes unfruitful**: Some people are like the seed that fell among the thorns. They receive the word but allow the interests and cares of this world to choke it out.

i. We might say this ground is *too* fertile. The word of God grows there, but so does everything else. And everything else soon begins to crowd out the word of God.

f. **The ones sown on good ground, those who hear the word, accept it, and bear fruit: some thirtyfold, some sixty, and some a hundred**: Some people are like the good ground, and they **accept** the word, **and bear fruit**, thus fulfilling the purpose of the seed.

i. This parable shows that when the word is received as it should be, *something happens* - fruit is produced. If nothing happens, then the word is not being received as it should.

ii. "This parable deals with the problem that is greatest of all to the thoughtful mind: how is it that the scribes and Pharisees can so misrepresent Him? And how is it that His kindred and disciples can totally fail to comprehend Him? Why does not the hearing of the doctrine produce the same result in every heart?" (Cole)

iii. "The Pharisees were not a button the better for all those heart-piercing sermons of our Saviour, nay, much the worse." (Trapp)

B. The responsibility of those who understand the Word of God.

1. (21-23) They are responsible to expose and publish the truth - that is, the word of God.

Also He said to them, "Is a lamp brought to be put under a basket or under a bed? Is it not to be set on a lampstand? For there is nothing hidden which will not be revealed, nor has anything been kept secret but that it should come to light. If anyone has ears to hear, let him hear."

a. **There is nothing hidden which will not be revealed**: By its very nature, light is meant to be revealed. Truth is the same way, and God promises that it will be revealed.

b. **But that it should come to light**: We must not hide this light. If you have the truth of God, you have a solemn responsibility to spread that truth in whatever way God gives you opportunity. It is just as someone who has the cure for a life-threatening disease has the moral responsibility to spread that cure. God didn't light your lamp so that it would remain hidden.

2. (24-25) When we hear the word, we become accountable; so we must take care how we hear.

Then He said to them, "Take heed what you hear. With the same measure you use, it will be measured to you; and to you who hear, more will be given. For whoever has, to him more will be given; but whoever does not have, even what he has will be taken away from him."

a. **Take heed what you hear**: Christians should be careful to put themselves under good teachers, teaching the whole counsel of God's Word. There are many reasons for choosing a church, but one of the big ones must be, "Jesus told me to **take heed what you hear**, and I know this church teaches the whole counsel of God's Word."

b. **With the same measure you use, it will be measured to you**: This is *why* it is important to **take heed what you hear**. God will respond to us as we have responded to Him and His word.

i. Charles Spurgeon said, "The hearer of the gospel will get measure for measure, and the measure shall be his own measure." And it works out just this way. To the one with no interest in the gospel, the preaching of the gospel seems uninteresting. To the one who wants to find fault with the church or the preacher, they find plenty of faults. On the other hand - the more blessed hand - those who hunger find food, and those who want the solid truth receive something from any faithful ministry.

c. **And to you who hear, more will be given**: When we hear the word of God, and receive it with gladness, more will be given to us from God's spiritual riches.

   i. **More will be given**: More what? More desire to hear. More understanding of what you hear. More personal possession of the blessings you hear about.

   ii. **More will be given**: Jesus reminds us that spiritual growth follows momentum, positive or negative. When we have the godly habits of receiving the word and living it, more is built on to that. When we lose those godly habits, they are extremely difficult to get back.

C. Two more kingdom parables.

1. (26-29) The parable of the growing seed.

And He said, "The kingdom of God is as if a man should scatter seed on the ground, and should sleep by night and rise by day, and the seed should sprout and grow, he himself does not know how. For the earth yields crops by itself: first the blade, then the head, after that the full grain in the head. But when the grain ripens, immediately he puts in the sickle, because the harvest has come."

   a. **As if a man should scatter seed**: When a farmer plants seed, and it grows **by night**, when he sees the seed sprouted in the morning, he has just worked as a partner with God. Man has done what he could do - plant the seed; and God has done what only He can do: grow the seed.

      i. This shows that the word of God works *invisibly* within us. God promised that His word would accomplish the purpose for which He sends it (Isaiah 55:11). So when you hear the word, it works in you - even as you sleep. In works in you spiritually, in a way that it invisible to our eyes.

      ii. "The secret of growth is in the seed, not in the soil nor in the weather nor in the cultivating. These all help, but the seed spontaneously works according to its own nature." (Robertson)

   b. **He himself does not know how**: *How* exactly the seed grows is a mystery to the farmer. Though it grows by a process he cannot see nor fully account for, he has faith in the growing process. So it is with the Kingdom of God: we work in partnership with God, yet the real work is left up to Him - we trust in a process we cannot see nor fully account for.

i. Because Jesus said that the Parable of the Soils was a key for understanding other parables (Mark 4:13), we can say that the **seed** He speaks of here represents the Word of God, as it did in the Parable of the Soils. Therefore, with this parable, Jesus shows the way the word of God works with hidden and mysterious power, just like a **seed**.

ii. The Bible isn't just an instruction manual or a list of rules to follow. It lives and works its life into us. The idea that a *preacher* lends life to God's Word is wrong; the only thing a preacher has to give to the word is a voice. Like a seed, the word of God has a hidden and mysterious power.

c. **The harvest has come**: Just as a field's crop may be unnoticed when first planted, but can't be missed when mature, so it is with the Kingdom of God. It has small beginnings and its root may be small, but when God develops the work it cannot be missed.

i. This is the glory of Jesus' work in us. It was prophetically said of Him, *a bruised reed He will not break, and smoking flax He will not quench* (Isaiah 42:3). Jesus takes something as small and insignificant as a seed, buries it, and makes it rise up to something glorious. Therefore, we should never despise the day of small things (Zechariah 4:10).

2. (30-34) The mustard seed.

Then He said, "To what shall we liken the kingdom of God? Or with what parable shall we picture it? *It is* like a mustard seed which, when it is sown on the ground, is smaller than all the seeds on earth; but when it is sown, it grows up and becomes greater than all herbs, and shoots out large branches, so that the birds of the air may nest under its shade." And with many such parables He spoke the word to them as they were able to hear *it*. But without a parable He did not speak to them. And when they were alone, He explained all things to His disciples.

a. **It grows up and becomes greater than all herbs, and shoots out large branches**: Some regard this as a beautiful picture of the church growing so large that it provides refuge for all of the world. But this mustard seed plant has grown into a monstrosity, and it harbors **birds** - who in the parables are emissaries of Satan, according to the foundational parable of the soils (Mark 4:13).

i. "The growth of the kingdom will not result in the conversion of the world. In fact, some of the growth will give opportunity for Satan to get in and go to work!" (Wiersbe)

ii. Jesus, in considering the growth of the work of God, reminded us that size and status are not necessarily benefits. Corrupt Christianity has been a curse to the world, being the form of godliness without the power.

c. **When they were alone, He explained all things to His disciples**: "This does not necessarily imply that the multitude understood nothing, but only that Jesus, by further talk, made the disciples understand *better*." (Expositor's)

D. Jesus calms a storm on the Sea of Galilee.

1. (35-39) Jesus rebukes the stormy Sea of Galilee.

On the same day, when evening had come, He said to them, "Let us cross over to the other side." Now when they had left the multitude, they took Him along in the boat as He was. And other little boats were also with Him. And a great windstorm arose, and the waves beat into the boat, so that it was already filling. But He was in the stern, asleep on a pillow. And they awoke Him and said to Him, "Teacher, do You not care that we are perishing?" Then He arose and rebuked the wind, and said to the sea, "Peace, be still!" And the wind ceased and there was a great calm.

a. **Let us cross over to the other side**: Jesus made a promise to His disciples. He didn't say, "Let us perish in the middle of the Sea of Galilee." He promised His disciples that they would **cross over to the other side**.

i. "The Lake of Galilee is 13 miles long at its longest, and 8 miles wide at its widest. At this particular part it was about 5 miles across." (Barclay)

ii. "Jonah ended up in a storm because of his disobedience, but the disciples got into a storm because of their *obedience* to the Lord." (Wiersbe)

b. **They took Him along in the boat as He was**: Jesus taught the multitude from a boat just off the shore of the Sea of Galilee. When the teaching was finished, He didn't return to shore. He just said to the disciples, "**Let us cross over to the other side**."

i. "Now the teaching was over; He was weary; He was craving for a period of rest. And so He bade His disciples to cross the lake, and that is the moment to which our text refers - they took Him even as He was... They had not waited till any cloaks were brought. They had not sent a messenger ashore. Weary, and probably hungry, they had taken Him even as He was." (Morrison)

ii. We must take Him as He was.

• Not as we wish Jesus was.

- Not as others may present Jesus.

- Not as you might see Him in the lives of others.

c. **And a great windstorm arose**: The Sea of Galilee is well known for its sudden, violent storms. The severity of this storm is shown by the reaction of the disciples (**we are perishing**). Several of the disciples were experienced fishermen on this very lake, and they were frightened and feared **perishing** in this storm.

d. **But He was in the stern, asleep on a pillow**: Jesus' true humanity is shown by His brief sleep on the boat. He became weary and sometimes caught a bit of sleep wherever He could.

i. Think of all the worries that might have kept Jesus awake. He could worry about the religious and political leaders who plotted against Him. He could worry about His family who thought He was crazy. He could worry about the overwhelming crowds with their overwhelming needs. He could worry about the disciples He chose. He could worry about the future, because He knew what His destiny was. With all these things to worry about, Jesus wasn't worried. He slept in a rocking boat.

ii. "The Lord's sleep was not only the sleep of weariness: it was also the rest of faith, for there is a rest of faith as well as a watch of faith." (Cole)

e. **And they awoke Him**: The wind didn't wake Him, the arguing of the disciples didn't wake Him, and water splashing over the boat didn't wake Him. But at the cry of His disciples He instantly awoke. Jesus is like the mother who sleeps through all kinds of racket, but at the slightest noise from her little baby, she instantly awakes.

f. **Teacher, do You not care that we are perishing?** Notice the "**we**." Their idea was, "Hey Jesus, You're in trouble here too. Maybe You had better wake up, get a bucket and start bailing along with us, because **we are perishing**!"

i. "It was not a request to Him to do anything; but a protest against His apparent indifference." (Morgan)

ii. The disciples were afraid, but at the same time there were several experienced fishermen among them. They knew they were in jeopardy (Luke 8:23) but probably felt they knew what to do. They worked hard at bailing out the water, at rowing in a certain rhythm, at piloting the boat in a certain direction. They were annoyed that Jesus didn't help them.

iii. "There may be both a sleeping Christ and a sleeping church, but neither Christ nor his church can perish. If our Lord be asleep, he is asleep near the helm - he has only to put his hand out and steer the vessel at once. He is asleep, but he only sleeps until we cry more loudly to him. When we get into such trouble that we cannot help ourselves and feel our entire dependence on him, then he will reveal his power." (Spurgeon)

g. **Then He arose and rebuked the wind**: Jesus didn't merely quiet the wind and the sea; He **rebuked the wind** and **the sea**. This, together with the disciples' fear and what Jesus will encounter at His destination, give the sense that Satan had a significant hand in this storm.

i. **Rebuked... "Peace, be still!"** The same terminology was used when Jesus rebuked and silenced demons. This was a spiritual battle as much as a weather crisis. "Jesus addressed the raging storm as a 'force' threatening him and his disciples. The force of the sea was muzzled as Jesus subdued it with his sovereign word of authority." (Lane)

ii. As well, Mark tells us **other little boats were also with Him**. When Jesus calmed the stormy Sea of Galilee, He did not only rescue Himself and the disciples, but all the others in the **little boats**.

2. (40-41) Jesus rebukes His disciples.

But He said to them, "Why are you so fearful? How *is it* that you have no faith?" And they feared exceedingly, and said to one another, "Who can this be, that even the wind and the sea obey Him!"

a. **Why are you so fearful? How is it that you have no faith?** Jesus didn't say, "Wow, what a storm!" Instead, He asked, "**Why is it that you have no faith?**" The storm could not disturb Jesus, but the unbelief of His disciples disturbed Him.

i. It was not their *fear of the storm* that made Jesus say they had **no faith**. A small boat in a big storm is a scary place, and the initial fear itself isn't wrong. What the disciples chose to *do* with the fear made all the difference.

ii. Jesus could say they had **no faith** because they did not believe His word. They each heard Jesus say, "*Let us go over to the other side of the lake*" (Mark 4:22). Jesus did not say, "Let's do the best we can and maybe we'll all drown." He promised a safe arrival, and the disciples *could have* chosen to trust in that promise, but they didn't. In this sense they had **no faith**.

iii. Jesus could say they had **no faith** because they accused Jesus of a lack of care towards them. When they woke Him, they said, "*Do you not care that we are perishing?*" (Mark 4:38) When we think Jesus doesn't care about us, it shows we have **no faith**, because we don't believe the truth about Jesus. It takes great faith to trust the sleeping Jesus, to know that He cares and works for us even when it does not *seem* like it. But this is the kind of trust God wants to build in us.

iv. Jesus could say they had **no faith** because they forgot the big picture. The disciples should have known that God would not allow the Messiah to perish in a boat crossing the Sea of Galilee. Could the story of Jesus possibly end with Him drowning in a boat accident on the Sea of Galilee? "Our fears are often intensely silly, and when we get over them, and ourselves look back upon them, we are full of shame that we should have been so foolish. Our Lord kindly censured their unbelief because it was unreasonable." (Spurgeon)

v. We could put the emphasis: **How is it that *you* have no faith?** Of all people, Jesus' own disciples should have had faith. Would Jesus put the same question to us? "After all I have done in you and for you, **how is it that *you* have no faith?**"

b. **They feared exceedingly**: The total calm of the sea should have filled them with peace, but instead, they were just as afraid when He calmed the storm as when they were in the midst of it.

c. **Who can this be, that even the wind and the sea obey Him!** The disciples ask a good question: **Who can this be?** It can only be the LORD, Jehovah, who only has this power and authority. *O LORD God of hosts, who is mighty like You, O LORD? Your faithfulness surrounds You. You rule the raging of the sea; when waves rise, You still them.* (Psalm 89:8-9)

i. In the span of a few moments, the disciples saw both the complete humanity of Jesus and the fullness of His deity. They saw Jesus for who He is: truly man and truly God.

ii. All this shows the abiding care Jesus has for His people. "There are many Christians today who seem to think the boat is going down! I am tired of the wailing of some of my friends who take that view. The boat cannot go down. Jesus is on board." (Morgan)

Mark 5 - Jesus Demonstrates His Authority

A. The authority of Jesus in the life of the Gadarene demoniac.

1. (1-8) The description of the demon-possessed man.

Then they came to the other side of the sea, to the country of the Gadarenes. And when He had come out of the boat, immediately there met Him out of the tombs a man with an unclean spirit, who had *his* dwelling among the tombs; and no one could bind him, not even with chains, because he had often been bound with shackles and chains. And the chains had been pulled apart by him, and the shackles broken in pieces; neither could anyone tame him. And always, night and day, he was in the mountains and in the tombs, crying out and cutting himself with stones. When he saw Jesus from afar, he ran and worshiped Him. And he cried out with a loud voice and said, "What have I to do with You, Jesus, Son of the Most High God? I implore You by God that You do not torment me." For He said to him, "Come out of the man, unclean spirit!"

    a. **Immediately there met Him out of the tombs a man with an unclean spirit**: This is the most detailed description of a demon-possessed man we have in the Bible. It is the classic profile of demonic possession.

- The man had been demon possessed for a *long time* (Luke 8:27).

- The man wore no clothes and lived like a sub-human, or like a wild animal (Luke 8:27).

- The man lived among the decaying and dead, contrary to Jewish law and human instinct (**dwelling among the tombs**).

- The man had supernatural strength (**chains pulled apart**).

- The man was tormented and self-destructive (**crying out and cutting himself with stones**).

- The man had uncontrollable behavior (**neither could anyone tame him**). Strangely, some Christians think that this is how the Holy

62

Spirit works: by overwhelming the operations of the body and making one do strange and grotesque things.

i. We can be sure that he did not start out this way. At one time this man lived among others in the village. But his own irrational, wild behavior convinced the villagers that he was demon possessed, or at least insane. They bound him with chains to keep him from hurting others, but he broke the chains time and again. Finally, they drove him out of town and he lived in the village cemetery, a madman among the tombs, hurting the only person he could - himself.

b. **Immediately there met Him**: When this man came to Jesus (Jesus did not seek out the man), Jesus said to the demon possessing the man, "**Come out of the man, unclean spirit!**"

c. **Jesus, Son of the Most High God**: This is what the demons said *in response* to Jesus' command to **come out of the man** (**for He said to them, "Come out of the man"**). This was a way they tried to *resist* the work of Jesus.

i. In the background of all this is the ancient superstition that you had spiritual power over another if you knew or said their exact name. This is why the unclean spirits addressed Jesus with this full title: **Jesus, Son of the Most High God**. According to the superstitions of the day, this was like a round of artillery fired at Jesus.

ii. "The full address is not a confession of Jesus' dignity but a desperate attempt to gain control over him or to render him harmless, in accordance with the common assumption of the period that the use of the precise name of an adversary gave one mastery over him." (Lane)

iii. Therefore, in their address of Jesus, they have the right theological facts, but they don't have the right heart. The demons inhabiting him had a kind of "faith" in Jesus. They knew the true identity of Jesus better than the religious leaders did. But it was not a faith or a knowledge of Jesus that could save (James 2:19).

d. **What have I to do with You... I implore You by God that You do not torment me**: This was the unclean spirit speaking, not the possessed man. The demon did not want to leave his host.

i. Demonic possession is when a demonic spirit *resides* in a human body, and at times the demon will show its own personality through the personality of the host body.

ii. Demonic possession is a reality today, though we must guard against either *ignoring* demonic activity or *over-emphasizing* supposed demonic activity.

e. **Do not torment me**: These demons considered it **torment** to be put out of this man's body. Demons want to inhabit human bodies for the same reasons a vandal wants a spray can, or a violent man wants a gun. A human body is a weapon that a demon can use in attacking God.

i. Demons also attack men because they hate the image of God in man. They attack that image by debasing man and making him grotesque - just as they did to this man in the country of the Gadarenes.

ii. Demons have the same goal in Christians: to wreck the image of God. But their tactics are restricted toward Christians because demonic spirits were "disarmed" by Jesus' work on the cross (Colossians 2:15). Yet demonic spirits certainly can both deceive and intimidate Christians, binding them with fear and unbelief.

2. (9-13) Jesus demonstrates His authority over evil spirits.

Then He asked him, "What *is* your name?" And he answered, saying, "My name *is* Legion; for we are many." Also he begged Him earnestly that He would not send them out of the country. Now a large herd of swine was feeding there near the mountains. So all the demons begged Him, saying, "Send us to the swine, that we may enter them." And at once Jesus gave them permission. Then the unclean spirits went out and entered the swine (there were about two thousand); and the herd ran violently down the steep place into the sea, and drowned in the sea.

a. **What is your name?** Jesus probably asked for the name so that *we* would know the full extent of the problem, knowing that the man was filled with many demons (**Legion**) and not just one. A Roman legion usually consisted of 6,000 men. This does not mean that the man was inhabited with 6,000 demons, but that he had many.

i. From the account as a whole, we see that Jesus was *not* playing into the ancient superstition about knowing a demon's name. In fact, Jesus showed that it was unnecessary for Him to know the name of the demon. When they replied "**Legion**," they really weren't saying a name, but simply trying to intimidate Jesus with a large number. **Legion** said, "There are a lot of us, we are organized, we are unified, we are ready to fight, and we are mighty."

ii. If it was important for Jesus to know their names, He could have demanded "name, rank, and serial number" for each of them one by one. But Jesus would not play into their superstitions. His power was greater than them. When it comes to demons and spiritual warfare, we must never be caught up in foolish and counter-productive superstitions.

iii. According to the superstitions of the day, the onlookers probably felt that the unclean spirits had the upper hand. They knew and declared a full name of Jesus. They evaded His request for their name. And finally, they hoped to frighten Jesus with their large number. But Jesus didn't buy into these ancient superstitions at all and easily cast the unclean spirits out of the afflicted man.

iv. "The answer may be evasive, the demons desiring to withhold their true names from Jesus in a desperate attempt to thwart his power. It is also possible that the name may have been selected to invoke the fear of a powerful name." (Lane)

b. **Also he begged Him earnestly that He would not send them out of the country**: Luke 8:31 tells us that the demons also *begged Him that He would not command them to go out into the abyss*. They did not want to become "inactive." "Lo, it is another hell to the devil to be idle, or otherwise than evil-occupied." (Trapp)

i. "Satan would rather vex swine than do no mischief at all. He is so fond of evil that he would work it upon animals if he cannot work it upon men." (Spurgeon)

ii. In Mark 5:7, the demons demonstrated that they knew who Jesus was. Here they demonstrate that they can "pray" to Jesus (**begged Him earnestly**). This shows that you can know who Jesus is and not surrender to Him. You can pray to Him and not surrender to Him.

c. **Send us to the swine, that we may enter them**: The demons wanted to enter the **swine** because demons are bent on destruction, and they *hate to be idle*. "The devil is so fond of doing mischief, that he will rather play at a small game than stand out." (Poole)

i. Notice that the demons can't even afflict *pigs* without the permission of God. "Since a demon cannot enter even into a *swine* without being *sent* by God himself, how little is the *power* or *malice* of them to be dreaded by those who have God for their portion and protector!" (Clarke)

d. **And at once Jesus gave them permission**: Instead of putting these unclean spirits completely out of commission, Jesus allowed this because the time of the total demonstration of His authority over demons had not yet come - it would come at the cross. Colossians 2:15 tells us that at the cross Jesus disarmed demons in their attacks on believers, He made a public spectacle of their defeat, and He triumphed over them in His work on the cross.

e. **The herd ran violently down the steep place into the sea, and drowned in the sea**: The destructive nature of demonic spirits was shown by their effect on the swine. They are like their leader, Satan whose desire is to *steal, and to kill, and to destroy.* (John 10:10)

> i. This shows another reason *why* Jesus allowed the demons to enter the pigs - because He wanted everyone to know what the real intention of these demons was. They wanted to destroy the man just as they destroyed the pigs. Because men are made in the image of God, they could not have their way as easily with the man, but their intention was just the same: to completely destroy him.

> ii. "'But the owners of the swine lost their property.' Yes, and learn from this how small value temporal riches are in the estimation of God. He suffers them to be lost, sometimes to disengage us from them through *mercy*; sometimes out of *justice*, to punish us for having *acquired* or *preserved* them either by *covetousness* or *injustice*." (Clarke)

3. (14-17) The reaction of the bystanders to the deliverance of the demon-possessed man.

So those who fed the swine fled, and they told *it* in the city and in the country. And they went out to see what it was that had happened. Then they came to Jesus, and saw the one *who had been* demon-possessed and had the legion, sitting and clothed and in his right mind. And they were afraid. And those who saw it told them how it happened to him *who had been* demon-possessed, and about the swine. Then they began to plead with Him to depart from their region.

a. **And they were afraid**: They were more afraid of a free man than a possessed man. When they saw the man **in his right mind**, sitting at the feet of Jesus, **they were afraid**.

> i. Part of their fear was found in the fact that their superstitions were shattered, and they didn't know what to make of it all. According to their superstitions, the demons should have had the upper hand over Jesus - but they didn't. They had a hard time accepting this.

b. **Then they began to plead with Him to depart from their region**: Before, they didn't seem to mind having a demon-possessed, tormented man in their midst. Yet they did mind having Jesus around, so they asked Him to leave - *and He did!*

> i. When people are more afraid of what Jesus will do in their lives than what Satan does in the moment, they often push Jesus away.

4. (18-20) The reaction of the man who had been delivered from demons.

And when He got into the boat, he who had been demon-possessed begged Him that he might be with Him. However, Jesus did not permit him, but said to him, "Go home to your friends, and tell them what great things the Lord has done for you, and how He has had compassion on you." And he departed and began to proclaim in Decapolis all that Jesus had done for him; and all marveled.

a. **He who had been demon-possessed begged Him that he might be with Him**: The man who had been set free by Jesus just wanted to be with Jesus. This man didn't want only what Jesus could do for him. The true change in his heart was shown by his desire to **be with** Jesus.

i. **He who had been demon possessed**: "That is a striking name for a man, 'he that had been possessed with the devil.' It would stick to him as long as he lived, and it would be a standing sermon wherever he went. He would be asked to tell the story of what he used to be and how the change came about. What a story for any man to tell!" (Spurgeon)

b. **Jesus did not permit him**: Jesus did not allow this because He knew that the man had a more important ministry with his own family and community.

i. Sometimes we have a hard time understanding the ways of God. The people of the city made an evil request: *they began to plead with Him to depart from their region*, and Jesus answered their prayer. The man **who had been demon possessed** made a godly request: **that he might be with Him**, and Jesus said no to that prayer.

ii. Of course, this was because this man could be a light among the people of these Gentile cities in a way that Jesus and the disciples could not. But it was also to cure the man of any superstitions. He might have thought that he had to stay close to Jesus to keep the demons from coming back. "Perhaps, too, his prayer was not answered, lest his fear should have been thereby sanctioned. If he did fear, and I feel morally certain that he did, that the devils would return, then, of course, he longed to be with Christ. But Christ took that fear from him, and as good as says to him, 'You do not need to be near me; I have so healed that you will never be sick again.'" (Spurgeon)

c. **What great things Jesus had done for him**: This was a great message to tell. This is a gospel we should all be able to preach. The man set free did, because **he departed and began to proclaim... all that Jesus had done for him**. His story showed the value of *one life* to Jesus, because this was the only reason why Jesus came to this side of the Sea of Galilee. His story also showed that with Jesus, *no one is beyond hope*, because if this man could be changed than anyone could.

> i. **Began to proclaim in Decapolis**: "The Decapolis was ten Greek cities on the eastern side of the sea of Galilee, including Damascus. It was to this gentile community that Jesus commanded this man to go and bear witness." (Stedman)

> ii. "Decapolis literally means The Ten Cities. Near to the Jordan and on its east side, there were ten cities mainly of rather a special character. They were essentially Greek. Their names were Scythopolis, which was the only one on the west side of the Jordan, Pella, Dion, Gerasa, Philadelphia, Gadara, Raphana, Kanatha, Hippos and Damascus." (Barclay) The spectacular remains of Scythopolis can be seen today.

> iii. "He was told to publish what great things *the Lord* had done for him. He went and published what great things *Jesus* had done for him. Did he make any mistake? Oh, no! It is but another name for the same Person: for Jesus is the Lord; and when you speak of him as divine, and talk of him in terms fit only for God, you do but speak rightly; for so he deserveth to be praised." (Spurgeon)

B. Jesus demonstrates His authority over sickness and death.

1. (21-24) A father asks Jesus to heal his daughter.

Now when Jesus had crossed over again by boat to the other side, a great multitude gathered to Him; and He was by the sea. And behold, one of the rulers of the synagogue came, Jairus by name. And when he saw Him, he fell at His feet and begged Him earnestly, saying, "My little daughter lies at the point of death. Come and lay Your hands on her, that she may be healed, and she will live." So *Jesus* went with him, and a great multitude followed Him and thronged Him.

> a. **A great multitude gathered to Him**: Jesus left the Gentile region around the Sea of Galilee, where He met the man possessed by many demons. Now He returned to the Jewish towns on **the other side**, and the large crowds immediately came to Jesus again.

> b. **One of the rulers of the synagogue came**: The *ruler of the synagogue* was somewhat like a modern day pastor. He managed both the spiritual and the business affairs of the synagogue. This man came in desperation to Jesus (**fell at His feet and begged Him earnestly**) because his daughter was **at the point of death**.

> > i. "As synagogue-ruler he was a lay official responsible for supervision of the building and arranging the service." (Lane)

c. **Come and lay Your hands on her, that she may be healed, and she will live**: This man had great confidence in Jesus and he believed that Jesus had all power to heal his daughter. But he also believed that Jesus should be there for it to happen (**come and lay Your hands on her**).

i. It may be that the man held a firm superstition in his mind, believing that the healer had to be present. It may be that he was just accustomed to thinking that way and never really thought about a person being healed in a different way. Whatever the reason, his thinking put Jesus in a box. "To heal my daughter, You have to **come and lay Your hands on her**."

ii. When a Roman Centurion came to Jesus in a similar situation (Luke 7:1-10), Jesus didn't even go to the centurion's house to heal the servant. He simply pronounced him healed from a distance. But here, Jesus did not demand that Jairus show the same faith the centurion had. Jesus responded to the faith Jairus had. Jesus asks us to give to Him *the faith that we have*.

iii. "This was weakness of faith, far short of that of the centurion, who yet was a Roman soldier; whereas Jairus was a learned Jew. Knowledge is therefore one thing, faith another; and the greatest scholars are not always the holiest men." (Trapp)

iv. Adam Clarke noticed four things displayed by Jairus that are necessary for answered prayer.

- We must put ourselves in the presence of Jesus (**one of the rulers of the synagogue came**).

- We must humble ourselves sincerely before Jesus (**he fell at His feet**).

- We must lay open our request with a holy earnestness (**and begged Him earnestly**).

- We must have total confidence in the power and the goodness of Jesus (**Come and lay Your hands on her, that she may be healed, and she will live**).

2. (25-34) A woman is healed of a hemorrhage.

Now a certain woman had a flow of blood for twelve years, and had suffered many things from many physicians. She had spent all that she had and was no better, but rather grew worse. When she heard about Jesus, she came behind *Him* in the crowd and touched His garment. For she said, "If only I may touch His clothes, I shall be made well." Immediately the fountain of her blood was dried up, and she felt in

her body that she was healed of the affliction. And Jesus, immediately knowing in Himself that power had gone out of Him, turned around in the crowd and said, "Who touched My clothes?" But His disciples said to Him, "You see the multitude thronging You, and You say, 'Who touched Me?'" And He looked around to see her who had done this thing. But the woman, fearing and trembling, knowing what had happened to her, came and fell down before Him and told Him the whole truth. And He said to her, "Daughter, your faith has made you well. Go in peace, and be healed of your affliction."

a. **A flow of blood for twelve years**: This woman was in a desperate condition. Her condition made her ceremonially and socially unclean, and this was a significant burden to live under for 12 years.

> i. According to the Jewish ideas of the time, if this woman touched anyone, she made him or her ceremonially unclean. This uncleanness did not allow them to take part in any aspect of Israel's worship (Leviticus 15:19-31).

> ii. "By the very law of her people, she was divorced from her husband, and could not live in her home; she was ostracized from all society, and must not come into contact with her old friends; she was excommunicated from the services of the synagogue, and thus shut out from the women's courts in the temple." (Morgan)

b. **Had suffered many things from many physicians**: She went to the doctors to get better, but only **suffered** worse - and became poorer. Luke the physician also tells us that she had *spent all her livelihood on physicians* (Luke 8:43). He knew how doctor bills could take all the money a family had.

> i. The ancient rabbis had many different formulas to help a woman afflicted like this. "Rabbi Jochanan says: '*Take of gum Alexandria, of alum, and of corcus hortensis, the weight of a zuzee each; let them be bruised together, and given in wine to the woman that hath an issue of blood.* But if this fail, *Take of Persian onions nine logs, boil them in wine, and give it to her to drink: and say,* Arise from thy flux. But should this fail, *Set her in a place where two ways meet, and let her hold a cup of wine in her hand; and let somebody come behind and affright her, and say,* Arise from thy flux. But should this do no good...'" (Clarke)

> ii. When a soul is sick today, they often go to different doctors and spend a great deal of time and money, only to **suffer many things from many physicians**. A sick soul may go to "Doctor Entertainment," but find no cure. They may pay a visit to "Doctor Success" but he is

no help in the long run. "Doctor Pleasure," "Doctor Self-Help," or "Doctor Religion" can't bring a real cure. Only "Doctor Jesus" can.

c. **If only I may touch His clothes, I shall be made well**: Because this woman's condition was embarrassing and because she was ceremonially unclean and would be condemned for touching Jesus or even being in a pressing crowd, she wanted to do this secretly. She would not openly ask Jesus to be healed, but she thought, "**If only I may touch His clothes, I shall be made well**."

> i. Since we have no evidence in the Bible that Jesus healed this way before, it seems that the woman acted at least partially on superstition. Her faith had elements of err and superstition, yet she did believe in the healing power of Jesus, and the border of His garment served as a point of contact for that faith. There were many things that we could find wrong with this woman's faith. Nevertheless, her faith was in *Jesus*, and the object of faith is much more important than the quality of faith.

> ii. "There was no magic in the garments of Jesus. Perhaps there was superstition in the woman's mind, but Jesus honoured her darkened faith as in the case of Peter's shadow and Paul's handkerchief." (Robertson)

> iii. Matthew 9:20 says she touched the *hem of His garment*, and that actually means one of the borders of the outer garment that all Jews wore. "Every devout Jew wore an outer robe with four tassels on it, one at each corner. These tassels were worn in obedience to the command in Numbers 15:38-40, and they were to signify to others, and to remind the man himself, that the wearer was a member of the chosen people of God." (Barclay)

d. **Immediately the fountain of her blood was dried up**: According to the thinking of the day, when this unclean woman touched Jesus it would make *Him* unclean. But because of the nature of Jesus and the power of God, that wasn't how it worked. When she touched His garment, Jesus wasn't made unclean; the woman was made whole. When we come to Jesus with our sin and lay it upon Him, it doesn't make Him a sinner, but it makes us clean.

e. **She felt in her body that she was healed of the affliction... immediately knowing in Himself that power had gone out of Him**: When the woman was healed, *both* the woman and Jesus knew it happened. She **felt in her body** that it happened, and Jesus felt **power had gone out of Him**.

i. It would be interesting to know what exactly "**power had gone out of Him**" means. This is the only healing or miracle in the ministry of Jesus - or anyone else in the Bible - that mentions this idea. From every other healing in the ministry of Jesus, we *don't* get the idea that God's healing power was communicated by a noticeable surge of power flowing through Jesus and into someone else. Yet on this occasion, *something* like that happened, even if we don't know how.

f. **Who touched My clothes?** Roberston says that Jesus more literally said, "Who touched me on my clothes." Her goal wasn't to touch the *clothes* of Jesus, but to touch Jesus. The clothes just happened to be the part of Jesus she could touch.

i. Because this woman was embarrassed and thought her uncleanness meant no one would let her touch Jesus, she tried to do it secretly. But God often brings His work out into the open, even if it may start secretly.

g. **And He looked around to see her who had done this thing**: This was *before* she revealed herself. Jesus knew all along exactly who touched Him and received the healing. He asked, "**Who touched My clothes?**" for the benefit of the *woman*, not because He didn't know who the person was.

i. The disciples were amazed that Jesus asked this question. Given the situation, **His disciples said to Him, "You see the multitude thronging You, and You say, 'Who touched Me?'"** But the disciples didn't understand the difference between *casual contact* with Jesus and *reaching out to touch Him in faith.*

ii. We can imagine someone who because of the press of the crowd bumped up against Jesus. When the woman's miracle was revealed, they might say, "I bumped into Jesus, I touched Him - yet I was not healed." But there is a huge difference between bumping into Jesus here and there and reaching out to touch Him in faith. You can come to church week after week and "bump into" Jesus. That isn't the same as reaching out to touch Him in faith.

iii. "It is not every contact with Christ that saves men; it is the arousing of yourself to come near to him, the determinate, the personal, resolute, believing touch of Jesus Christ which saves." (Spurgeon)

iv. "Augustine long ago said of this story, 'Flesh presses, faith touches.'... He can always distinguish between the jostle of a curious mob, and the agonized touch of a needy soul." (Morgan)

h. **But the woman, fearing and trembling, knowing what had happened to her, came and fell down before Him and told Him the whole truth:**

Jesus made her go through this although He knew who she was, and she knew who she was. It might seem that His only purpose was to *embarrass* this poor woman before others, but that wasn't the purpose at all.

i. Jesus did it so that *she* would know she was healed. It is true that Mark tells us **she felt in her body that she was healed of the affliction**, but this woman was like any other person. Soon she would begin to doubt and fear, wondering if she really was healed. She would wonder when the ailment might return. But Jesus told her "**Go in peace, and be healed of your affliction.**" Jesus called her out so that *she* would absolutely know that she was healed.

ii. Jesus did it so that *others* would know she was healed. This woman had an ailment that no one could see and that made her a public outcast. It would sound suspicious to many if she just announced that she was healed. They would think that she made it up just to be considered "clean" again. Jesus called her out so that *others* would absolutely know that she was healed.

iii. Jesus did it so that she would know *why* she was healed. When Jesus said, "**Daughter, your faith has made you well,**" it showed the woman that it really wasn't touching the clothing of Jesus that healed her. Instead, it was her **faith** in Jesus and what He could do for her.

iv. Jesus did it because He didn't want her to think she *stole* a blessing, that she could never look Jesus in the eye again. She didn't steal anything; she received it by faith and Jesus wanted her to know that.

v. Jesus did it so that *Jairus* could see this woman's faith and be encouraged regarding his daughter. Jesus "called her out" to *encourage someone else* in faith.

vi. Jesus did it because He wanted to bless her in a special way. He called her "**Daughter.**" Jesus never called any other person by this name. Jesus wanted her to come forth and hear this special name of tenderness. When Jesus calls us forward, it is because He has something special to give us.

vii. "It seemed cruel, but it was really kind. It sent her home with loftier thoughts of Him. She would never talk of the wonder of the tassel; she would always talk of the wonder of the Lord. Permitted to walk away without confession, she would have said exultantly, 'I've found a cure.' *Now* the woman cried, 'I've found a friend.'" (Morrisson)

viii. Jesus may ask us to do things that seem embarrassing today. He doesn't ask us to do them just because He wants to embarrass us. There is also a higher purpose even if we can't see it. But if avoiding embarrassment is the most important thing in our life, then pride is our god. We are more in love with ourselves and with our self-image than we are in love with Jesus.

i. **Came and fell down before Him and told Him the whole truth**: When we come to Jesus, we must tell Him **the whole truth**.

> i. We must tell Him **the whole truth** about our *sin*. We come to Him as the Great Physician and He asks, "What seems to be the problem?" So don't leave anything out.

> ii. We must tell Him **the whole truth** about all our *suffering*. He wants to know where it hurts, so tell Him.

> iii. We must tell Him **the whole truth** about the *other doctors and cures* we tried.

> iv. We must tell Him **the whole truth** about all our *hopes*, because He wants to know what He can do for us.

j. **Daughter, your faith has made you well. Go in peace, and be healed of your affliction**: This whole account is so wonderful that later Christians couldn't help but embellish the story. Some said the woman's name was Berenice, and others said it was Veronica. One said outside her door she set up a statute of her bowing down before Jesus, and at the foot of the statue a strange plant grew that could miraculously heal diseases.

> i. Poor Jairus! During all this, his daughter laid ill at home, her life slipping away. It was torture to see Jesus take time out to minister to this woman while his daughter suffered. God is never slow, but He often *seems* slow to the sufferer.

3. (35-36) Jesus calls Jairus to an extreme faith with an extreme promise.

While He was still speaking, *some* came from the ruler of the synagogue's *house* who said, "Your daughter is dead. Why trouble the Teacher any further?" As soon as Jesus heard the word that was spoken, He said to the ruler of the synagogue, "Do not be afraid; only believe."

a. **Your daughter is dead**: Jairus' heart sank when he heard this. He must have thought, "I knew this was taking too long. I knew Jesus shouldn't have wasted His time on this silly woman. Now the situation is beyond hope."

b. **Do not be afraid; only believe**: Jesus told Jairus to do two things. First, to stop being **afraid**. It sounds almost cruel for Jesus to say this to a man who just lost his daughter, but Jesus knew that *fear* and *faith* don't go together. Before Jairus could really trust Jesus, he had to *decide* to put away fear. Second, Jesus told Jairus to **only believe**. Don't try to **believe** and be afraid at the same time. Don't try to **believe** and figure it all out. Don't try to **believe** and make sense of the delay. Instead, **only believe**.

i. Jairus was supposed to **believe** the word of Jesus. Everything else told him the situation was hopeless, but the word of Jesus brought hope.

4. (37-43) Jesus raises Jairus' daughter from the dead.

And He permitted no one to follow Him except Peter, James, and John the brother of James. Then He came to the house of the ruler of the synagogue, and saw a tumult and those who wept and wailed loudly. When He came in, He said to them, "Why make this commotion and weep? The child is not dead, but sleeping." And they ridiculed Him. But when He had put them all outside, He took the father and the mother of the child, and those *who were* **with Him, and entered where the child was lying. Then He took the child by the hand, and said to her, "Talitha, cumi," which is translated, "Little girl, I say to you, arise." Immediately the girl arose and walked, for she was twelve years** *of age.* **And they were overcome with great amazement. But He commanded them strictly that no one should know it, and said that** *something* **should be given her to eat.**

a. **He permitted no one to follow Him except Peter, James, and John**: Often these three are considered the "inner circle" of Jesus' disciples. Yet it could be just as true that Jesus knew He had to keep a special eye on these three.

b. **The child is not dead, but sleeping**: Jesus wasn't out of touch with reality when He said this. He wasn't playing make-believe. He said this because He knew a higher reality, a spiritual reality that was more certain and powerful than death itself.

c. **A tumult and those who wept and wailed loudly**: In that day it was customary to hire professional mourners to add to the atmosphere of grief and pain at a funeral. But the professional mourners only grieved superficially. Notice how quickly they turned from weeping to ridicule (**they ridiculed Him**).

i. **They ridiculed Him**: "Note imperfect tense. They kept it up." (Robertson)

ii. "Since even the poorest man was required by common custom to hire a minimum of two fluteplayers and one professional mourner in the event of his wife's death, it is probable that one who held the rank of synagogue-ruler would be expected to hire a large number of professional mourners." (Lane)

d. **When He had put them all outside**: Jesus would have nothing to do with these people who don't believe His promises. He drove them out so that they would not discourage the faith of Jairus.

e. **Little girl, I say to you, arise**: Jesus spoke to a dead girl as if she were alive, and He did this because He is God. Romans 4:17 says that God *gives life to the dead and calls those things which do not exist as though they did.* Jesus spoke to this girl with the power of God and she was raised from the dead.

f. **They were overcome with great amazement**: Jesus didn't fail Jairus, and He didn't fail the woman who needed healing. But in ministering to both, He needed to stretch the faith of Jairus extra far.

  i. In all this we see how the work of Jesus is different, yet the same, among each individual. If Jesus can touch each need so personally, He can touch our needs the same way.

  - Jairus had 12 years of sunshine that were about to be extinguished. The woman had 12 years of agony that seemed hopeless to heal.

  - Jairus was an important man, the ruler of the synagogue. The woman was a nobody. We don't even know her name.

  - Jairus was probably wealthy because he was an important man. The woman was poor because she spent all her money on doctors.

  - Jairus came publicly. The woman came secretly.

  - Jairus thought Jesus had to do a lot to heal his daughter. The woman thought all she needed was to touch Jesus' garment.

  - Jesus responded to the woman immediately. Jesus responded to Jairus after a delay.

  - Jairus' daughter was healed secretly. The woman was healed publicly.

Mark 6 - Rejection, Opinions and Miracles

A. Rejection in Jesus' hometown.

1. (1-3) Jesus' countrymen are offended at Him.

Then He went out from there and came to His own country, and His disciples followed Him. And when the Sabbath had come, He began to teach in the synagogue. And many hearing *Him* were astonished, saying, "Where *did* this Man *get* these things? And what wisdom *is* this which is given to Him, that such mighty works are performed by His hands! Is this not the carpenter, the Son of Mary, and brother of James, Joses, Judas, and Simon? And are not His sisters here with us?" And they were offended at Him.

a. **Where did this Man get these things?** In His hometown, Jesus faced a crowd that wondered how He became so powerful in both word and works. Jesus left Nazareth as a carpenter. He came back as a rabbi, complete with a group of disciples. It isn't hard to see how the Nazareth locals would wonder, "What happened to Jesus?"

b. **Is this not the carpenter**: This was not a compliment. It was a way of pointing out that Jesus had no formal theological training. He was never a formal disciple of a rabbi, much less a prominent rabbi.

i. Throughout the centuries, some people have thought that Jesus' employment as a **carpenter** somehow discredited His message. In ancient Rome, there was a terrible persecution under the Emperor Julian. At that time, a philosopher mocked a Christian, asking him "What do you think the carpenter's son is doing now?" The Christian wisely answered, "He is building a coffin for Julian."

c. **The carpenter**: The word **carpenter** was actually much broader than just one who works with wood. It had the idea of "a builder." Jesus may have worked with stone as much as with wood, because stone was a much more common building material in that time and place.

i. It is wonderful to think that our Lord - of all the professions He could have been - chose to be a *carpenter*. God is a builder, and He knows how to build in our lives - and He knows how to finish the job.

ii. A few things Jesus learned as a carpenter:

- He learned that there is a lot of potential in a log.
- He learned it takes work and time to make something useable.
- He learned that the finest things are made from the hardest wood.

d. **The Son of Mary**: This also was not a compliment. "The additional phrase 'the son of Mary' is probably disparaging. It was contrary to Jewish usage to describe a man as the son of his mother, even when she was a widow, except in insulting terms. Rumors to the effect that Jesus was illegitimate appear to have circulated in his own lifetime and may lie behind this reference as well." (Lane)

i. "How much of suspicion and contempt may have lurked behind that particular description of Him?" (Morgan)

ii. The lack of mention of Joseph perhaps implies that he died when Jesus was young; Jesus probably stayed at home to support His family until the youngest children were old enough to support the family.

e. **His sisters**: We know that Jesus had brothers (Mark 3:31), but now we also learn that He had **sisters**. Mary did not remain a virgin after she gave birth to Jesus.

f. **And they were offended at Him**: These neighbors of Jesus were "too familiar" with Jesus. They knew *little enough* about Him to think that they knew *everything* about Him.

2. (4-6) Jesus' reaction to the rejection by His own countrymen.

But Jesus said to them, "A prophet is not without honor except in his own country, among his own relatives, and in his own house." Now He could do no mighty work there, except that He laid His hands on a few sick people and healed *them*. And He marveled because of their unbelief. Then He went about the villages in a circuit, teaching.

a. **A prophet is not without honor, except in his own country**: Jesus accepted rejection as price a faithful prophet must pay, though it must have hurt Him badly to be rejected by friends and neighbors.

b. **He could do no mighty work**: His work was limited in this climate of unbelief. In this sense, Jesus' power was limited by the unbelief of His countrymen.

i. This was in respect to God's principle of partnership with man. God may work with *no* belief, but not with *un*belief.

c. **He marveled because of their unbelief**: Jesus was amazed at their unbelief. Our inability to believe God and trust Him is indeed amazing.

i. Jesus only **marveled** at Jewish unbelief and Gentile faith (Luke 7:9). Would Jesus marvel at your faith or your unbelief? "Unbelief must needs be a monstrous sin, that puts Christ to the marvel." (Trapp)

ii. We never read that Jesus marveled at art or architecture or even the wonders of creation. He never marveled at human ingenuity or invention. He didn't marvel at the piety of the Jewish people or the military dominance of the Roman Empire. But Jesus did marvel at faith - when it was present in an unexpected place, and when it was absent where it should have been.

d. **He went about the villages in a circuit, teaching**: Jesus did not let this rejection by His countrymen debilitate Him. Jesus got on with the business of teaching and ministry.

3. (7-13) The twelve are sent out preaching.

And He called the twelve to *Himself*, and began to send them out two *by* two, and gave them power over unclean spirits. He commanded them to take nothing for the journey except a staff; no bag, no bread, no copper in *their* money belts; but to wear sandals, and not to put on two tunics. Also He said to them, "In whatever place you enter a house, stay there till you depart from that place. And whoever will not receive you nor hear you, when you depart from there, shake off the dust under your feet as a testimony against them. Assuredly, I say to you, it will be more tolerable for Sodom and Gomorrah in the day of judgment than for that city!" So they went out and preached that *people* should repent. And they cast out many demons, and anointed with oil many who were sick, and healed *them*.

a. **And began to send them out two by two**: In the Gospel of John, Jesus said, *as the Father has sent Me, I also send you* (John 20:21). Here, Jesus sent out His disciples to do the same things that He did: preach, heal the sick, and free people from demonic possession.

b. **He commanded them to take nothing for the journey**: The disciples didn't need fancy equipment to preach a simple message. Too much stuff would get in the way of their urgent message.

i. There was a rule from the Jewish rabbis that you could not enter the temple area with a staff, shoes, or a moneybag, because you wanted to avoid even the appearance of being engaged in any other business than the service of the Lord. The disciples were engaged in such holy work (preaching the gospel and bringing God's healing) that they could not give the impression that they have any other motive.

c. **No bag, no bread, no copper in their money belts**: Traveling light kept them dependent upon God. They had to trust the Lord for everything if they didn't take much with them. If the preacher doesn't trust God, how can he tell others to trust Him?

d. **And whoever will not receive you nor hear you, when you depart from there, shake off the dust under your feet as a testimony against them**: Their job as preachers wasn't to change people's minds. They were to persuasively present the message; but if their audience didn't receive it, they didn't receive it - and they could leave, and **shake the very dust from your feet** as they left.

 i. In that day, if Jewish people had to go in or through a Gentile city, as they left they would shake the dust off their feet. It was a gesture that said, "We don't want to take anything from this Gentile city with us." Essentially, Jesus told them to regard a Jewish city that rejects their message as if it were a Gentile city.

e. **It will be more tolerable for Sodom and Gommorah in the day of judgment**: The implication is that some will be judged more severely than others **in the day of judgment**. Of course, none will have it good in hell; but perhaps some will have it worse than others will.

f. **So they departed**: They actually did it. We can hear Jesus' word to us all day long, but something is missing until we *do* it.

g. **They went out and preached**: To preach simply means to *proclaim*, to tell others in the sense of announcing news to them. Some of the best and most effective preaching never happens inside a church. It happens when followers of Jesus are one-on-one with others, telling about what Jesus did for them.

 i. Morgan on **preached that people should repent**: "First they preached that men should repent. That is a declaration that needs careful consideration. It does not mean that they told men to repent, but that they preached in such a way as to produce repentance."

 ii. "When the apostles went out to preach to men, they did not *create* a message; they *brought* a message." (Barclay)

h. **And anointed with oil many who were sick, and healed them**: The other reference to anointing with oil for healing is in James 5:14-15. We know that anointing with oil was a picture of an outpouring of the Holy Spirit, but it may also have had a medicinal purpose in that day.

i. "It is possible that the use of oil (olive oil) as a medicine is the basis of the practice... It was the best medicine of the ancients and was used internally and externally... The very word *aleipho* can be translated rub or anoint without any ceremony." (Robertson)

B. The death of John the Baptist.

1. (14-16) Herod hears of Jesus' ministry and is perplexed.

Now King Herod heard *of Him,* for His name had become well known. And he said, "John the Baptist is risen from the dead, and therefore these powers are at work in him." Others said, "It is Elijah." And others said, "It is the Prophet, or like one of the prophets." But when Herod heard, he said, "This is John, whom I beheaded; he has been raised from the dead!"

a. **King Herod**: Actually, Emperor Augustus denied the title "king" to Herod. Goaded by the ambitious Herodias, Herod pressed for the title again and again until he so offended the emperor's court that he was dismissed as a traitor. Mark used the title **King Herod** because it was the *local* custom to call him king, or more likely he used it *ironically*. All his ancient readers would remember the character of this man.

b. **It is Elijah**: Some people thought Jesus was **Elijah**, because it was prophesied Elijah would come before the Messiah did (Malachi 4:5). Others thought He was **the Prophet** whom Moses said would come after him (Deuteronomy 18:15).

c. **This is John, whom I beheaded; he has been raised from the dead**: Herod feared Jesus was John the Baptist. Herod's confusion came from his own guilty conscience. It is hard to see clearly who Jesus is when we are in sin and rebellion.

2. (17-29) The sordid death of John the Baptist.

For Herod himself had sent and laid hold of John, and bound him in prison for the sake of Herodias, his brother Philip's wife; for he had married her. For John had said to Herod, "It is not lawful for you to have your brother's wife." Therefore Herodias held it against him and wanted to kill him, but she could not; for Herod feared John, knowing that he *was* a just and holy man, and he protected him. And when he heard him, he did many things, and heard him gladly. Then an opportune day came when Herod on his birthday gave a feast for his nobles, the high officers, and the chief *men* of Galilee. And when Herodias' daughter herself came in and danced, and pleased Herod and those who sat with him, the king said to the girl, "Ask me whatever you want, and I will give *it* to you." He also swore to her, "Whatever you ask

me, I will give you, up to half of my kingdom." So she went out and said to her mother, "What shall I ask?" And she said, "The head of John the Baptist!" Immediately she came in with haste to the king and asked, saying, "I want you to give me at once the head of John the Baptist on a platter." And the king was exceedingly sorry; *yet,* because of the oaths and because of those who sat with him, he did not want to refuse her. Immediately the king sent an executioner and commanded his head to be brought. And he went and beheaded him in prison, brought his head on a platter, and gave it to the girl; and the girl gave it to her mother. When his disciples heard *of it,* they came and took away his corpse and laid it in a tomb.

a. **Herod himself had sent and laid hold of John, and bound him in prison**: Herod imprisoned John for his bold rebuke of his sin. At the same time, Herod did not want to kill John out of fear of the multitudes - and because he knew that John was a **just and holy man**.

i. "More weak than cruel, Herod listened to John with an undeniable fascination. John's word left him perplexed, and in anguish. Yet he found a strange pleasure in the authoritative preaching of this holy man, whose stringent life gave added power to his probing word. Too weak to follow John's counsel, he nevertheless had to listen." (Lane)

b. **For John had said to Herod, "It is not lawful for you to have your brother's wife."** When he preached repentance, John did not spare the rich and powerful. He called Herod and his wife Herodias to repent, because Herodias had been the wife of Herod's brother Philip.

i. John Trapp tells of another bold confrontation of sin in a king: "So Latimer presented for a new-year's gift to King Henry VIII a New Testament, with a napkin, having this posy about it, Whoremongers and adulterers God will judge."

c. **And when Herodias' daughter herself came in and danced, and pleased Herod and those who sat with him**: Herodias' daughter shamelessly danced before Herod and friends, winning favor and a special request.

i. "With immodest gesticulations and trippings on the toe, wherewith the old fornicator was so inflamed, that he swore she should have anything of him." (Trapp)

ii. "Such dancing was an almost unprecedented thing for women of rank, or even respectability. It was mimetic and licentious, and performed by professionals." (Robertson)

d. **So she went out and said to her mother, "What shall I ask?" And she said, "The head of John the Baptist!"** The immediate reply of Herodias showed that the mother had this planned out all along. She knew her husband and she knew the situation, and knew she could get what she wanted this way.

i. "The girl's question implies by the middle voice that she is thinking of something for herself. She was no doubt unprepared for her mother's ghastly reply." (Robertson)

e. **And the king was exceedingly sorry; yet, because of the oaths and because of those who sat with him, he did not want to refuse her**: Because Herod was afraid to cross his wife or lose face before his friends, he did something he knew to be wrong.

i. "The depth of distress experienced by Herod at Salome's request for the head of John the Baptist is expressed graphically by the Greek word *perilypos*, 'greatly distressed'. This is the same word used to describe Jesus' agony in Gethsemane (Mark 14:34)." (Wessell)

ii. "Neither was it long ere this tyrant Herod had his payment from heaven." (Trapp) In order to take his brother's wife Herodias, Herod put away his first wife, a princess from a neighboring kingdom to the east. Her father was offended, and came against Herod with an army, defeating him in battle. Then his brother Agrippa accused him of treason against Rome, and he was banished into the distant Roman province of Gaul, where Herod and Herodias committed suicide.

C. Jesus displays His power over the laws of nature.

1. (30-34) Jesus' compassion on the multitude.

Then the apostles gathered to Jesus and told Him all things, both what they had done and what they had taught. And He said to them, "Come aside by yourselves to a deserted place and rest a while." For there were many coming and going, and they did not even have time to eat. So they departed to a deserted place in the boat by themselves. But the multitudes saw them departing, and many knew Him and ran there on foot from all the cities. They arrived before them and came together to Him. And Jesus, when He came out, saw a great multitude and was moved with compassion for them, because they were like sheep not having a shepherd. So He began to teach them many things.

a. **Come aside by yourselves to a deserted place and rest a while**: The disciples came back from a successful time of ministry, being sent by Jesus into the towns of Galilee (Mark 6:7-12). When they returned, Jesus knew they needed a time of **rest**. Jesus knew when it was time to work, and He knew when it was time to **rest**.

> i. Jesus knew the importance of hard work better than anyone did. He said, *I must work the works of Him who sent Me while it is day; the night is coming when no one can work.* (John 9:4) At the same time, He knew that we can only be most effective at work when we also take time for rest. Jesus and the disciples were constantly busy (**there were many coming and going, and they did not even have time to eat**), so Jesus took them away to a **deserted place** for some rest.

> ii. "*Rest* is necessary for those who *labour,* and a *zealous* preacher of the Gospel will as often stand in need of it as a *galley slave.*" (Clarke)

b. The multitudes saw them departing, and many knew Him and ran there on foot from all the cities: Perhaps the multitude was rude and demanding. The disciples wanted to send them away (Mark 6:36), but Jesus **was moved with compassion for them**.

> i. The disciples often saw the crowds as *work,* and as constant *demands,* especially at a time like this when their well-deserved rest was interrupted by the multitude. But Jesus saw them and was **moved with compassion**. Each face reflected a need, a hunger, or a hurt. Being a thoroughly others-centered person, Jesus cared more about the needs of someone else than he cared about His own needs.

c. Because they were like sheep without a shepherd: Jesus knew that without a shepherd, sheep were in a lot of trouble. They can't fend for themselves against predators and have a hard time finding the food and water they need. Jesus was **moved with compassion** for the people among the crowd because He knew their pressing demands were prompted by great needs.

d. So He began to teach them many things: As a faithful Shepherd, Jesus took care of their most pressing need. He fed them with the Word of God.

2. (35-44) Jesus feeds the multitude.

When the day was now far spent, His disciples came to Him and said, "This is a deserted place, and already the hour *is* late. Send them away, that they may go into the surrounding country and villages and buy themselves bread; for they have nothing to eat." But He answered and said to them, "You give them something to eat." And they said to Him, "Shall we go and buy two hundred denarii worth of bread and give them *something* to eat?" But He said to them, "How many loaves do you have? Go and see." And when they found out they said, "Five, and two fish." Then He commanded them to make them all sit down in groups

on the green grass. So they sat down in ranks, in hundreds and in fifties. And when He had taken the five loaves and the two fish, He looked up to heaven, blessed and broke the loaves, and gave *them* to His disciples to set before them; and the two fish He divided among *them* all. So they all ate and were filled. And they took up twelve baskets full of fragments and of the fish. Now those who had eaten the loaves were about five thousand men.

a. **Send them away... for they have nothing to eat**: Both Jesus and the disciples saw exactly the same need among the multitude. The disciple's solution was to get rid of the need by getting rid of the needy. Jesus saw a different solution and wanted the disciples to see it also (**You give them something to eat**).

b. **Shall we go and buy two hundred denarii worth of bread and give them something to eat?** It's hard to know if the disciples were *angry* or just *couldn't believe* what Jesus said. Clearly, they thought spending about a year's income to feed this multitude for one meal was not only impossible but also a waste.

i. Understandably, it never entered their minds that Jesus might provide for the multitude with a miracle. God has resources that we know nothing about, so we can trust Him and be at peace even when we can't figure out how He will provide.

ii. Jesus' suggestion must have seemed so *extravagant* to the disciples. "Jesus if we had that kind of money, we would never spend it on one meal for this crowd. They annoy us, and they would be hungry again in a few hours. Shouldn't the money be spent on something else?" But Jesus will perform an extravagant miracle because He wanted to sit down to a dinner with the multitude - because He loved them.

c. **How many loaves do you have? Go and see**: God's way of provision always begins with *what we already have*. He wants us to use what we already have wisely. Don't foolishly pray for more from God if you don't use what He already has given you in a godly way.

i. What they did have was almost laughable. **Five loaves** and **two fish** were about enough for one or two people, because they were small loaves and small fishes. Even though the amount was tiny, Jesus still started with what they had.

d. **Then He commanded them to make them all sit down in groups on the green grass**: Jesus did this because these people were like *sheep without a shepherd*, and Jesus acted like their shepherd. The Good Shepherd *makes me lie down in green pastures*. (Psalm 23:2)

e. **So they sat down in ranks, in hundreds and in fifties**: Jesus *organized* the multitude. He didn't want a mob scene; He wanted to have a nice dinner with these people. God likes organization, especially when it comes to managing what He provides for us.

i. The ancient Greek word for **groups** "is a very pictorial word. It is the normal Greek word for the rows of vegetables in the vegetable garden. When you looked at the little groups, as they sat there in their orderly rows, they looked for all the world like the rows of vegetables in a series of garden plots." (Barclay)

f. **He looked up to heaven, blessed and broke the loaves**: When Jesus **blessed** before the meal, He didn't bless the food; He **blessed** God for supplying it. The idea of praying before a meal isn't to bless the food; it is to bless God in the sense of thanking and honoring Him for blessing *us* with the food.

i. "Jesus faithfully followed the accepted form: he took the bread in his hands, pronounced the blessing, broke the bread into pieces and distributed it. The only deviation from normal practice was that while praying Jesus looked toward heaven rather than downward, as prescribed." (Lane)

g. **So they all ate and were filled**: Jesus miraculously multiplied the loaves and fishes, until far more than 5,000 were fed. Seemingly, the miracle happened in the hands of Jesus.

i. It really seems too extravagant. Why feed the multitude until they were **filled** and can't eat any more? Why not just give them a little meal? Wouldn't that be enough? No. Jesus had people He loved over for dinner, and there will always be *more* than enough food. That's how much Jesus loved them and loves us.

ii. Jesus provided extravagantly, yet simply. As long as He was making food miraculously, He could have provided steak and lobster and any number of other great things. But He simply gave people bread and fish. When Jesus provides, don't be surprised if He provides simply.

iii. If someone left hungry, it was either because they refused the bread from Jesus or because the apostles didn't distribute the bread to everyone. Jesus supplied plenty for everybody to eat a good meal. But everybody had to eat for *himself*. Sometimes when we attend a spiritual meal, we gather food for everyone else except ourselves.

iv. The assurance that Jesus can provide - even miraculously - for all of our needs should be precious to us; it was to the earliest Christians.

On the walls of the catacombs, and other places of early Christian art, loaves and fishes are common pictures.

h. **And they took up twelve baskets full of fragments and of the fish**: Jesus could have just left this behind, but He didn't. Jesus generously provides, but He doesn't want things wasted. It isn't because Jesus is cheap or doesn't trust for future provision; He simply knew that wastefulness didn't glorify the God of all provision.

3. (45-46) Jesus departs for prayer.

Immediately He made His disciples get into the boat and go before Him to the other side, to Bethsaida, while He sent the multitude away. And when He had sent them away, He departed to the mountain to pray.

a. **He sent the multitude away**: Jesus loved the multitude, but he was not obsessed with crowds. He knew when to kindly tell them to go home (**He sent the multitude away**).

b. **He departed to the mountain to pray**: A long, difficult day spent ministering to the spiritual and physical needs of the multitude left Jesus exhausted. But that hard day drove Jesus *to prayer*, not *from prayer*.

4. (47-52) Jesus walks on the water.

Now when evening came, the boat was in the middle of the sea; and He *was* alone on the land. Then He saw them straining at rowing, for the wind was against them. Now about the fourth watch of the night He came to them, walking on the sea, and would have passed them by. And when they saw Him walking on the sea, they supposed it was a ghost, and cried out; for they all saw Him and were troubled. But immediately He talked with them and said to them, "Be of good cheer! It is I; do not be afraid." Then He went up into the boat to them, and the wind ceased. And they were greatly amazed in themselves beyond measure, and marveled. For they had not understood about the loaves, because their heart was hardened.

a. **The boat was in the middle of the sea**: Jesus sent the disciples across the Sea of Galilee (Mark 6:45). As Jesus prayed in the heights above the Sea of Galilee, **He saw them straining at the rowing** as they attempted to cross the lake in the face of the **wind**. Unknown to the disciples, Jesus saw their difficulty and cared for them.

i. It was difficult to get across because *a great wind was blowing* (John 6:18). They had rowed for much of the night and had only come about halfway across the lake (John 6:19).

ii. "The apostolic crew rowed, and rowed, and rowed, and it was no fault of theirs that they made no progress, 'for the wind was contrary unto them.' The Christian man may make little or no headway, and yet it may be no fault of his, for the wind is contrary. Our good Lord will take the will for the deed, and reckon our progress, not by our apparent advance, but by the hearty intent with which we tug at the oars." (Spurgeon)

iii. **About the fourth watch of the night** is somewhere around 3 a.m.

b. **He came to them, walking on the sea**: Jesus almost walked casually because He **would have passed them by**. Jesus came over to them only after they responded with fear and **cried out**.

c. **He went up into the boat to them**: As Jesus got into the boat with them, miraculously the boat was instantly carried over to the other side (John 6:21). Jesus rescued His disciples from working in futility. This was a miracle meant to assure them that He was in fact in control and that He would always lovingly be there to help them fulfill what He commanded.

i. "He came walking on the waves; and so he puts all the swelling storms of life under his feet. Christians, why be afraid?" (Augustine)

ii. We also know that it was on this occasion that Peter got out of the boat, walking on the water to Jesus (Matthew 14:28-31). There is reason - from history and subtle clues, not explicitly from the Scriptures - to believe that Peter was the main source for Mark's gospel. If this was the case, Peter may have left out the story because he didn't want to be exalted for walking on the water - or to be humbled for sinking.

iii. "Mark does not give the incident of Peter's walking on the water and beginning to sink. Perhaps Peter was not fond of telling that story." (Robertson)

5. (53-56) Jesus heals many in unusual ways.

When they had crossed over, they came to the land of Gennesaret and anchored there. And when they came out of the boat, immediately the people recognized Him, ran through that whole surrounding region, and began to carry about on beds those who were sick to wherever they heard He was. Wherever He entered into villages, cities, or in the country, they laid the sick in the marketplaces, and begged Him that they might just touch the hem of His garment. And as many as touched Him were made well.

a. **As many as touched Him were made well**: With this description of the healing ministry of Jesus, Mark concludes a brief section where we see the power of Jesus over the laws of nature. Normally, five thousand are not fed by one small lunch. Normally, men don't walk on water. Normally, the sick are not instantly healed. None of this is normal, except by the power of God.

Mark 7 - Declaring Food and People Clean

A. A dispute about ritual washings.

1. (1-5) Religious leaders from Jerusalem come to find fault and to ask questions about the failure of the disciples to observe ceremonial washings.

Then the Pharisees and some of the scribes came together to Him, having come from Jerusalem. Now when they saw some of His disciples eat bread with defiled, that is, with unwashed hands, they found fault. For the Pharisees and all the Jews do not eat unless they wash *their* hands in a special way, holding the tradition of the elders. *When they come* from the marketplace, they do not eat unless they wash. And there are many other things which they have received and hold, *like* the washing of cups, pitchers, copper vessels, and couches. Then the Pharisees and scribes asked Him, "Why do Your disciples not walk according to the tradition of the elders, but eat bread with unwashed hands?"

a. **Having come from Jerusalem**: This was another official delegation of religious leaders **from Jerusalem**, coming to evaluate the ministry of Jesus. We saw a previous delegation in Mark 3:22, and they pronounced a harsh condemnation against Jesus. This delegation **from Jerusalem** already made up their mind about Jesus and looked for something to confirm their opinon.

i. The *concept* of evaluating Jesus' ministry was fine. In outward appearance, these men protected Israel from a potential false prophet or false messiah. But the way they *actually evaluated* Jesus was all wrong. First, they already made up their mind about Jesus. Second, they did not evaluate Jesus against the measure of God's Word. They evaluated Him against the measure of their religious traditions.

b. **But eat bread with unwashed hands**: The religious leaders meant elaborate ceremonial washings, not washing for the sake of cleanliness. The observant Jews of that time strictly observed a rigid and extensive ritual for washing before meals.

i. The hand washing described here was *purely ceremonial*. It wasn't enough to properly clean your hands if they were very dirty. You would have to first wash your hands to make them clean, and then perform the ritual to make them *spiritually clean*. They even had an accompanying prayer to be said during the ritual washing: "Blessed be Thou, O Lord, King of the universe, who sanctified us by the laws and commanded us to wash the hands." (Cited in Lane)

ii. "The biblical mandate that the priests had to wash their hands and feet prior to entering the Tabernacle (Exodus 30:19; 40:12) provided the foundation for the wide-spread practice of ritual washings in Palestinian and diaspora Judaism." (Lane)

c. **Why do Your disciples not walk according to the tradition of the elders**: These washings were commanded by **tradition**, not by Scripture. The religious leaders *knew* this, yet they still criticized the disciples for not obeying these traditions.

i. In Judaism of that time they honored the *written law*. But there was also the *oral law*, which was written down, but was man's tradition and interpretation on top of the *written law*. Many Jewish leaders of Jesus' time honored the *oral law* even more than the *written law*.

ii. "Rabbi Eleazer said, 'He who expounds the Scriptures in opposition to the tradition has no share in the world to come'... The *Mishna*, a collection of Jewish traditions in the *Talmud*, records, 'It is a greater offense to teach anything contrary to the voice of the Rabbis than to contradict Scripture itself.'" (Wiersbe)

iii. "The Jews have several ordinary sayings, that show in what esteem they had these traditions, as *If the scribes say our right hand is our left, and our left hand is our right, we are to believe them*. And, *There is more in the words of the scribes than the words of the law*... The Jewish Rabbi Jose saith, *He sinneth as much as who eateth with unwashen hands, as he that lieth with an harlot*." (Trapp)

iv. "There had grown up a great body of traditions; traditions which in the first place were intended to be interpretations of the law, and applications of the law to local circumstances; traditions which in the second place became interpretations of traditions, and applications of traditions; and the traditions in the third place, which were interpretations of interpretations of interpretations of traditions!" (Morgan)

v. "It was Jesus' failure to support the validity of the oral law which made him an object of concerted attack by the scribes." (Lane)

d. **For the Pharisees and all the Jews do not eat unless they wash their hands in a special way, holding the tradition of the elders**: For these ceremonial washings, special stone vessels of water were kept because ordinary water might be unclean. To **wash** your **hands in a special way**, you started by taking at least enough of this water to fill one and one-half egg shells. Then you poured the water over your hands, starting at the fingers and running down towards your wrist. Then you cleansed each palm by rubbing the fist of the other hand into it. Then you poured water over your hands again, this time from the wrist towards the fingers.

i. A *really* strict Jew would do this not only before the meal, but also between each course. And the rabbis were deadly serious about this. They said that bread eaten with unwashed hands was no better than excrement. One rabbi who once failed to perform the ritual washing was excommunicated. Another rabbi was imprisoned by the Romans, and he used his ration of water for ceremonial cleansing instead of drinking, nearly dying of thirst. He was regarded as a great hero for this sacrifice.

ii. It's easy for us to think these religious leaders, or this whole religious culture was really stupid and phony for their emphasis on traditions like this. But we don't realize how subtly these things emerge and how spiritual they seem to be, especially in the beginning. Many rituals or traditions seem to be built on unshakable spiritual logic:

- Doesn't God want us to honor Him in everything we do?
- Didn't God command the priests to wash their hands before serving Him?
- Shouldn't every faithful follower of God have the same devotion as a priest?
- Isn't every meal sacred to God?
- Shouldn't we take every opportunity to make ourselves pure before the Lord?
- Doesn't God say, *Who may ascend into the hill of the LORD? Or who may stand in His holy place? He who has clean hands and a pure heart* (Psalm 24:3-4).

iii. When the questions are put this way, it's easy to say, "Yes, yes, yes," until you have agreed with the logic supporting the tradition. But if in the end you have a word of man, a tradition of man, a ritual of man, that has the same weight as the Word of God, you're wrong. Your "spiritual logic" doesn't matter. You are then wrong.

2. (6-9) Exalting man's tradition over God's will.

He answered and said to them, "Well did Isaiah prophesy of you hypocrites, as it is written:

'This people honors Me with *their* lips,
But their heart is far from Me.
And in vain they worship Me,
Teaching *as* doctrines the commandments of men.'

For laying aside the commandment of God, you hold the tradition of men; the washing of pitchers and cups, and many other such things you do." He said to them, "*All too* well you reject the commandment of God, that you may keep your tradition."

a. **You hypocrites**: Jesus spoke so strongly because these leaders were far too concerned with trivial matters like ritual washing. When they focused on these trivial traditions, they excluded everyone who didn't keep the traditions, and so they discouraged them from coming to God.

i. The Living Bible paraphrases Isaiah's quote: *These people speak very prettily about the Lord but they have no love for Him at all. Their worship is a farce, for they claim God commands the people to obey their petty rules.*

b. **This people honors Me with their lips**: Yes, they honored God **with their lips**; but in fact, God said of them **their heart is far from Me**. It is possible to have the *image* of being religious or spiritual, but actually be far from God. This was exactly the case with these religious leaders.

i. This is the whole idea behind the word **hypocrite**. The word in the ancient Greek language referred to "an actor" or "someone who wears a mask." The image they promote is more important to them than what they actually are.

ii. Would God say something similar to us?

- They attend church, **but their heart is far from Me**.
- They read their Bible, **but their heart is far from Me**.
- They pray eloquently, **but their heart is far from Me**.
- They contribute money, **but their heart is far from Me**.
- They do ministry, **but their heart is far from Me**.
- They love to sing, **but their heart is far from Me**.
- They talk to others about Jesus, **but their heart is far from Me**.

c. **Teaching as doctrines the commandments of men**: This is one of the pillars of legalism. Taking a commandment or opinion of men and teaching or promoting it as a doctrine from God is what supports legalism. It gives man's word the same weight as God's word.

> i. Not everything in the Christian life is a matter of right and wrong. Some things - many things - are simply matters of personal conscience before God. The Scriptures do not command ritual washing before meals. If you want to do it, then fine. Do it unto the Lord and without a sense of spiritual superiority before your brothers and sisters. If don't want to do it, fine also. Don't do it unto the Lord, and don't look down upon those whose conscience compels them to do the ritual washing.

d. **You reject the commandment of God**: This is another pillar of legalism. It would be bad enough to *add* the commandments of men to the word of God. But almost without fail, the legalist or religious hypocrite goes the next step - to **reject the commandment of God** and to **keep your tradition**. In doing this, they *subtract* the real essence and focus of God's word.

> i. "To the spiritual mind, it is a question of unceasing wonder that men should be so ready to follow and even fearlessly contend for the authority of human traditions, while they are just as ready to ignore the plain teachings of the Word of God." (Ironside)

3. (10-13) An example of how their traditions dishonored God: the practice of not helping your parents with "devoted" goods.

"For Moses said, 'Honor your father and your mother'; and, 'He who curses father or mother, let him be put to death.' But you say, 'If a man says to his father or mother, "Whatever profit you might have received from me *is* Corban";' (that is, a gift *to God*), then you no longer let him do anything for his father or his mother, making the word of God of no effect through your tradition which you have handed down. And many such things you do."

a. **For Moses said**: The Old Testament clearly laid out the responsibility of children to **honor** their parents. When children are young and in their parent's household, they are also responsible to *obey* their parents. But even when they are no longer responsible to *obey*, they are still responsible to **honor**.

b. **Whatever profit you might have received from me is Corban**: In this practice, a son could say that his possessions or savings were **Corban** - that is, especially devoted to God - and therefore unavailable to help his parents.

c. **Making the word of God of no effect through your tradition**: Through this, a son could completely disobey the command to **honor your father**

or mother and do it while being ultra-religious. Jesus called this **making the word of God of no effect through your tradition**.

4. (14-16) Jesus speaks to the multitude about the mere image of religion.

When He had called all the multitude to *Himself,* **He said to them, "Hear Me, everyone, and understand: There is nothing that enters a man from outside which can defile him; but the things which come out of him, those are the things that defile a man. If anyone has ears to hear, let him hear!"**

a. **There is nothing that enters a man from the outside which can defile him**: This is not to say that there are not defiling things that we can take into ourselves (such as pornography). But in this specific context, Jesus spoke about ceremonial cleanliness in regard to food, and He anticipated the time when under the New Covenant all foods would be declared kosher (Acts 10:15).

b. **The things which come out of him, those are things that defile a man**: The fundamental principle is simple. Eating with unclean hands or any other such thing that we put into us is not defiling. Rather, *what comes out of us* defiles and reveals that we have unclean (defiled) hearts.

i. "Although it may not seem so now, this passage, when it was first spoken, was well-nigh the most revolutionary passage in the New Testament." (Barclay)

5. (17-23) Jesus speaks to His disciples about religious externalism.

When He had entered a house away from the crowd, His disciples asked Him concerning the parable. So He said to them, "Are you thus without understanding also? Do you not perceive that whatever enters a man from outside cannot defile him, because it does not enter his heart but his stomach, and is eliminated, *thus* **purifying all foods?" And He said, "What comes out of a man, that defiles a man. For from within, out of the heart of men, proceed evil thoughts, adulteries, fornications, murders, thefts, covetousness, wickedness, deceit, lewdness, an evil eye, blasphemy, pride, foolishness. All these evil things come from within and defile a man."**

a. **Are you thus without understanding also?** In response to the parable, Jesus amplified the point made to the multitudes. We are defiled from the *inside out* rather than from the *outside in*, and this is particularly true of ceremonial things like foods.

b. **For from without, out of the heart of men, proceed evil**: God is far more concerned with what comes *out* of us than what goes *into* us. This is *especially* true when it comes to foods and traditions and rituals.

c. **Evil thoughts, adulteries, fornications**: This is a 13-part list that exposes the kind of evil that lives in the human heart. You don't need to travel a long distance to find the source of these sins. You don't need to conduct an exhaustive search. All you need to do is look at your own heart. "The source from which these rivers of pollution proceed is the natural heart of man. Sin is not a splash of mud upon man's exterior, it is a filth generated within himself." (Spurgeon)

> i. "I sicken as I think how man has plagued his fellow-men by his sins. But I will not go through the list, nor need I: the devil has preached upon this text this week, and few have been able to escape the horrible exposition." (Spurgeon)

d. **Evil thoughts**: "Every outward act of sin is preceded by an inward act of choice; therefore Jesus begins with the evil thought from which the evil action comes." (Barclay)

e. **Blasphemy**: "When this is used of words against man, it means *slander*; when it is used of words against God, it means *blasphemy*. It means insulting man or God." (Barclay)

B. Two wonderful examples of the healing power of Jesus.

1. (24-26) A Gentile woman's request.

From there He arose and went to the region of Tyre and Sidon. And He entered a house and wanted no one to know *it*, but He could not be hidden. For a woman whose young daughter had an unclean spirit heard about Him, and she came and fell at His feet. The woman was a Greek, a Syro-Phoenician by birth, and she kept asking Him to cast the demon out of her daughter.

a. **He entered a house and wanted no one to know it**: Jesus traveled some 50 miles to the north to visit these Gentile cities (**the region of Tyre and Sidon**). This was unusual in Jesus' ministry because His focus was on *the lost sheep of Israel* (Matthew 15:24).

> i. It also shows that Jesus did not obey the Jewish traditions that said a faithful Jew would have *nothing* to do with Gentiles and would *never* enter a Gentile's house.

> ii. "The previous incident shows Jesus wiping out the distinction between clean and unclean foods. Can it be that here, in symbol, we have him wiping out the difference between clean and unclean people? Just as a Jew would never soil his lips with forbidden foods, so he would never soil his life by contact with the unclean Gentile." (Barclay)

iii. **Wanted no one to know it**: At the same time, Jesus didn't want to needlessly offend people. He knew that the time for breaking down the wall between Jew and Gentile by bringing them into one body (the church) was still in the future. So while not keeping His presence in **the region of Tyre and Sidon** strictly secret, He did not want it publicized.

b. **But He could not be hidden**: It is a glorious principle - Jesus cannot **be hidden**. Anytime Jesus is present *at all*, He finds a way to touch lives, because He cannot be hidden.

c. **She came and fell at His feet... she kept asking Him to cast the demon out of her daughter**: This woman came to intercede for her daughter, and she is a picture of an intercessor because she made her daughter's needs her own.

2. (27-30) Jesus responds to the woman's request.

But Jesus said to her, "Let the children be filled first, for it is not good to take the children's bread and throw *it* to the little dogs." And she answered and said to Him, "Yes, Lord, yet even the little dogs under the table eat from the children's crumbs." Then He said to her, "For this saying go your way; the demon has gone out of your daughter." And when she had come to her house, she found the demon gone out, and her daughter lying on the bed.

a. **Let the children be filled first, for it is not good to take the children's bread and throw it to the little dogs**: Jesus seemed to discourage the woman, reminding her that **the children** (the Jewish people) get priority over the **little dogs** (Gentiles like her).

i. In that day, Jews often called Gentiles "dogs" in a very derogatory way. "To the Greek, the word *dog* meant a shameless and audacious woman; it was used exactly with the connotation that we use the word *bitch* to-day. To the Jews it was equally a term of contempt." (Barclay)

ii. Yet Jesus did not use the normal word for "dogs." Instead He softened it into **little dogs** - essentially, reminding the woman of her place as a Gentile, yet not wanting to push her completely away. "In Greek, diminutives are characteristically affectionate. Jesus took the sting out of the word." (Barclay)

b. **Yes, Lord, yet even the little dogs under the table eat from the children's crumbs**: The woman responded with great faith. First, she accepted her low place before Jesus by not debating the reference to **little dogs**. Second, she asked Jesus to deal with her on her own low level (**even the little dogs under the table eat**). She therefore received from Jesus.

i. We need to see the power of coming to God as we are, and letting Him make true His promises to those weak and unclean. If the woman had responded, "Who are you calling a dog?" she would not have received from Jesus what her daughter needed. Her humble, faith-filled submission to Jesus brought the victory. "Nothing appealed to our blessed Lord more than faith coupled with humility." (Ironside)

ii. Clarke praised the prayer of this woman and showed it had nine notable features: "1. It is short; 2. humble; 3. full of faith; 4. fervent; 5. modest; 6. respectful; 7. rational; 8. relying only on the mercy of God; 9. persevering."

3. (31-37) The healing of a deaf and dumb man.

Again, departing from the region of Tyre and Sidon, He came through the midst of the region of Decapolis to the Sea of Galilee. Then they brought to Him one who was deaf and had an impediment in his speech, and they begged Him to put His hand on him. And He took him aside from the multitude, and put His fingers in his ears, and He spat and touched his tongue. Then, looking up to heaven, He sighed, and said to him, "Ephphatha," that is, "Be opened." Immediately his ears were opened, and the impediment of his tongue was loosed, and he spoke plainly. Then He commanded them that they should tell no one; but the more He commanded them, the more widely they proclaimed *it*. And they were astonished beyond measure, saying, "He has done all things well. He makes both the deaf to hear and the mute to speak."

a. **They begged Him to put His hand on him**: This was another example of intercession. The friends of this troubled man came and brought his need to Jesus.

b. **He took him aside... put His fingers in his ears, and He spat and touched his tongue**: Jesus used a curious manner in healing this man. Throughout His ministry, Jesus used many different ways of healing. He healed with a word, healed without a word, healed in response to one's faith, healed in response to the faith of another, healed those who asked, and healed those He approached. Jesus didn't want to be tied down to any "one method" to show that His power was not dependent on any method but on the sovereign power of God.

i. Many people cared about this man, and perhaps many had prayed for his healing. But no one ever stuck their fingers in his ears and spit on his tongue like this. Jesus did something completely new to catch this man's attention because He could not catch his attention with words. "Through touch and the use of spittle Jesus entered into the mental world of the man and gained his confidence." (Lane)

ii. Undoubtedly, Jesus knew there was something special in His manner that would minister to this man. "He adapts His method to the peculiar circumstances of need of the one with whom He is dealing. I am quite convinced if we could perfectly know these men we should discover the reason for the method. In each case Christ adapted Himself to the need of the man." (Morgan)

c. **He sighed**: "Behold, 'a Man of sorrows, and acquainted with grief!' Behold a Man exercising a ministry full of healing power and elemental light; but never forget that this service was costly." (Morgan)

i. "The 'sigh' was an inward groan, our Lord's compassionate response to the pain and sorrow sin has brought into the world. It was also a prayer to the Father on behalf of the handicapped man. (The same word is used in connection with prayer in Romans 8:23, and the noun in Romans 8:26)." (Wiersbe)

d. **Immediately his ears were opened, and the impediment of his tongue was loosed, and he spoke plainly**: The ancient Greek word for **impediment in his speech** is *mogilalon* and is only used here in the New Testament. It is a word that is also used once in the Septuagint translation of the Old Testament, in Isaiah 35:5-6: *Then the eyes of the blind shall be opened, and the ears of the deaf shall be unstopped. Then the lame shall leap like a deer, and the tongue of the <u>dumb</u> [mogilalon] sing. For waters shall burst forth in the wilderness, and streams in the desert.* Mark wants us to know that the Messiah was here, bringing the glorious benefits of His rule.

i. "Mark's use of an extremely rare word to describe the man's speech defect is almost certainly an allusion to Isaiah 35:5 which celebrates God as the one who comes in order to unstop the ears of the deaf and to provide song for the man of inarticulate speech." (Lane)

e. **He has done all things well**: Jesus does **things well**. There is no shoddy, slip-shod work with Him. It is true of *creation*, but it is even truer of His work of *redemption*.

Mark 8 - Who Is Jesus?

A. Feeding the four thousand.

1. (1-4) Jesus gives the disciples an opportunity for faith.

In those days, the multitude being very great and having nothing to eat, Jesus called His disciples *to Him* and said to them, "I have compassion on the multitude, because they have now continued with Me three days and have nothing to eat. And if I send them away hungry to their own houses, they will faint on the way; for some of them have come from afar." Then His disciples answered Him, "How can one satisfy these people with bread here in the wilderness?"

> a. **I have compassion on the multitude**: The situation was similar to the recent feeding of the five thousand. We see both a hungry multitude and a compassionate Jesus, so Jesus presented the dilemma to the disciples: what do we do?

> b. **How can one satisfy these people with bread here in the wilderness?** We can imagine Jesus hoping one of the disciples might say, "Jesus, You did this before. You can do the same kind of work again." Jesus hoped they would regard His past faithfulness as a promise to meet their present need.

2. (5-10) Jesus and the disciples feed the multitude.

He asked them, "How many loaves do you have?" And they said, "Seven." So He commanded the multitude to sit down on the ground. And He took the seven loaves and gave thanks, broke *them* and gave *them* to His disciples to set before *them*; and they set *them* before the multitude. They also had a few small fish; and having blessed them, He said to set them also before *them*. So they ate and were filled, and they took up seven large baskets of leftover fragments. Now those who had eaten were about four thousand. And He sent them away,

immediately got into the boat with His disciples, and came to the region of Dalmanutha.

a. **How many loaves do you have?** Jesus asked them to give up their *own food* this time. Before they used the food of the little boy, but this time Jesus made the disciples give.

b. **So He commanded the multitude to sit down**: "He intended them not only a running banquet, a slight come-off, but a full feast, a good meal, and therefore bade them sit down and feed their fill." (Trapp)

c. **Broke them and gave them to the His disciples to set before them**: Jesus did what He only could do - the creative miracle. But Jesus left to the disciples to do what they could do - the distribution of the bread.

d. **They also had a few small fish**: It seems that the disciples kept the fish from Jesus until they saw He could multiply the bread. They needed to see that we are safe giving *everything* to Jesus.

i. "Why were these not mentioned before? Could it be that they had been withheld by the doubting disciples until they saw how the bread was multiplied? Apparently, the fishes were blessed separately and then distributed as the bread had been." (Ironside)

e. **So they ate and were filled, and they took up seven large baskets of leftover fragments**: At the end of the meal, they gathered more bread than they had to begin with. This was miraculous provision. The **seven *large* baskets** showed that God provided out of His abundance.

i. Some scholars argue this specific miracle never happened. They claim that this was merely a retelling of the feeding of the 5,000. Their main argument is, "how could the disciples forget Jesus' previous work so quickly?" Yet even mature Christians, having experienced God's power and provision, sometimes go on to act in unbelief. This wasn't so surprising after all.

B. The leaven of the Pharisees.

1. (11-12) The Pharisees ask for a sign from heaven.

Then the Pharisees came out and began to dispute with Him, seeking from Him a sign from heaven, testing Him. But He sighed deeply in His spirit, and said, "Why does this generation seek a sign? Assuredly, I say to you, no sign shall be given to this generation."

a. **Seeking from Him a sign from heaven**: In the mind of the Pharisees, this was not a request for another miracle of the type Jesus had already done. They asked for a dramatic sign from the sky, something similar Elijah's fire from heaven (1 Kings 18).

i. **Testing Him**: This was not a friendly encounter. The word **tested** could be translated *tempted*. The Pharisees tempted Jesus to perform a miraculous sign just as Satan tempted Him to do so in the wilderness.

b. **He sighed deeply in His spirit**: This attack and the unbelief it showed distressed Jesus. He was amazed at the unbelief and audacity of these religious leaders. "The sigh physical, its cause spiritual - a sense of irreconcilable enmity, invincible unbelief, and coming doom." (Bruce)

i. This demand for a "special" sign was an extreme example of the arrogance and pride of the Pharisees towards Jesus. Essentially, they said, "You have done a lot of small-time miracles. Come on up to the big leagues and really show us something."

c. **No sign shall be given to this generation**: Jesus refused because His miracles are not done with the intention of convincing hardened unbelievers. Instead, Jesus did miracles to show the power of God in the context of mercy. Those who believe that if people see enough signs they will come to faith presume to know more than Jesus did. He condemned the generation who sought a sign.

2. (13-15) Jesus warns of the *leaven* of the Pharisees and Herod.

And He left them, and getting into the boat again, departed to the other side. Now the disciples had forgotten to take bread, and they did not have more than one loaf with them in the boat. Then He charged them, saying, "Take heed, beware of the leaven of the Pharisees and the leaven of Herod."

a. **Beware of the leaven of the Pharisees**: This leaven wasn't merely yeast, but a pinch of dough left over from the previous batch, as in the making of sourdough bread. This was how bread was commonly leavened in the ancient world, and a little pinch of dough from the old lump could make a whole new lump of dough rise and "puff up." So, the work of leaven was considered an illustration of the work of sin and pride. The presence of a little can corrupt a large amount.

i. "Sometimes the Jew used the word leaven much as we would use the term *original sin*, or the natural evil of human nature." (Barclay)

b. **Take heed, beware**: Jesus essentially said, "Beware of the evil way the Pharisees and Herod think of the Kingdom of the Messiah, for in a short time I will reveal the truth of it to you." Both Herod and the Pharisees idealized the Kingdom as domineering power and authority. Herod saw it more as political power and authority, and the Pharisees saw it as more spiritual power and authority, but they still saw the kingdom in this high-minded way.

3. (16-21) Jesus questions the twelve about their lack of understanding.

And they reasoned among themselves, saying, *"It is* because we have no bread." But Jesus, being aware of *it,* said to them, "Why do you reason because you have no bread? Do you not yet perceive nor understand? Is your heart still hardened? Having eyes, do you not see? And having ears, do you not hear? And do you not remember? When I broke the five loaves for the five thousand, how many baskets full of fragments did you take up?" They said to Him, "Twelve." "Also, when I broke the seven for the four thousand, how many large baskets full of fragments did you take up?" And they said, "Seven." So He said to them, "How *is it* you do not understand?"

a. **It is because we have no bread**: When Jesus spoke of the *leaven of the Pharisees and the leaven of Herod,* the disciples didn't relate it to a spiritual idea at all. All they could think of was the bread that goes in the stomach, not the bread that goes in the soul.

b. **Do you not yet perceive nor understand?** Jesus confronted His disciples over their lack of understanding. From this we know that they *could have* done better than this. They could have understood more if they applied themselves more.

c. **Do you not remember?** Their understanding should have been based on seeing what Jesus already did. We can always take the past faithfulness of God as a promise for His continued love and care.

i. This is one of the situations where we wish we had a recording of Jesus' words to hear what tone of voice He used. Was it a tone communicating *anger, concern,* or *frustration?* We know that even when Jesus confronted His disciples, He did it in *love.*

4. (22-26) Blind eyes are opened.

Then He came to Bethsaida; and they brought a blind man to Him, and begged Him to touch him. So He took the blind man by the hand and led him out of the town. And when He had spit on his eyes and put His hands on him, He asked him if he saw anything. And he looked up and said, "I see men like trees, walking." Then He put *His* hands on his eyes again and made him look up. And he was restored and saw everyone clearly. Then He sent him away to his house, saying, "Neither go into the town, nor tell anyone in the town."

a. **He had spit on his eyes and put His hands on him**: Adam Clarke had an interesting perspective on this: "It is likely that this was done merely to *separate* the *eyelids*; as, in certain cases of blindness, they are found always gummed together. It required a *miracle* to restore the *sight*, and this was done in consequence of Christ having laid his hands upon the blind man: it required *no* miracle to *separate* the *eyelids*, and, therefore, *natural means* only were employed - this was done by rubbing them with spittle."

b. **He put His hands on his eyes again**: This is the only "gradual" or "progressive" healing described in the ministry of Jesus. It is another example of the variety of healing methods Jesus used.

> i. Jesus probably choose this method at this time as an illustration to His disciples, showing them then that their spiritual blindness - shown in the previous passage - will be healed, but only gradually.

C. Jesus reveals His mission.

1. (27-30) Peter confesses Jesus as the Messiah.

Now Jesus and His disciples went out to the towns of Caesarea Philippi; and on the road He asked His disciples, saying to them, "Who do men say that I am?" So they answered, "John the Baptist; but some *say*, Elijah; and others, one of the prophets." He said to them, "But who do you say that I am?" Peter answered and said to Him, "You are the Christ." Then He strictly warned them that they should tell no one about Him.

a. **Who do men say that I am?** Jesus did not ask this question because He didn't know who He was or because He had a twisted dependence on the opinion of others. He asked this question as an introduction to a more important follow-up question.

b. **John the Baptist; but some say, Elijah; and others, one of the prophets**: People who thought that Jesus was *John the Baptist* didn't know much about Him, and they didn't know that Jesus and John had ministered at the same time. But both John and **Elijah** were national reformers who stood up to the corrupt rulers of their day.

> i. Perhaps in seeing Jesus as **John the Baptist** or Elijah, people hoped for a political messiah who would overthrow the corrupt powers oppressing Israel.

c. **But who do you say that I am?** It was fine for the disciples to know what *others* thought about Jesus. But Jesus had to ask them, as individuals, what *they* believed about Jesus.

d. **You are the Christ**: Peter knew the opinion of the crowd - though complimentary towards Jesus - wasn't accurate. Jesus was much more than John the Baptist, or Elijah, or a prophet. He was more than a national reformer, more than a miracle worker, more than a prophet. Jesus is **the Christ**, the Messiah.

i. Calling Jesus the Messiah was right on the mark but easily misunderstood. In the thinking of most people in Jesus' day, the Messiah was a political and national superman. "Toward the close of the OT period, the word 'anointed' assumed a special meaning. It denoted the ideal king anointed and empowered by God to deliver his people and establish his righteous kingdom." (Wessel)

2. (31-32a) Jesus reveals His mission plainly: to come and die, and then rise again.

And He began to teach them that the Son of Man must suffer many things, and be rejected by the elders and chief priests and scribes, and be killed, and after three days rise again. He spoke this word openly.

a. **That the Son of Man must suffer many things**: This was the necessary work of the Messiah and it was predicted in passages like Isaiah 53:3-12. He **must** die, and He **must** after His death **rise again**.

i. The suffering and death of Jesus was a **must** because of two great facts: *man's sin* and *God's love*. While His death was the ultimate example of man's sin against God, it was also the supreme expression of God's love to man.

b. **He spoke this word openly**: This was an unbelievable shock to anyone expecting or hoping that Jesus was the national and political messiah. It is as if an American presidential candidate announced toward the end of his campaign that he would go to Washington to be rejected and executed.

i. "A suffering Messiah! Unthinkable! The Messiah was a symbol of strength, not weakness." (Wessel)

ii. "Sometimes the Messiah was thought of as a king of David's line, but more often he was thought of as a great, super-human figure crashing into history to remake the world and in the end to vindicate God's people... The Messiah will be the most destructive conqueror in history, smashing his enemies into utter extinction." (Barclay)

3. (32b-33) Peter rebukes Jesus; Jesus rebukes Peter.

And Peter took Him aside and began to rebuke Him. But when He had turned around and looked at His disciples, He rebuked Peter, saying, "Get behind Me, Satan! For you are not mindful of the things of God, but the things of men."

a. **Peter took Him aside and began to rebuke Him**: Peter's intent was love for Jesus, but he was unwittingly used of Satan. You don't have to be demon possessed for Satan to use you, and we need to be on guard lest we are unwittingly used.

i. Matthew 16:17-19 gives us a little more insight into this passage. We read there that after Peter made the confession of faith recorded in Mark 8:29 (*You are the Christ*), Jesus then *answered and said to him, "Blessed are you, Simon Bar-Jonah, for flesh and blood has not revealed this to you, but My Father who is in heaven."* Jesus went on to further build up Peter after that complimentary word. It's not hard to see Peter following these steps:

- Peter confessed Jesus as the Messiah.
- Jesus complimented Peter, telling him that God revealed this to him.
- Jesus told of His impending suffering, death, and resurrection.
- Peter felt that wasn't right, and he believed that he heard from God.
- Peter rebuked Jesus.

ii. We can infer that if Peter was bold enough to **rebuke** Jesus, he was confident that God told him what was right and that Jesus was wrong. Where it all broke down was that Peter was far too confident in his ability to hear from God.

- What Peter said didn't line up with the Scriptures.
- What Peter said was in contradiction to the spiritual authority over him.

b. **Get behind Me, Satan!** This was a strong rebuke from Jesus, yet entirely appropriate. Though a moment before Peter spoke as a messenger of God, he then spoke as a messenger of **Satan**. Jesus knew there was a satanic purpose in discouraging Him from His ministry on the cross, and Jesus would not allow that purpose to succeed.

i. We can be sure that Peter *was not aware* that he spoke for Satan, just as a moment before he was not aware that he spoke for God. It is often much easier to be a tool of God or of the devil than we want to believe.

c. **You are not mindful of the things of God, but the things of men**: Jesus exposed how Peter came into this satanic way of thinking. He didn't make a deliberate choice to reject God and embrace Satan; he simply let his mind settle on **the things of men** instead of **the things of God**, and Satan took advantage of it.

i. Peter is a perfect example of how a sincere heart coupled with man's thinking can often lead to disaster.

ii. Peter's rebuke of Jesus was evidence of the *leaven* mentioned in Mark 8:15. With his mind on **the things of men**, Peter saw the Messiah only as the embodiment of power and strength, instead of as a suffering servant. Because Peter couldn't handle a suffering Messiah, he rebuked Jesus.

4. (34) In light of His mission, Jesus warns those who want to follow Him.

When He had called the people to *Himself*, with His disciples also, He said to them, "Whoever desires to come after Me, let him deny himself, and take up his cross, and follow Me."

a. **Let him deny himself, and take up his cross**: It was bad enough for the disciples to hear that Jesus would suffer, be rejected, and die on a cross. Now Jesus told them that they had to do the same thing

b. **Deny himself, and take up his cross**: Everybody knew what Jesus meant when He said this. Everyone knew that the cross was an unrelenting instrument of death. The **cross** had no other purpose.

i. The **cross** wasn't about religious ceremonies; it wasn't about traditions and spiritual feelings. The cross was a way to execute people. In these 20 centuries after Jesus, we sanitized and ritualized the cross. How would we receive it if Jesus said, "Walk down death row daily and follow Me"? Taking up your cross wasn't a journey; it was a one-way trip.

ii. "Cross bearing does not refer to some irritation in life. Rather, it involves the way of the cross. The picture is of a man, already condemned, required to carry his cross on the way to the place of execution, as Jesus was required to do." (Wessel)

iii. "Every Christian must be a Crucian, said Luther, and do somewhat more than those monks that made themselves wooden crosses, and carried them on their back continually, making all the world laugh at them." (Trapp)

c. Jesus makes **deny himself** equal with **take up his cross**. The two express the same idea. The cross wasn't about self-promotion or self-affirmation. The person carrying a cross knew they couldn't save themselves.

i. "Denying self is not the same as self-denial. We practice self-denial when, for a good purpose, we occasionally give up things or activities. But we deny self when we surrender ourselves to Christ and determine to obey His will." (Wiersbe)

ii. Denying self means to live as an others-centered person. Jesus was the only person to do this perfectly, but we are to follow in His steps (**and follow Me**). This is following Jesus at its simplest: He carried a cross, and walked down death row; so must those who follow Him.

5. (35-9:1) Why we must take up our cross and follow Jesus.

"**For whoever desires to save his life will lose it, but whoever loses his life for My sake and the gospel's will save it. For what will it profit a man if he gains the whole world, and loses his own soul? Or what will a man give in exchange for his soul? For whoever is ashamed of Me and My words in this adulterous and sinful generation, of him the Son of Man also will be ashamed when He comes in the glory of His Father with the holy angels." And He said to them, "Assuredly, I say to you that there are some standing here who will not taste death till they see the kingdom of God present with power."**

a. **Whoever loses his life for My sake and the gospel's will save it**: We must follow Jesus this way because it is the only way that we will ever find life. It sounds strange to say, "You will never live until you walk down death row with Jesus," but that is the idea. You can't gain resurrection life without dying first.

   i. You don't lose a seed when you plant it, though it seems dead and buried. Instead, you set the seed free to be what it was always intended to be.

b. **What will it profit a man if he gains the whole world, and loses his own soul?** Avoiding the walk down death row with Jesus means that we may gain the **whole world**, and end up losing everything.

   i. Jesus Himself had the opportunity to gain the world by worshipping Satan (Luke 4:5-8), but He found life and victory in obedience instead.

   ii. Amazingly, the people who live this way before Jesus are the ones who are really, genuinely happy. Giving our life to Jesus all the way and living as an others-centered person does not take away from our life, it adds to it.

c. **For whoever is ashamed of Me and My words in this adulterous and sinful generation, of him the Son of Man also will be ashamed**: It isn't easy to walk death row with Jesus. It means that we have to associate ourselves with someone who was despised and executed. Yet if we are **ashamed** of Him, He will be **ashamed** of us.

   i. "If Jesus Christ had come into the world as a mighty and opulent man, clothed with earthly glories and honours, he would have had a multitude of partisans, and most of them *hypocrites*." (Clarke)

ii. Jesus is coming again **in glory**, and if we will rebel against the world, the flesh, and the devil, we will share in the glory.

iii. Most people think of following Jesus as conforming to the establishment. Actually, Jesus called us to rebel against the established order of this world. We are called to rebel against the tyranny of the flesh, against the fear and conformity of the world, against the traditions of man. Jesus encourages a slave rebellion, where the slaves of sin, Satan, and the world rebel against their masters.

d. **Some standing here... will not taste death until they see the kingdom of God present with power**: Walking with Jesus doesn't just mean a life of death and crosses. It also means a life of the power and glory of the kingdom of God. Jesus promised some of His disciples glimpses of that power and glory.

i. "The unveiling of Jesus' glory in the presence of the three disciples corresponds to the assurance that *some will see*." (Lane)

Mark 9 - The Transfiguration

A. Jesus is transfigured.

1. (2-3) Jesus is transfigured before His disciples.

Now after six days Jesus took Peter, James, and John, and led them up on a high mountain apart by themselves; and He was transfigured before them. His clothes became shining, exceedingly white, like snow, such as no launderer on earth can whiten them.

> a. **Peter, James, and John**: Most people assume that Jesus took these three aside on this and other occasions because they were special favorites of the Lord. It could have also been that they were the three most likely to get into trouble, so He kept them close to keep an eye on them.

> b. **Led them up on a high mountain apart by themselves**: What started as a mountain retreat quickly changed as the glory of Jesus shone forth and Jesus was transformed right before the eyes of the disciples (**He was transfigured before them**).

>> i. Matthew said that Jesus' *face shone like the sun* (Matthew 17:2), and both Matthew and Mark used the word **transfigured** to describe what happened to Jesus. For this brief time, Jesus took on an appearance more appropriate for the King of Glory than for a humble man.

> c. **He was transfigured before them**: Mark did his best to describe for us what Jesus looked like - no doubt, through the eyes of Peter. Basically, Jesus' whole appearance shone forth in glorious, bright light - **his clothes became shining** and whiter than anything seen on this earth.

>> i. If we're not careful, we think of the transfiguration as just a bright light shined on Jesus. But this wasn't a light coming on Jesus from the outside. "The word *transfigured* describes a change on the outside that comes from the inside. It is the opposite of 'masquerade,' which is an outward change that does not come from within." (Wiersbe)

ii. This was not a *new* miracle, but the temporary pause of an ongoing miracle. The real miracle was that Jesus, most of the time, could *keep* from displaying His glory. "For Christ to be glorious was almost a less matter than for him to restrain or hide his glory. It is forever his glory that he concealed his glory; and that, though he was rich, for our sakes he became poor." (Spurgeon)

d. **Transfigured before them**: Jesus did this because He just told His disciples that He was going the way of the cross (Mark 8:31) and that spiritually they should follow Him in the way of the cross (Mark 8:34-38). It was easy for them to lose confidence in Jesus after such a negative statement.

i. But now, as Jesus displayed His glory as King over all God's Kingdom, the disciples knew that Jesus knew what He was doing. If He was to suffer, be rejected and killed, He was still in control.

ii. Jesus also dramatically showed that cross bearers would be glory receivers. The *goal* isn't the cross. The cross is the *path* to the goal, and the goal is the glory of God.

2. (4) Elijah and Moses appear with Jesus.

And Elijah appeared to them with Moses, and they were talking with Jesus.

a. **Elijah appeared to them with Moses**: Both **Elijah** and **Moses** represent those who are caught up to God (Jude 9 and 2 Kings 2:11). Moses represents those who die and go to glory, and Elijah represents those who are caught up to heaven without death (as in 1 Thessalonians 4:13-18).

i. They also represent the Law (**Moses**) and the Prophets (**Elijah**). The sum of Old Testament revelation comes to meet with Jesus at the Mount of Transfiguration.

ii. They also figure together in the future fulfillment of prophecy. **Elijah** and **Moses** are likely connected to the witnesses of Revelation 11:3-13.

iii. Right in front of them, the disciples saw evidence of life beyond this life. When they saw Moses and Elijah, they knew that Moses had passed from this world 1,400 years before and Elijah had passed some 900 years before. Yet there they were, alive in glory before them. It gave them confidence in Jesus' claim to resurrection.

iv. It seems that the disciples just knew that this was Elijah and Moses. This shows us that we will know each other when we get to heaven. We won't know *less* in heaven than we do on earth.

b. **They were talking with Jesus**: Elijah and Moses were interested in the outworking of God's plan through Jesus. They spoke about what Jesus *was about to accomplish at Jerusalem* (Luke 9:31).

3. (5-10) Peter's unwise offer to build three tabernacles to honor Jesus, Moses, and Elijah, and the Father's response.

Then Peter answered and said to Jesus, "Rabbi, it is good for us to be here; and let us make three tabernacles: one for You, one for Moses, and one for Elijah"; because he did not know what to say, for they were greatly afraid. And a cloud came and overshadowed them; and a voice came out of the cloud, saying, "This is My beloved Son. Hear Him!" Suddenly, when they had looked around, they saw no one anymore, but only Jesus with themselves. Now as they came down from the mountain, He commanded them that they should tell no one the things they had seen, till the Son of Man had risen from the dead. So they kept this word to themselves, questioning what the rising from the dead meant.

a. **Let us make three tabernacles: one for You, one for Moses, and one for Elijah**: When Peter saw Jesus in His glory, he must have said to himself: "This is good. This is how it should be. Forget this business about suffering, being rejected, and crucified. Let's build some tabernacles so we can live this way with the glorified Jesus all the time."

b. **Because he did not know what to say**: We often get into trouble when we speak like Peter did, not knowing what to say. We also see that Peter spoke out of *fear* (**for they were greatly afraid**). We say many foolish things without thinking and out of fear.

i. "Peter was openhearted, bold, enthusiastic. To my mind, there is something very lovable about Peter; and, in my opinion, we need more Peters in the church of the present day. Though they are rash and impulsive, yet there is fire in them, and there is steam in them, so that they keep us going." (Spurgeon)

ii. Luke tells us that Peter, James, and John were all asleep, and when they awoke they saw Jesus transfigured with Elijah and Moses. "Peter, suddenly awakened from sleep in time to see the glory fade, was garrulous in his terror, as some men are." (Cole)

iii. What Peter said was foolish because he put Jesus on an equal level with Elijah and Moses - one tabernacle for each! But Jesus isn't just another Moses or Elijah, or even a *greater* Moses or Elijah. Jesus is the Son of God.

iv. **For they were greatly afraid**: Being in the presence of God's glory isn't necessarily a pleasant experience - especially when we are like

Peter, not really glorifying God. Sometimes the glory of God is shown in the way that He corrects us.

c. **And a cloud came and overshadowed them**: This is a familiar cloud, the cloud of God's glory traditionally known as the *Shekinah*.

- It was the pillar of cloud that stood by Israel in the wilderness (Exodus 13:21-22).

- It was the cloud of glory that God spoke to Israel from (Exodus 16:10).

- It was from this cloud of glory that God met with Moses and others (Exodus 19:9, 24:15-18, Numbers 11:25, 12:5, 16:42).

- It was the cloud of glory that stood by the door of the Tabernacle (Exodus 33:9-10).

- It was from this cloud that God appeared to the High Priest in the Holy Place inside the veil (Leviticus 16:2).

- It was from this cloud God appeared to Solomon when the temple was dedicated, so filling the temple that the priests could not continue (1 Kings 8:10-11, 2 Chronicles 5:13-14).

- It was the cloud of Ezekiel's vision, filling the temple of God with the brightness of His glory (Ezekiel 10:4).

- It was the cloud of glory that overshadowed Mary when she conceived Jesus by the power of the Holy Spirit (Luke 1:35).

- It was the cloud of glory that received Jesus into heaven at His ascension (Acts 1:9).

- It was the cloud that will display the glory of Jesus Christ when He returns in triumph to this earth (Luke 21:27).

d. **This is My beloved Son. Hear Him!** The voice from the cloud of glory made it clear that Jesus was not on the same level as Elijah and Moses. He is the **beloved Son** - so **Hear Him!**

i. This word from heaven answered the disciples' doubts after the revelation of the suffering Messiah. It assured them that the plan was all right with God the Father also.

e. **He commanded them that they should tell no one the things they had seen, till the Son of Man had risen from the dead**: After it was all over, Peter, John and James **kept this word to themselves** - after all, who would believe them?

i. But the event left a lasting impression on these men. Peter related what happened in 2 Peter 1:16-18, how the voice from God saying,

"**This is My beloved Son. Hear Him!**" still rang in his ears, confirming who Jesus was.

ii. As impressive as this experience was, it in itself did not change the lives of the disciples as much as being born again did. Being born again by the Spirit of God is the great miracle, the greatest display of the glory of God ever.

iii. "It is a better thing for a man to live near to Christ, and to enjoy his presence, than it would be for him to be overshadowed with a bright cloud, and to hear the divine Father himself speaking out of it." (Spurgeon)

4. (11-13) The problem of Elijah coming first: a question based on Malachi 4:5-6.

And they asked Him, saying, "Why do the scribes say that Elijah must come first?" Then He answered and told them, "Indeed, Elijah is coming first and restores all things. And how is it written concerning the Son of Man, that He must suffer many things and be treated with contempt? But I say to you that Elijah has also come, and they did to him whatever they wished, as it is written of him."

a. **Why do the scribes say**: The coming of Elijah before the Messiah was clearly prophesied in Malachi 4:5-6. So the disciples wondered, "If Jesus is the Messiah, then where is Elijah?"

b. **Elijah does come first**: Jesus told them that the Elijah prophecy in Malachi would indeed be fulfilled. Though Jesus did not say this here, the prophecy of Elijah's coming had to do with Jesus' *second* coming, not His first, and Elijah would likely return in connection with one of the two witnesses as Revelation 11:2-13.

i. **How is it written concerning the Son of Man, that He must suffer**: Jesus here drew attention to the contrast between His first and second comings. The disciples were well aware of the prophecies concerning the glory of the Messiah; Jesus asked them to consider the prophecies concerning His suffering and that He **must be treated with contempt**.

c. **But I say to you that Elijah has also come**: While it was true that Elijah was yet to come in reference to the second coming of Jesus, there was also a sense in which **Elijah has also come** - in the person of John the Baptist.

i. John was not a reincarnation of Elijah, but he did minister in the role and spirit of Elijah. John the Baptist was a type or a picture of Elijah.

B. Jesus casts out a difficult demon from a boy.

1. (14-18) The disciples are unable to cast out a demon.

And when He came to the disciples, He saw a great multitude around them, and scribes disputing with them. Immediately, when they saw Him, all the people were greatly amazed, and running to *Him,* greeted Him. And He asked the scribes, "What are you discussing with them?" Then one of the crowd answered and said, "Teacher, I brought You my son, who has a mute spirit. And wherever it seizes him, it throws him down; he foams at the mouth, gnashes his teeth, and becomes rigid. So I spoke to Your disciples, that they should cast it out, but they could not."

a. **Scribes disputing with them**: From the context, it is reasonable to assume that scribes criticized the disciples for their inability to help the demon-possessed boy. "One wonders why these same scribes, instead of further embarrassing the crestfallen disciples before the crowd, did not set about exorcising the demon themselves, as a proof of orthodoxy." (Cole)

i. This kind of conflict was exactly what Peter wanted to avoid by staying up on the mountain of transfiguration (Mark 9:5). But it couldn't be that way. They simply had to come down off the mountain and deal with what they found.

ii. "He found disputing scribes, a distracted father, a demon-possessed boy, and defeated disciples... He silenced the scribes, He comforted the father, He healed the boy, He instructed the disciples." (Morgan)

b. **A mute spirit**: In the eyes of contemporary Jewish exorcists, this was a particularly difficult - if not impossible - demon to cast out. This was because they believed that you had to learn a demon's name before you could cast it out, and if a demon made someone mute, you could never learn his name.

c. **Wherever it seizes him, it throws him down; he foams at the mouth, gnashes his teeth, and becomes rigid**: The boy displayed signs that many today would regard as evidence of epilepsy, but Jesus perceived that they were caused by demonic possession. Surely, *some* of whom we diagnose as physically or mentally ill today are actually demon possessed.

i. "Jesus addresses the demon as a separate being from the boy as he often does. This makes it difficult to believe that Jesus was merely indulging popular belief in a superstition. He evidently regards the demon as the cause in this case of the boy's misfortune." (Robertson)

d. **That they should cast it out, but they could not**: This particular case of demon possession was too much for the disciples, though Jesus had given them authority over unclean spirits (Mark 6:7).

i. Apparently some demons are stronger - that is, more stubborn or intimidating than others. Ephesians 6:12 seems to describe different ranks of demonic beings, and it isn't a stretch to think that some ranks might be more powerful than others are.

2. (19-27) Jesus delivers the boy.

He answered him and said, "O faithless generation, how long shall I be with you? How long shall I bear with you? Bring him to Me." Then they brought him to Him. And when he saw Him, immediately the spirit convulsed him, and he fell on the ground and wallowed, foaming at the mouth. So He asked his father, "How long has this been happening to him?" And he said, "From childhood. And often he has thrown him both into the fire and into the water to destroy him. But if You can do anything, have compassion on us and help us." Jesus said to him, "If you can believe, all things *are* possible to him who believes." Immediately the father of the child cried out and said with tears, "Lord, I believe; help my unbelief!" When Jesus saw that the people came running together, He rebuked the unclean spirit, saying to it, "Deaf and dumb spirit, I command you, come out of him and enter him no more!" Then *the spirit* cried out, convulsed him greatly, and came out of him. And he became as one dead, so that many said, "He is dead." But Jesus took him by the hand and lifted him up, and he arose.

a. **O faithless generation, how long shall I be with you?** When Jesus describes a **faithless generation**, He might refer to the contentious scribes, to the desperate father, or to the unsuccessful disciples.

b. **And when he saw Him, immediately the spirit convulsed him, and he fell on the ground**: When Jesus came near, the demon inside the boy knows that his time was short. He wanted to do as much damage as he could before he left.

c. **But if you can do anything**: The man seemed unsure if Jesus could do anything. But the "if" wasn't in regard to what Jesus could do. The "if" was in regard to the man's faith. So Jesus told him, **if you can believe, all things are possible to him who believes**. When we trust God as true and all His promises as true, **all things** He promises **are possible**.

d. **Lord, I believe; help my unbelief**: The poor father in this account was challenged by Jesus' exhortation for faith. He did believe in Jesus' power to deliver his boy - after all, why else would he have come to Jesus? But he also recognized his doubts. So, he tearfully plead with Jesus: **Lord, I believe; help my unbelief!**

i. In this case, the man's **unbelief** was not a rebellion against or a rejection of God's promise. He did not *deny* God's promise; he *desired* it. However, it just seemed too good to be true. Thus he said, "**help my unbelief!**"

ii. **Help my unbelief** is something a man can only say by *faith*. "While men have no faith, they are unconscious of their unbelief; but, as soon as they get a little faith, then they begin to be conscious of the greatness of their unbelief." (Spurgeon)

e. **Then the spirit cried out, convulsed him greatly, and came out of him**: Jesus had no difficulty whatsoever in dealing with the demon, even though the demon made a final display of his terrible strength. Knowing he must leave, the demon did the most damage he could before he left. But it was not lasting damage.

3. (28-29) Why were the disciples unsuccessful?

And when He had come into the house, His disciples asked Him privately, "Why could we not cast it out?" So He said to them, "This kind can come out by nothing but prayer and fasting."

a. **Why could we not cast it out?** Jesus revealed the reason for their weakness: it was due to a lack of **prayer and fasting**.

b. **This kind can come out by nothing but prayer and fasting**: It isn't that **prayer and fasting** make us more worthy to cast out demons. It is that prayer and fasting draw us closer to the heart of God, and they put us more in line with His power. They are an expression of our total dependence on Him.

i. Jesus already gave them the authority to cast out demons (Mark 3:14-15). Yet, "The authority that Jesus had given them was effective only if exercised by faith, but faith must be cultivated through spiritual discipline and devotion." (Wiersbe)

ii. This total dependence on God is the remedy for many spiritual problems. To be disappointed in yourself is to have trusted in yourself.

C. On to Jerusalem.

1. (30-32) Jesus reminds His disciples of His mission.

Then they departed from there and passed through Galilee, and He did not want anyone to know *it*. For He taught His disciples and said to them, "The Son of Man is being betrayed into the hands of men, and they will kill Him. And after He is killed, He will rise the third day." But they did not understand this saying, and were afraid to ask Him.

a. **He did not want anyone to know it**: This was probably because Jesus did not want the Galilean multitude to cling to Him and to hinder this important trip to Jerusalem.

b. **The Son of Man is being delivered into the hands of men, and they will kill Him**: Jesus clearly told His disciples of this destiny back in Mark 8:31. Now, as they departed from Galilee towards Jerusalem, they headed towards the destiny Jesus spoke of.

c. **But they did not understand this saying**: The disciples couldn't "process" what Jesus said about His destiny in Jerusalem - to die and then rise again. Unfortunately, they **were afraid to ask**.

2. (33-34) The dispute on the road.

Then He came to Capernaum. And when He was in the house He asked them, "What was it you disputed among yourselves on the road?" But they kept silent, for on the road they had disputed among themselves who *would be the* greatest.

a. **They had disputed among themselves who would be the greatest**: It seems that this was the favorite debating topic among the disciples. They all counted on Jesus to take over the world as King Messiah, and the debate was about who was most worthy to be Jesus' chief associate.

b. **But they kept silent**: This was an embarrassed silence. It showed that they were ashamed of their obsession with greatness. It was a healthy sense of shame and proved that some of the message of Jesus was sinking into their hearts.

3. (35-37) True greatness in the kingdom of God.

And He sat down, called the twelve, and said to them, "If anyone desires to be first, he shall be last of all and servant of all." Then He took a little child and set him in the midst of them. And when He had taken him in His arms, He said to them, "Whoever receives one of these little children in My name receives Me; and whoever receives Me, receives not Me but Him who sent Me."

a. **He sat down**: This was important because by sitting down, Jesus showed that he was going to teach. "When a Rabbi was teaching as a Rabbi, as a master teaches his scholars and disciples, when he was really making a pronouncement, he sat to teach. Jesus deliberately took up the position of a Rabbi teaching his pupils before he spoke." (Barclay)

b. **If anyone desires to be first, he shall be last of all and servant of all**: The question at hand was, "Who would be the greatest?" Jesus could have answered the question, "Hey dummies - *I'm* the greatest." But Jesus did not put the focus on Himself. For an example of greatness, Jesus put forth the **last** and the **servant**.

i. Of course, Jesus *is* the greatest in the kingdom. So when He said **last** and **servant**, He was really describing Himself - and He accurately expressed His nature. He was truly **first** yet made Himself **last of all and servant of all** for our sake.

ii. Jesus challenged us to be **last of all**. The desire to be praised and to gain recognition should be foreign to a follower of Jesus. Jesus wants us to embrace **last** as a choice, allowing others to be preferred before us, and not only because we are *forced* to be last.

iii. Jesus challenges us to be the **servant of all**. In the worldly idea of power, a great man is distinguished by how many people serve him. In ancient China, it was fashionable for wealthy men to grow their fingernails so long that their hands were unusable for basic tasks. This demonstrated that they did not need to do *anything* for themselves; a servant was always there to wait on them. The world may think of this as greatness, but God does not. Jesus declared that true greatness is shown not by how many serve you, but by how many you serve.

iv. "It was not that Jesus abolished ambition. Rather he recreated and sublimated ambition. For the ambition to rule he substituted the ambition to serve. For the ambition to have things done for us he substituted the ambition to do things for others." (Barclay)

c. **He took a little child and set him in the midst of them**: Jesus drew their attention to His nature by presenting a child as an example. In that day, children were regarded more as property than individuals. It was understood that they were to be seen and not heard. Jesus said that the way we receive people regarded like **children** shows how we would receive Him (**whoever receives one of these little children in My name receives Me**).

i. Children are not threatening. We aren't afraid of meeting a 5-year old in a dark alley. When we have a tough, intimidating presence, we aren't like Jesus.

ii. Children are not good at deceiving. They don't do a very good job at fooling their parents. When we are good at hiding ourselves and deceiving others, we aren't like Jesus.

d. **Whoever receives one of these little children in My name receives Me**: Because Jesus is **last of all and servant of all** and like a child, when we honor and receive a child - or someone who is a servant like Jesus - we honor and receive Jesus Himself.

4. (38-42) True greatness isn't cliquish; it has an inclusive instinct.

Now John answered Him, saying, "Teacher, we saw someone who does not follow us casting out demons in Your name, and we forbade him

because he does not follow us." But Jesus said, "Do not forbid him, for no one who works a miracle in My name can soon afterward speak evil of Me. For he who is not against us is on our side. For whoever gives you a cup of water to drink in My name, because you belong to Christ, assuredly, I say to you, he will by no means lose his reward. But whoever causes one of these little ones who believe in Me to stumble, it would be better for him if a millstone were hung around his neck, and he were thrown into the sea."

a. **Teacher, we saw someone**: It had to frustrate Jesus' disciples that these other followers of Jesus successfully cast out demons when they had just failed (Mark 9:18). No wonder John wanted them to stop.

i. "We may therefore safely imagine that this was either one of John the Baptist's disciples, who, at his master's command, had believed in Jesus, or one of the *seventy*, whom Christ had sent out, Luke 10:1-7, who, after he had fulfilled his commission, had retired from accompanying the other disciples; but as he still held fast his faith in Christ and walked in good conscience, the influence of his Master still continued with him, so that he could cast out demons as well as the other disciples." (Clarke)

b. **For he who is not against us is on our side**: There are many that may be wrong in some aspect of their presentation or teaching, yet they still set forth Jesus in some manner. Let God deal with them. Those who are not *against* a Biblical Jesus are still *for* Him, at least in some way.

i. Paul saw many men preaching Jesus from many motives, some of them evil - yet he could rejoice that Christ was preached (Philippians 1:15-18).

c. **For whoever gives you a cup of water to drink in My name**: Because of this principle of unity, it is appropriate to show kindness to others in the name of Jesus. Even **a cup of water**, if given in the nature of Jesus, will be rewarded.

i. Nothing could seem more petty than giving a mere **cup of water**. But God remembers the heart, not only the gift itself.

d. **Whoever causes one of these little ones who believe in Me to stumble**: If a small act of kindness towards others done in Jesus' name will be eternally remembered, so will any cause for stumbling. And the punishment is severe: **it would be *better* for him if a millstone were hung around his neck, and he were thrown into the sea.**

i. In that day, there were two different sizes of millstones. The smaller one was used by a woman to grind a small amount of grain. The larger one was turned by a donkey to grind a larger amount of grain. Jesus refered to the larger kind of **millstone** here.

ii. Some Christians think nothing of drawing young, weak Christians into their own little squabbles and divisions. They themselves emerge without much damage, but the **little ones** they brought with them into the squabble often end up shipwrecked.

5. (43-48) The urgency to enter God's kingdom.

If your hand causes you to sin, cut it off. It is better for you to enter into life maimed, rather than having two hands, to go to hell, into the fire that shall never be quenched; where

'Their worm does not die,
And the fire is not quenched.'

And if your foot causes you to sin, cut it off. It is better for you to enter life lame, rather than having two feet, to be cast into hell, into the fire that shall never be quenched; where

'Their worm does not die,
And the fire is not quenched.'

And if your eye causes you to sin, pluck it out. It is better for you to enter the kingdom of God with one eye, rather than having two eyes, to be cast into hell fire; where 'Their worm does not die, and the fire is not quenched.'

a. **If your hand makes you sin, cut it off**: Tragically, some have taken these words of Jesus in a sense He did not intend and have cut off their hands or have mutilated themselves in some other way in a mistaken battle against sin.

i. The problem with taking Jesus' words literally here is that bodily mutilation does not go *far enough* in controlling sin. Sin is more a matter of the heart than of any particular limb or organ, and if I cut off my right hand, my left is still ready to sin. If I completely dismember my body, I can still sin in my mind and in my heart.

ii. "This was not a demand for physical self-mutilation, but in the strongest manner possible Jesus speaks of the costliest sacrifices." (Lane)

b. **It is better for you to enter into life maimed, rather than having two hands, to go to hell**: With this exhortation, Jesus tried to correct a big misunderstanding on the part of the disciples. They thought of the kingdom mainly in terms of reward, not in terms of sacrifice.

i. Essentially, Jesus restates what Mark recorded in 8:34-35: that if we try to save our lives, we will lose them, and to follow Jesus means to pick up our cross and follow Him.

c. **To go to hell, into the fire that shall never be quenched**: The word **hell** is an ancient Greek translation of the Hebrew word for "Valley of Hinnom." This was a place outside Jerusalem's walls desecrated by Molech worship and human sacrifice, thus turned into the dump where rubbish and refuse were burned. The smoldering fires and festering worms made it a graphic and effective picture of the fate of the damned.

i. This place is also called the "lake of fire" in Revelation 20:13-15, a place prepared for the devil and his angels (Matthew 25:41).

ii. **That shall never be quenched**: "A child with a spoon may sooner empty the sea than the damned accomplish their misery. A river of brimstone is not consumed by burning." (Trapp)

d. **Where their worm does not die**: "It seems that every one has *his* worm, his *peculiar remorse* for the evils he did, and for the grace he rejected; while the *fire*, the state of excruciating torment, is *common* to all. Reader! May the living God save *thee* from this *worm*, and from this *fire!*" (Clarke)

i. "This worm (say divines) is only a continual remorse and furious reflection of the soul upon its own willful folly, and now woeful misery. Oh, consider this before thy friends be scrambling for thy goods, worms for thy body, devils for thy soul." (Trapp)

ii. The message of Jesus was clear: knowing how terrible hell is, it is worth any sacrifice to avoid. Therefore, we cannot think of the kingdom of God just in the context of reward; we must also think in terms of sacrifice.

6. (49-50) Jesus speaks of salt and fire.

"For everyone will be seasoned with fire, and every sacrifice will be seasoned with salt. Salt *is* good, but if the salt loses its flavor, how will you season it? Have salt in yourselves, and have peace with one another."

a. **For everyone will be seasoned with fire**: Jesus declared that His followers will be **seasoned with fire** and that **every sacrifice will be seasoned with salt**. The salt must retain its **flavor**, and this will bring **peace** among us.

b. **Everyone will be seasoned with fire, and every sacrifice will be seasoned with salt**: This passage has led to many different interpretations.

i. The first main interpretation is that **fire** refers to tribulation and suffering; these things accompany the "living sacrifice" (Romans 12:1) of the disciple. Since Old Testament sacrifices always included salt

(Leviticus 2:13), Jesus is saying, "Just as every sacrifice under the law required salt, so the living sacrifice My followers bring to Me must be seasoned with suffering and tribulations."

ii. The other main interpretation is that **fire** refers to the Holy Spirit. As His presence in our lives "seasons" us, it purifies, preserves, and adds flavor to our lives, thus making our "living sacrifice" acceptable to God.

Mark 10 - Jesus Teaches on Marriage, Riches, and Service

A. Marriage and divorce.

1. (1-2) A test from the Pharisees: **is it lawful for a man to divorce his wife?**

Then He arose from there and came to the region of Judea by the other side of the Jordan. And multitudes gathered to Him again, and as He was accustomed, He taught them again. The Pharisees came and asked Him, "Is it lawful for a man to divorce *his* wife?" testing Him.

a. **Is it lawful for a man to divorce his wife?** Divorce was a controversial topic in Jesus' day, with two main schools of thought centered around two of its most famous proponents. The first was the school of Rabbi Hillel (a lenient and popular view) and the school of Rabbi Shammai (a strict and unpopular view).

b. **Is it lawful for a man to divorce his wife?** The real point of the Pharisees' question is made clear by Matthew's account: *Is it lawful for a man to divorce his wife for just any reason?* (Matthew 19:3) If the question is, "**is it lawful?**," then **lawful** is understood by *for just any reason*.

i. The debate centers around the Mosaic law that gave permission for divorce in Deuteronomy 24:1: *When a man takes a wife and marries her, and it happens that she finds no favor in his eyes because he has found some uncleanness in her, and he writes her a certificate of divorce, puts it in her hand, and sends her out of his house.* The debate among the rabbis tried to answer the question "What constitutes *uncleanness?*"

ii. Rabbi Shammai understood that *uncleanness* meant sexual immorality and said that was the only valid reason for divorce. But Rabbi Hillel understood *uncleanness* to mean *any* sort of discretion, even to the point of burning the breakfast being valid grounds for divorce.

iii. William Barclay described the teaching of Rabbi Hillel on divorce and the term *uncleanness* in Deuteronomy 24:1, "They said that it could mean if the wife spoiled a dish of food, if she spun in the streets, if she talked to a strange man, if she spoke disrespectfully of her husband's relations in his hearing, if she was a brawling woman (who was defined as a woman whose voice could be heard in the next house). Rabbi Akiba even went the length of saying that it meant if a man found a woman who was fairer in his eyes than his wife was."

c. **Testing Him**: The Pharisees tried to get Jesus to speak against Moses or against popular thought; they hoped to catch Him in a trap.

2. (3-9) Jesus emphasizes marriage and God's plan in marriage.

And He answered and said to them, "What did Moses command you?" They said, "Moses permitted *a man* to write a certificate of divorce, and to dismiss *her."* And Jesus answered and said to them, "Because of the hardness of your heart he wrote you this precept. But from the beginning of the creation, God 'made them male and female.' 'For this reason a man shall leave his father and mother and be joined to his wife, and the two shall become one flesh'; so then they are no longer two, but one flesh. Therefore what God has joined together, let not man separate."

a. **What did Moses command you?** Jesus emphasized the heart of the matter in Deuteronomy 24:1. Moses did not **command** divorce; Moses **permitted** it. This went against the teaching of Rabbi Hillel, who taught that it was a *righteous duty* to divorce your wife if she displeased you in any way.

i. The rabbis of that day had a saying, "If a man has a bad wife, it is a religious duty to divorce her." Jesus went against this way of thinking.

b. **Because of the hardness of your heart he wrote you this precept**: The Mosaic law granting divorce was a concession to the **hardness of your heart**. It was never commanded by God but permitted because of the **hardness** of the offending party (in the cruelty of their unfaithfulness to their spouse). It was also permitted because of the **hardness** of the offended party (being unable to perfectly forgive and restore a damaged relationship).

i. The law of Deuteronomy 24:1 was really given as a *protection* to the divorced wife. "Moses permitted divorce providing a certificate of divorce was given to the wife... Its primary function was to provide a degree of protection for the woman who had been repudiated by her husband." (Lane)

c. **But from the beginning of the creation**: Jesus now transitioned from a talk about *divorce* to a talk about *marriage*. The problem was not that they did not understand the law about divorce. The problem was that they did not understand what God said about *marriage*.

i. This emphasis on marriage rather than divorce is a wise approach for anyone interested in keeping a marriage together. Divorce cannot be seen as an option when things are hard. Marriage is like a mirror; it reflects what we put into it. If someone has divorce readily in his or her mind as a convenient option, divorce will be much more likely.

ii. **From the beginning**: It's striking that Jesus took us back to the beginning to learn about marriage. Today many want to say, "We live in different times" or "The rules are different today" or "We need a modern understanding." Yet Jesus knew that the answers were in going back to the beginning.

d. **From the beginning of the creation, God made them male and female**: God's real purpose for marriage is not fulfilled in divorce but only in seeing God's original plan for marriage. In saying, "**God made them**," Jesus asserted God's ownership over marriage; it is God's institution, not man's, so *His* rules apply.

e. **And the two shall become one flesh**: By bringing the issue back to the foundation of marriage, Jesus made it plain that couples must forsake their singleness (**a man shall leave his father and mother**) and come together in a **one flesh** relationship that is both a fact (**they are**) and a goal (**shall become**).

i. The term **joined to his wife** has the idea of *gluing two things together*. "Be glued to her... A husband ought to be as firm to his wife as to himself." (Trapp)

ii. The term Jesus uses for **joined together** is literally *yoked together*. Like two animals yoked together, couples must work together and head the same way to really be joined the way God wants them to be joined.

iii. Here there is a new and overriding unity. The bond between a husband and wife should be even stronger than the bond between parent and child. The marriage bond should be stronger than the blood-bond. "And the law of God was not, that a man should forsake his wife whenever he had a mind to it, but that he should rather forsake his father and mother than his wife; loving his wife as his own body." (Poole)

iv. "Not only meaning that they should be considered as *one* body, but also as two souls in one body, with a complete union of interests, and an indissoluble partnership of life and fortune, comfort and support, desires and inclinations, joys and sorrows." (Clarke)

f. **What God has joined together**: Next, Jesus reminded the Pharisees that marriage is spiritually binding before God. Marriage is not merely a social contract, and as God has joined He will keep together.

i. In using the terms **joined together** and **separate**, Jesus reminded us that divorce is really like an amputation. Sometimes in the most extreme circumstances, amputation may be the right thing to do. But the patient must first have a diagnosis worthy of such an extreme solution.

3. (10-12) Jesus clarifies the point for His disciples.

In the house His disciples also asked Him again about the same *matter*. So He said to them, "Whoever divorces his wife and marries another commits adultery against her. And if a woman divorces her husband and marries another, she commits adultery."

a. **His disciples also asked Him again about the same matter**: This is not a 1-verse teaching of all there is to know about divorce and remarriage. Jesus clearly followed up His remarks made earlier in the chapter, where He indicated that God *did* permit (not command) divorce in the case of sexual immorality. Here, Jesus answered the question, "Then what about a divorce gained on *other* grounds?"

b. **Whoever divorces his wife and marries another commits adultery against her**: We can only understand this passage by taking into account *the whole counsel of God* (Acts 20:27). In Matthew's more complete recording of this teaching, he noted how Jesus said, *"And I say to you, whoever divorces his wife, except for sexual immorality, and marries another, commits adultery; and whoever marries her who is divorced commits adultery"* (Matthew 19:9). With this answer, Jesus interpreted the meaning of the word *uncleanness* in Deuteronomy 24:1, showing that divorce (and the freedom to remarry) was only permitted in the case of *sexual immorality*.

i. The ancient Greek word for *sexual immorality* is *porneia*. It is a broad word and it covers a wide span of sexual impropriety. One may be guilty of *porneia* without actually having consummated an act of adultery.

ii. To this permission for divorce, Paul added the case of abandonment by an unbelieving spouse (1 Corinthians 7:15).

iii. Note that incompatibility, not loving each other anymore, brutality, and misery are not grounds for divorce, though they may be proper grounds for a separation and consequent celibacy within marriage.

c. **Commits adultery against her**: The reason why a person who does not have a legitimate divorce **commits adultery** upon remarrying (as well as their new spouse) is because they *are not* divorced in the eyes of God. Since their old marriage is still valid, they are actually guilty of bigamy and adultery.

i. We must come to grips with the fact that marriage, as a promise made to God, our spouse and the world, is a binding promise, and cannot be broken at our own discretion. There are certain cases where God allows the promise to be dissolved, but it is up to God and not us.

d. **If a woman divorces her husband and marries another, she commits adultery**: This statement of Jesus shows why it is important to take the *whole counsel of God* on any given topic. If this were the only passage on divorce and remarriage in the Bible, then we should say that if anyone divorces for any reason, they then commit adultery and therefore God never permits remarriage in the case of divorce. But taking the *whole counsel of God* into account, it is impossible to say this.

i. There are some that neglect the *whole counsel of God* and say that God never allows remarriage after divorce. But when we see what the entire Bible says on the subject, we see that if a divorce is made on Biblical grounds (adultery or abandonment by an unbelieving spouse), there is *full right* to remarry.

ii. If a divorce is not based on Biblical grounds - the kind of **divorce** Jesus referred to here - then there is no right to remarry. This is because as far as God is concerned, *the marriage is still together*, and to marry another would be **adultery**.

iii. This means that as God looks down from heaven, He does not have three categories: single, married, and divorced. He has two categories: single and married. You are either bound under a marriage vow or you are not. If you are bound, you can't marry another. If you are not bound, you are free to marry in the Lord. Understanding the *whole counsel of God* on this subject frees people from the stigma of "divorced" in the church.

4. (13-16) Jesus blesses the children and uses them as an example of how we must receive the kingdom of God.

Then they brought little children to Him, that He might touch them; but the disciples rebuked those who brought *them*. But when Jesus saw

it, He was greatly displeased and said to them, "Let the little children come to Me, and do not forbid them; for of such is the kingdom of God. Assuredly, I say to you, whoever does not receive the kingdom of God as a little child will by no means enter it." And He took them up in His arms, put *His* hands on them, and blessed them.

a. **They brought little children to Him**: The ancient Greek word used for **brought** (*prosphero*) suggests that they brought their children to Jesus for dedication. "The word is commonly used of sacrifices, and suggests here the idea of *dedication.*" (Bruce)

b. **Let the little children come to Me**: Children love to come to Jesus, and it says something about Him that children loved Him and that He loved children. Children don't love mean, sour people.

c. **The disciples rebuked those who brought them**: Because children love to come to Jesus, we should never block the way - or fail to provide them a way. We know more about Jesus than the women of Judea did. Is there any good reason for us to not bring our own children to Jesus?

i. This is a duty for children's ministry workers and especially for *parents.* The prayers and words of a parent can mean so much in the salvation of a child. Long into his adult life, Charles Spurgeon recalled the prayers of his mother for him: "Then came a mother's prayer, and some of the words of a mother's prayer we shall never forget, even when our hair is grey. I remember on one occasion her praying thus: 'Now, Lord, if my children go on in their sins, it will not be from ignorance that they perish, and my soul must bear a swift witness against them at the day of judgment if they lay not hold of Christ.' That thought of a mother's bearing swift witness against me, pierced my conscience and stirred my heart."

ii. It is especially important to bring children to Jesus when we remember they have a whole life in front of them to serve God with. "Will you be very angry if I say that a boy is more worth saving than a man? It is infinite mercy on God's part to save those who are seventy; for what good can they now do with the [burnt] end of their lives? When we get to be fifty or sixty, we are almost worn out, and if we have spent all our early days with the devil, what remains for God? But these dear boys and girls - there is something to be made out of them. If now they yield themselves to Christ they may have a long, happy, and holy day before them in which they may serve God with all their hearts. Who knows what glory God may have of them? Heathen lands may call them blessed. Whole nations may be enlightened by them." (Spurgeon)

d. He took them up in His arms, put His hands on them, and blessed them: Jesus simply yet powerfully **blessed them**. The ancient Greek verb is emphatic, literally meaning to *fervently bless*.

i. How could children receive such a blessing from Jesus? Because children can receive the blessing of Jesus without trying to make themselves worthy of it or pretending they do not need it. We need to receive God's blessing the same way.

e. For of such is the kingdom of God: Children are not only for blessing; they are also examples of how we must enter the kingdom with a child*like* faith, not with a child*ish* faith. We must come to God with a faith that trusts God just like a little child trusts his father - and leave all the problems up to daddy.

i. The emphasis isn't that children are humble and innocent, because sometimes they aren't. But the emphasis is on the fact that children will **receive** and don't feel they have to *earn* everything they get. Children are in a place where often all they can do is **receive**. They don't refuse gifts out of self-sufficient pride. So we must **receive the kingdom of God as a little child** - because we surely will **by no means enter it** by what we *do* or *earn*.

B. Jesus teaches on riches.

1. (17-18) An eager man questions Jesus.

Now as He was going out on the road, one came running, knelt before Him, and asked Him, "Good Teacher, what shall I do that I may inherit eternal life?" So Jesus said to him, "Why do you call Me good? No one *is* good but One, *that is,* God."

a. **Good Teacher**: This title was never applied to other Rabbis in Jesus' day because it implied sinlessness, a complete goodness. Jesus and everyone else recognized that He was being called by a unique title.

i. "There is no instance in the whole Talmud of a rabbi being addressed as 'Good Master.'" (Plummer, cited in Geldenhuys) Only God was called *good* by ancient rabbis.

b. **Why do you call Me good?** This was not Jesus denying His deity. Instead, He invited the young man to reflect upon it. It is as if Jesus said, "do you really know what you are saying when you **call Me good?**"

c. **What shall I do that I may inherit eternal life?** The focus of the man's question is **what shall I *do***. He thought eternal life was a matter of earning and deserving, not of relationship. As he bowed down on his knees in front of Jesus, the mere closeness of that relationship made him closer to salvation than anything he could **do**. He didn't want Jesus to be his savior; he wanted Jesus to show him the way to be his own savior.

> i. The man really didn't know who *he* was also. He thought that he was righteous and didn't really know the kind of person he was. When you don't know who Jesus really is, you probably don't know who you are either. And knowing Jesus comes first.

2. (19-22) Jesus' counsel to the young man.

"You know the commandments: 'Do not commit adultery,' 'Do not murder,' 'Do not steal,' 'Do not bear false witness,' 'Do not defraud,' 'Honor your father and your mother.'" And he answered and said to Him, "Teacher, all these things I have kept from my youth." Then Jesus, looking at him, loved him, and said to him, "One thing you lack: Go your way, sell whatever you have and give to the poor, and you will have treasure in heaven; and come, take up the cross, and follow Me." But he was sad at this word, and went away sorrowful, for he had great possessions.

a. **You know the commandments**: Being a Jew, this man knew the commandments. Jesus was careful to quote to him only those commandments from what is often called the second table of the law, addressing how we treat one another.

> i. Each one of these commandments is pure, just, and good. The world would be a much better place if everyone lived by just the five commandments Jesus mentioned here.

b. **Teacher, all these things I have kept from my youth**: In his reply, this ruler said of himself that he had kept all these commandments, and that he has done so since his youth. This was *possible* according to the way these commandments were commonly interpreted but *impossible* according to the true meaning of God for these commandments.

> i. In Philippians 3:6, Paul said he thought he had kept all the commandments as a religious Jew. He wrote of his thinking at that time that he was *concerning the righteousness which is in the law,* [he was] *blameless.*

> ii. Yet in the Sermon on the Mount, Jesus gave us the real meaning of the law - it goes to the heart, not just to actions. You can have a heart filled with adultery even if you never commit it; a heart filled with murder even if you never do it; a heart that steals even if you never steal. God looks at the heart as well as the actions.

> iii. The man *should* have responded, "There is no way I have kept or can keep the law of God completely. *I need a savior.*"

c. **Then Jesus, looking at him, loved him, and said to him**: Jesus was filled with loving compassion for this man because his life was so empty. He had climbed to the top of the ladder of success, only to find his ladder leaned against the wrong building.

d. **One thing you lack**: Instead of challenging the man's fulfillment of the law (which Jesus had every right to do), Jesus instead took him further down his own path. "So you want to find fulfillment and salvation by *doing* for God? Then here, *do* it all." Jesus wanted the man to see the futility of finding fulfillment or salvation through *doing*, but the man wouldn't see it.

i. He also did not choose to love God more than his wealth, even though Jesus specifically promised him *treasure in heaven*. The man was more interested in the earthly treasure of men than in God's heavenly treasures. This man was essentially an idolater. Wealth was his god instead, the true God of the Bible. He put money first.

e. **Come, take up the cross, and follow Me**: This man, like all men by nature, had an orientation towards a works-righteousness; he asked, "**what shall I *do***." If we really want to do the works of God, it must begin with believing on Jesus, whom the Father has sent (John 6:29).

i. Jesus' purpose wasn't to make the man sad; yet he could only be happy by doing what Jesus told him to do. So, he **went away grieved**. Many people have almost everything, yet they are *grieved*.

3. (23-27) The difficulty of riches.

Then Jesus looked around and said to His disciples, "How hard it is for those who have riches to enter the kingdom of God!" And the disciples were astonished at His words. But Jesus answered again and said to them, "Children, how hard it is for those who trust in riches to enter the kingdom of God! It is easier for a camel to go through the eye of a needle than for a rich man to enter the kingdom of God." And they were greatly astonished, saying among themselves, "Who then can be saved?" But Jesus looked at them and said, "With men *it is* impossible, but not with God; for with God all things are possible."

a. **How hard it is for those who have riches to enter the kingdom of God... the disciples were astonished at His words**: We are like the disciples. We have a hard time seeing how riches could hinder us from the kingdom of God. We tend to think that riches can only bring blessing and good.

i. The words of Jesus amazed the disciples because they assumed that wealth was always a sign of God's blessing and favor. They thought that the rich were *especially* saved.

b. **For those who have riches**: We often excuse ourselves from what Jesus said here because we don't consider ourselves rich. Yet compared to this rich young ruler, each one of us enjoys more luxuries and comforts than he did.

c. **Children, how hard it is for those who trust in riches to enter the kingdom of God!** Riches present a difficulty because they tend to make us satisfied with this life instead of longing for the age to come. It is also true that riches must often be acquired at the expense of acquiring God.

> i. We may contrast the *dependence* of a child with the *independence* of a rich man. Jesus indicated that it was much more likely that the child would inherit the kingdom of God instead of the rich man.

> ii. Perhaps more importantly, the wealthy man is often a successful *doer*. He has *done well*, so he is rich. It is very easy for him to think that salvation and his relationship with the Lord is also a matter of successful *doing*, when really it is about humble *receiving*.

d. **It is easier for a camel to go through the eye of a needle than for a rich man to enter the kingdom of God**: With man, salvation is like a camel going through the eye of a needle. With God, it is possible.

> i. "The camel was the largest animal found on Palestinian soil. The violent contrast between the largest animal and the smallest opening expresses what, humanly speaking, is impossible or absurd." (Lane)

> ii. "Attempts have been made to explain Jesus' words about the *camel* and the *eye of a needle* in terms of a camel shuffling through a small postern gate, or by reading *kamilon* 'cable' for *kamelon* 'camel'. Such 'explanations' are misguided. They miss the point that Jesus is using a humourous illustration." (Morris)

e. **With God all things are possible**: However, God's grace is sufficient to save the rich man. Biblically speaking we have the examples of people like Zaccheus, Joseph of Arimathea, and Barnabas, and through history many more examples.

4. (28-31) Our reward and the solution to the problem of riches.

Then Peter began to say to Him, "See, we have left all and followed You." So Jesus answered and said, "Assuredly, I say to you, there is no one who has left house or brothers or sisters or father or mother or wife or children or lands, for My sake and the gospel's, who shall not receive a hundredfold now in this time; houses and brothers and sisters and mothers and children and lands, with persecutions; and in the age to come, eternal life. But many *who are* first will be last, and the last first."

a. **See, we have left all and followed You**: In contrast to the rich young ruler, the disciples *had* **left all** to follow Jesus; what will be their reward? This question seems typical of Peter.

> i. Of course there is a special honor for the disciples. They will have a special place in the judgment, probably in the sense of administration in the millennial Kingdom. The apostles also had the honor of helping to provide a singular foundation for the church (Ephesians 2:20) and will have a special tribute in the New Jerusalem (Revelation 21:14).

b. **There is no one who has left house or brothers... who shall not receive a hundredfold**: There will be universal honor for all who sacrifice for Jesus' sake. Whatever is given up for Him will be returned many times over, in addition to **eternal life**.

> i. **Hundredfold** is obviously not literal. Otherwise, Jesus promised a hundred mothers and a hundred wives.

c. **But many who are first will be last, and the last first**: This was the qualifying remark regarding the apostle's reward. All who sacrifice for the Lord will be rewarded, but God's way and timing of rewarding may not match up with man's way and timing of being rewarded. When God rewards, expect the unexpected.

> i. As the text continues in Matthew 20:1-16, Jesus taught the parable of the landowner and the workers - a powerful illustration of God's right and ability to reward in unusual (though never in unfair) ways.

> ii. "In the final account, it shall be found that no man has been a loser through giving up anything for the Lord Jesus Christ though he has his own method of deciding who are to be first and who are to be last." (Spurgeon)

5. (32-34) Jesus again announces His coming fate in Jerusalem.

Now they were on the road, going up to Jerusalem, and Jesus was going before them; and they were amazed. And as they followed they were afraid. Then He took the twelve aside again and began to tell them the things that would happen to Him: "Behold, we are going up to Jerusalem, and the Son of Man will be betrayed to the chief priests and to the scribes; and they will condemn Him to death and deliver Him to the Gentiles; and they will mock Him, and scourge Him, and spit on Him, and kill Him. And on the third day He will rise again."

a. **They were amazed... they were afraid**: As they drew near to Jerusalem, the disciples sensed the danger of their mission. Jesus was a wanted man and yet **Jesus was going before them**. Therefore, the disciples **were**

amazed at the *courage* of Jesus and **they were afraid** of the fate awaiting them all in Jerusalem.

i. We sometimes don't think enough about the *courage* of Jesus. It took a tremendous amount of bravery for Him to walk straight towards His fate at Calvary and to walk *in front of* the disciples. The courage of Jesus is especially amazing in light of our frequent cowardice as Christians, afraid to stand out for Jesus. He wasn't afraid to stand out for us.

ii. **As they followed they were afraid**: At the same time, the disciples are to be commended for continuing to follow Jesus. It is true they **were afraid**, but it is also true that **they followed**.

b. **They will condemn Him to death and deliver Him to the Gentiles**: Jesus already told His disciples that He would be crucified and rise again the third day (Mark 8:31). This is the first time in the Gospel of Mark where Jesus revealed that they would **deliver Him to the Gentiles**. This was an additional insult and betrayal.

i. "Delivery to the Gentiles reveals that Jesus will be held in contempt by his own countrymen, for the Gentiles are the last people to whom the Messiah of the people of God should be handed over." (Lane)

c. **And they will mock Him, and scourge Him, and spit on Him, and kill Him**: Significantly, Jesus mentioned the *shame* of His suffering. Jesus suffered the most terrible emotional humiliation in His death, and it was done out of love for us.

i. This sharing in the shame of Jesus marked the early church and was evidence of their commitment and strength. Acts 5:41 says, *So they departed from the presence of the council, rejoicing that they were counted worthy to suffer shame for His name.* It's not that the disciples rejoiced in the shame itself, because Jesus didn't rejoice in the shame itself (Hebrews 12:2). Instead they rejoiced in identifying with Jesus and gladly suffered shame if they had to.

C. True greatness in God's kingdom.

1. (35-37) James and John request positions of status.

Then James and John, the sons of Zebedee, came to Him, saying, "Teacher, we want You to do for us whatever we ask." And He said to them, "What do you want Me to do for you?" They said to Him, "Grant us that we may sit, one on Your right hand and the other on Your left, in Your glory."

a. **Grant us that we may sit, one on Your right hand and the other on Your left, in Your glory**: Despite the continual declaration of His coming suffering, the disciples still thought that when Jesus got to Jerusalem, He would establish a political kingdom. Here, James and John asked for positions of high status in Jesus' administration - which they anticipated would be installed soon.

i. The place of honor was the seat on the right. The place of second honor was the seat on the left (1 Kings 2:19, Psalm 110:1). They asked for the two most prestigious places in Jesus' administration.

b. **Teacher, we want You to do for us whatever we ask**: This was no doubt an outgrowth of the continual topic of conversation among the disciples. They often spoke about which one among them was the greatest (Mark 9:33-34). James and John feel confident they will be the greatest, so they asked Jesus to confirm their opinion by appointing them to high positions now.

2. (38-41) Jesus' reply: think in terms of sacrifice, not self-glory.

But Jesus said to them, "You do not know what you ask. Are you able to drink the cup that I drink, and be baptized with the baptism that I am baptized with?" They said to Him, "We are able." So Jesus said to them, "You will indeed drink the cup that I drink, and with the baptism I am baptized with you will be baptized; but to sit on My right hand and on My left is not Mine to give, but *it is for those* for whom it is prepared." And when the ten heard *it*, they began to be greatly displeased with James and John.

a. **You do not know what you ask**: Since James and John still worked under carnal ideas regarding the kingdom of God, they really had no idea what it would take to be great in the kingdom. Yet it was not because Jesus had not told them.

b. **Are you able to drink the cup that I drink**: As it would turn out, both James and John took the **cup** and were **baptized** in suffering, but they each experienced the suffering in different ways.

i. James was the first apostle to be martyred (Acts 12:1-2). According to tradition, John was never martyred, though he survived an attempted murder by immersion in a vat of boiling oil (according to reasonably reliable church history).

ii. "In popular Greek usage the vocabulary of baptism was used to speak of being overwhelmed by disaster or danger, and a similar metaphorical use of submersion is present in Scripture." (Lane) Passages like Psalm 42:7, Psalm 93:3, and Psalm 69:2 reflect this idea.

c. **You will indeed drink the cup that I drink**: Perhaps when Jesus said this a big smile came over the face of James and John. They thought they had won something, and so did the other disciples (**when the ten heard it, they began to be greatly displeased with James and John**). However, it is doubtful that Jesus smiled because He knew what the baptism they asked for was all about. He knew that it was a baptism of suffering.

3. (42-45) Jesus describes true greatness.

But Jesus called them to *Himself* and said to them, "You know that those who are considered rulers over the Gentiles lord it over them, and their great ones exercise authority over them. Yet it shall not be so among you; but whoever desires to become great among you shall be your servant. And whoever of you desires to be first shall be slave of all. For even the Son of Man did not come to be served, but to serve, and to give His life a ransom for many."

a. **Those who are considered rulers over the Gentiles lord it over them**: Their desire for position and status showed they didn't know the nature of Jesus yet, in respect to leadership and power. Those who exercise power or authority in the church today as "lording it over" others still don't understand the Jesus style of leadership and life.

i. **Yet it shall not be so among you** is a stinging rebuke to the manner in which the modern church looks to the world for both its substance and style. Plainly, the church is not to operate the way the world does.

b. **Whoever desires to become great among you shall be your servant**: In the Kingdom community, status, money, and popularity are not the prerequisites for leadership. Humble service is the greatest (and only) prerequisite, as displayed by Jesus' own ministry.

c. **Just as the Son of Man did not come to be served, but to serve**: Real ministry is done for the benefit of those ministered to, not for the benefit of the minister. Many people are in the ministry for what they can receive (either materially or emotionally) from their people instead of for what they can give.

d. **And to give His life a ransom for many**: This is one of the great claims Jesus made about Himself and His ministry. He is the one who stands in the place of guilty sinners and offers Himself as a substitute for them.

i. "The ransom metaphor sums up the purpose for which Jesus gave his life and defines the complete expression of his service. The prevailing notion behind the metaphor is that of deliverance by purchase, whether a prisoner of war, a slave, or a forfeited life is the object to be delivered. Because the idea of equivalence, or substitution, was proper to the concept of a ransom, it became an integral element in the vocabulary of redemption in the OT. It speaks of a liberation which connotes a servitude or an imprisonment from which man cannot free himself." (Lane)

4. (46-52) On the way to Jerusalem, a blind man is healed.

Now they came to Jericho. As He went out of Jericho with His disciples and a great multitude, blind Bartimaeus, the son of Timaeus, sat by the road begging. And when he heard that it was Jesus of Nazareth, he began to cry out and say, "Jesus, Son of David, have mercy on me!" Then many warned him to be quiet; but he cried out all the more, "Son of David, have mercy on me!" So Jesus stood still and commanded him to be called. Then they called the blind man, saying to him, "Be of good cheer. Rise, He is calling you." And throwing aside his garment, he rose and came to Jesus. So Jesus answered and said to him, "What do you want Me to do for you?" The blind man said to Him, "Rabboni, that I may receive my sight." Then Jesus said to him, "Go your way; your faith has made you well." And immediately he received his sight and followed Jesus on the road.

a. **He cried out all the more, "Son of David, have mercy on me!"** Blind Bartimaeus didn't have much tact, but he did have persistence and determination. People tried to shut him up, but they couldn't because he really wanted a touch from Jesus.

i. The persistent and energetic nature of Bartimaeus' prayer is a good example of prayer. He wasn't discouraged because no one led him to Jesus. Those who told him to stay away did not discourage him.

ii. "Take the gates of heaven and shake them with thy vehemence, as though thou wouldst pull them up post and bar and all. Stand at Mercy's door, and take no denial. Knock, and knock, and knock again, as though thou wouldst shake the very spheres, but what thou wouldst obtain an answer to thy cries. 'The kingdom of heaven suffereth violence, and the violent take it by force.' Cold prayers never win God's ear. Draw thy bow with thy full strength, if thou wouldst send thy arrow up so high as heaven." (Spurgeon)

b. **Have mercy on me!** The blind man knew what he needed from Jesus - **mercy**. He didn't come thinking that God owed him. All he wanted from Jesus was mercy.

c. **What do you want Me to do for you?** It might seem that the need of Bartimaeus was obvious. Yet Jesus had a deliberate purpose in the question. There was real power in both the asking and in the answer of Jesus. God may ask us the same question, and we should be able to articulate an answer that glorifies Him.

d. **Rabboni, that I may receive my sight**: The title **Rabboni** "is a strengthened form of 'Rabbi,' and means 'my lord,' 'my master.'" (Lane) When Bartimaeus said this, he expressed his humble submission towards Jesus.

> i. The specific nature of Bartimaeus' request is a good example for our prayers. "**Have mercy on me**" is general, but his prayer moved from the general to the specific request, "**that I may receive my sight.**"

> ii. "Rest assured that those are the best prayers in all respects, if they be earnest and sincere, which go most directly to the point. You know there is a way of praying in the closet, and praying in the family, in which you do not ask for anything. You say a great many good things, introduce much of your own experience, review the doctrines of grace very thoughtfully, but you do not ask for anything in particular. Such prayer is always uninteresting to listen to, and I think it must be rather tedious to those who offer it." (Spurgeon)

e. **Go your way; your faith has made you well**: The **faith** of the blind man saved him because it was a specific kind of faith.

- It was faith that was determined to reach Jesus (**he cried out all the more**).
- It was faith that knew who Jesus was (**Son of David**).
- It was faith that came humbly to Jesus (**have mercy on me**).
- It was faith that humbly submitted to Jesus (**Rabboni**).
- It was faith that could tell Jesus what it wanted (**that I may receive my sight**).

f. **Immediately he received his sight and followed Jesus**: Now healed and saved, blind Bartimaeus then **followed Jesus**. The way of Jesus became his way. This was especially significant when we consider where Jesus was going at this time - to Jerusalem where a cross waited for Him.

> i. First Jesus told Bartimaeus, **go your way**. Then, Bartimaeus **followed Jesus**. He made Jesus' way his own way, and was follower of Him. Bartimaeus must have figured, "Now that I have my sight, I always want to look upon Jesus."

> ii. "Apply to the Son of David; lose not a moment; he is *passing by*, and thou art *passing* into *eternity*, and probably wilt never have a more favourable opportunity than the present." (Clarke)

Mark 11 - Jesus Comes to Jerusalem

A. The triumphal entry.

1. (1-6) Preparation for the entry.

Now when they drew near Jerusalem, to Bethphage and Bethany, at the Mount of Olives, He sent two of His disciples; and He said to them, "Go into the village opposite you; and as soon as you have entered it you will find a colt tied, on which no one has sat. Loose it and bring *it*. And if anyone says to you, 'Why are you doing this?' say, 'The Lord has need of it,' and immediately he will send it here." So they went their way, and found the colt tied by the door outside on the street, and they loosed it. But some of those who stood there said to them, "What are you doing, loosing the colt?" And they spoke to them just as Jesus had commanded. So they let them go.

a. **Now when they drew near to Jerusalem**: If all we had was the Gospel of Mark, we might think this was Jesus' first journey to Jerusalem. But the Gospel of John tells us of many previous trips. Jesus, like any devout Jewish man, went to Jerusalem for as many of the major feasts as He possibly could.

b. **At the Mount of Olives, He sent two of His disciples**: As Jesus prepared to enter Jerusalem, He carefully and deliberately sent His disciples to make arrangements for His arrival into the city. Since the time was short before His crucifixion, Jesus left nothing to chance.

c. **You will find a colt tied, on which no one has sat**: With this, Jesus established that He would enter Jerusalem riding on **a colt**. He deliberately chose a young horse, not a stallion, not a donkey, and not coming on foot. This is because in that day, to come riding a **colt** - as opposed to a mighty war-horse - was to come as a man of peace. Jesus didn't come to Jerusalem as a conquering general, but as a suffering (though triumphant) servant.

i. The Rabbis of Jesus' day had several different theories regarding how the Messiah would come to Jerusalem. Based on Daniel 7:13, some thought the Messiah would come as a majestic conqueror. Based on Zechariah 9:9, some thought that the Messiah would come in a lowly and humble way, riding on a colt.

ii. In the days of Jesus, some Rabbis reconciled these by saying that the Messiah would come humbly to an *unworthy* Israel but mightily to a *worthy* Israel. Since Israel considered itself worthy, they only looked for a triumphant, conquering Messiah.

iii. **On which no one had sat**: "To Jesus it made no difference that this was an unbroken colt. He was the Creator come into this scene as a Man, and as such all the lower creatures were subject to Him." (Ironside)

d. **They spoke to them just as Jesus had commanded. So they let them go**: Apparently, Jesus had pre-arranged this with the colt owner, and the disciples were just instructed to say, "It's for Jesus," if they were questioned. They did as Jesus said, and it was fine.

2. (7-11) Praise for Jesus.

Then they brought the colt to Jesus and threw their clothes on it, and He sat on it. And many spread their clothes on the road, and others cut down leafy branches from the trees and spread *them* on the road. Then those who went before and those who followed cried out, saying:
"Hosanna!
'Blessed *is* He who comes in the name of the LORD!'
Blessed *is* the kingdom of our father David
That comes in the name of the Lord!
Hosanna in the highest!"

And Jesus went into Jerusalem and into the temple. So when He had looked around at all things, as the hour was already late, He went out to Bethany with the twelve.

a. **And many spread their clothes on the road, and others cut down leafy branches from the trees and spread them on the road**: We like this slice from the life of Jesus because it simply *feels* so right. For much of Jesus' ministry, He was despised and rejected of men. Often the adoring crowds followed Him only for what they could *get* from Him, and most of His audience rejected any kind of personal commitment to Jesus. All of that was different on this day.

i. On this day, they lavished attention and honor on Jesus. They used their clothes as a saddle for Jesus and as a red carpet for the colt He rode on. Considering the expense and value of clothing in that day, this was generous praise.

b. **Then those who went before and those who followed cried out, saying: "Hosanna! 'Blessed is He who comes in the name of the LORD!'"** For most of His ministry, Jesus did everything He could to *discourage* people from publicly celebrating Him as the Messiah. Here Jesus went out of His way to invite public praise and adoration as the Messiah.

i. In fact, when the religious leaders of His day objected, He told them *"I tell you that if these should keep silent, the stones would immediately cry out."* (Luke 19:40)

ii. The statements from the crowd came from Psalm 118:19-29. In this, their praise was *Scriptural*. It is important that we praise God *as He wants to be praised*. So if God says we are to come to Him with words (Hosea 14:2), then that is how we come. If God says we are to come to Him with song (Psalm 100:2), then that is how we should come. If God says we are to come to Him with hands raised up (Psalm 134:2), that is how we come. The whole point in worship is to do *what pleases God*, not what pleases us, but the beautiful truth is that when we please God, we find ourselves wonderfully pleased.

iii. We call this event the "Triumphal Entry," but it was a strange kind of triumph. If you spoke of Jesus' Triumphal Entry to a Roman, they would have laughed at you. For them, a Triumphal Entry was a honor granted to a Roman general who won a complete and decisive victory and had killed at least 5,000 enemy soldiers. When the general returned to Rome, they had an elaborate parade. First came the treasures captured from the enemy, then the prisoners. His armies marched by unit by unit, and finally the general rode in a golden chariot pulled by magnificent horses. Priests burned incense in his honor and the crowds shouted his name and praised him. The procession ended at the arena, where some of the prisoners were thrown to wild animals for the entertainment of the crowd. *That* was a Triumphal Entry, not a Galilean Peasant sitting on a few coats set out on a pony.

c. **When He looked around at all things**: Jesus came as the Messiah to Jerusalem, not as a mighty general to conquer the Romans. He came first to look at the standing of the people of God, and to make an inspection. In the rest of Mark 11, we see the results of this inspection.

i. Malachi 3:1-3 speaks prophetically of the Messiah coming to the temple in careful assessment.

ii. We see again the *courage* of Jesus because He didn't hide from the authorities. John 11:57 makes it clear that there was a price on Jesus' head and the authorities were looking for Him. Despite that threat, Jesus came into Jerusalem in the most public way possible.

B. The lesson of the fig tree.

1. (12-14) Jesus curses a fig tree.

Now the next day, when they had come out from Bethany, He was hungry. And seeing from afar a fig tree having leaves, He went to see if perhaps He would find something on it. When He came to it, He found nothing but leaves, for it was not the season for figs. In response Jesus said to it, "Let no one eat fruit from you ever again." And His disciples heard *it*.

a. **Seeing from afar a fig tree having leaves, He went to see if perhaps He would find something on it**: Essentially, the tree was a picture of false advertising, **having leaves** but no figs. Ordinarily this is not the case with these fig trees, which normally do not have leaves without also having figs.

i. **For it was not the season for figs**: It wasn't that the fig tree didn't have figs because it wasn't supposed to. The problem is that it *had leaves* but didn't have figs. The leaves said, "There are figs here," but the figs weren't there.

ii. There were many trees with only leaves, and these were not cursed. There were many trees with neither leaves nor fruit, and these were not cursed. This tree was cursed because it professed to have fruit, but did not.

b. **In response Jesus said to it, "Let no one eat fruit from you ever again"**: The tree was cursed for its *pretense* of leaves, not for its *lack* of fruit. Like Israel in the days of Jesus, it had the outward form but no fruit. In this picture, Jesus warned Israel - and us - of God's displeasure when we have the *appearance* of fruit but not the fruit itself. God isn't pleased when His people are all leaves and no fruit.

i. In all works in the ministry of Jesus, this is the only destructive miracle. The Old Testament is filled with miracles of destruction and judgment, but Jesus most perfectly showed us the nature of God. If this was the only miracle of its kind, we must see there was a great and important lesson in it. God doesn't approve when there is profession without reality, talk without walk.

ii. "There is no more warrant for criticizing our Lord for destroying a tree for the purpose of teaching, than there is for objecting to a

Christmas tree for our children, or the plucking of petals from a flower in a lesson on botany." (Morgan)

3. (15-19) The temple cleansed.

So they came to Jerusalem. Then Jesus went into the temple and began to drive out those who bought and sold in the temple, and overturned the tables of the money changers and the seats of those who sold doves. And He would not allow anyone to carry wares through the temple. Then He taught, saying to them, "Is it not written, 'My house shall be called a house of prayer for all nations'? But you have made it a 'den of thieves.'" And the scribes and chief priests heard it and sought how they might destroy Him; for they feared Him, because all the people were astonished at His teaching. When evening had come, He went out of the city.

a. **Then Jesus went into the temple and began to drive out those who bought and sold in the temple**: The temple area was filled with profiteers who worked in cooperation with the priests and robbed the pilgrims by forcing them to purchase approved sacrificial animals and currencies at inflated prices.

i. Every Jewish male had to pay a yearly temple tax - an amount equaling about two days' pay. It had to be paid in the currency of the temple, and the money exchangers made the exchange into temple money at outrageous rates.

b. **Those who bought and sold in the temple**: They did this in the outer courts of the temple, the only area where Gentiles could worship and pray. Therefore, this place of prayer was made into a marketplace, and a dishonest one at that. God intended the temple to be a **house of prayer for all nations**, but they had made it **a den of thieves**.

i. **A den of thieves** is a place where **thieves** associate and hide. It is a sorry, shameful condition when the house of God becomes a place where unrepentant and active sinners can associate and hide.

4. (20-24) Return to the cursed fig tree.

Now in the morning, as they passed by, they saw the fig tree dried up from the roots. And Peter, remembering, said to Him, "Rabbi, look! The fig tree which You cursed has withered away." So Jesus answered and said to them, "Have faith in God. For assuredly, I say to you, whoever says to this mountain, 'Be removed and be cast into the sea,' and does not doubt in his heart, but believes that those things he says will be done, he will have whatever he says. Therefore I say to you, whatever

things you ask when you pray, believe that you receive *them*, and you will have *them*."

a. **Have faith in God**: Jesus explained that this miracle was really the result of a prayer made in faith, and He encouraged His marveling disciples to have this kind of faith, trusting that God would hear them also.

b. **In God**: Jesus made it clear that prayer must be offered in faith, and faith must be **in God**. Faith is trust, confidence, and reliance upon someone or something.

i. Some, using Greek transliterations, have said Jesus was really saying that we must "*Have God's faith.*" But Greek scholars object to this understanding of the phrase "**have faith in God**."

- "Objective genitive *theou* [God] as in Gal. 3:26; Rom. 3:22, 26." (Robertson) God is the *object* of faith in this sentence.

- "The word 'God' is in the genitive case, showing here the object of faith." (Wuest)

- "Faith *in* God, genitive objective as in Rom. iii. 22 and Heb. vi. 2." (Expositor's)

ii. The grammatical *case* of the word **God** in this passage is the objective genitive. The *objective case* refers to what *receives* the action of the verb *have*; it is not in a *possessive* case, which would indicate that we are to "have God's faith."

c. **Whoever says to this mountain, "Be removed"**: **Mountain** was a popular figure of speech for any insurmountable problem; Jesus said that as we believe, God could overcome any obstacle.

i. "The phrase about removing mountains was a quite common Jewish phrase. It was a regular, vivid phrase for *removing difficulties*." (Barclay)

ii. This promise of God's answer to the prayer made in faith was made to disciples, not to the multitude. "Nor should we interpret Mark 11:24 to mean, 'If you pray hard enough and *really believe*, God is obligated to answer your prayer no matter what you ask.' That kind of faith is not faith in God; rather it is nothing but faith in faith, or faith in feelings." (Wiersbe)

5. (25-26) Prayer and forgiveness.

"And whenever you stand praying, if you have anything against anyone, forgive him, that your Father in heaven may also forgive you your trespasses. But if you do not forgive, neither will your Father in heaven forgive your trespasses."

a. **Whenever you stand praying, if you have anything against anyone, forgive him**: A lack of faith is not the only obstacle to effective prayer. Refusing to forgive or holding on to bitterness can also hinder our prayer.

> i. The point may also be that this is an area where we need great faith. Sometimes a hard and unforgiving heart is bigger than any mountain.

b. **Whenever you stand praying, if you have anything against anyone**: This means that we are never to place religious duty or ministry ahead of good relationships with people. We are to set things right first, and then continue on in prayer. We are to do what Paul commanded in Romans 12:18: *If it is possible, as much as depends on you, live peaceably with all men.*

c. **If you do not forgive, neither will your Father in heaven forgive your trespasses**: The forgiven heart will forgive others. If we have hard, unforgiving hearts, it calls into question if we have ever received or appreciated the forgiveness God offers us.

C. By what authority?

1. (27-28) The religious leaders question Jesus.

Then they came again to Jerusalem. And as He was walking in the temple, the chief priests, the scribes, and the elders came to Him. And they said to Him, "By what authority are You doing these things? And who gave You this authority to do these things?"

a. **As He was walking in the temple, the chief priests, the scribes, and the elders came to Him**: Jesus wasn't looking to debate the religious leaders. He wanted to teach the people and tell them about God's good news. But the questioners came to Him, and He was more than able to handle them.

b. **By what authority are You doing these things?** Jesus was extremely courageous by boldly entering Jerusalem and driving out the corrupt merchants from the temple courts. Now **the chief priests, the scribes, and the elders** wanted to know what right He had to do such things.

2. (29-33) Jesus answers their question with a question.

But Jesus answered and said to them, "I also will ask you one question; then answer Me, and I will tell you by what authority I do these things: The baptism of John; was it from heaven or from men? Answer Me." And they reasoned among themselves, saying, "If we say, 'From heaven,' He will say, 'Why then did you not believe him?' But if we say, 'From men'"; they feared the people, for all counted John to have been a prophet indeed. So they answered and said to Jesus, "We do not know." And Jesus answered and said to them, "Neither will I tell you by what authority I do these things."

a. **I will also ask you one question**: When Jesus asked them to answer the question regarding John the Baptist, He was not evading their question. If John really was from God, then he was right about Jesus and Jesus was indeed the Messiah. If what John said was true, then Jesus had all authority.

> i. "It was not a dodge, but a home thrust that cleared the air and defined their attitude both to John and Jesus. They rejected John as they now reject Jesus." (Robertson)

b. **We do not know**: Their response to His question exposed the fact that these men were not sincere seekers of truth. They cared more about scoring rhetorical points in debate and in pleasing the crowds than in knowing the truth.

> i. "The whole story is a vivid example of what happens to men who will not face the truth. They have to twist and wriggle and in the end get themselves into a position in which they are so helplessly involved that they have nothing to say." (Barclay) It is more difficult at first to face the truth and admit wrong, but it is the only path with a real *future*.

Mark 12 - Jesus Debates the Authorities

A. The story of the tenant farmers.

1. (1-8) A parable about a landowner and his tenants.

Then He began to speak to them in parables: "A man planted a vineyard and set a hedge around *it*, dug *a place for* the wine vat and built a tower. And he leased it to vinedressers and went into a far country. Now at vintage-time he sent a servant to the vinedressers, that he might receive some of the fruit of the vineyard from the vinedressers. And they took *him* and beat him and sent *him* away empty-handed. Again he sent them another servant, and at him they threw stones, wounded *him* in the head, and sent *him* away shamefully treated. And again he sent another, and him they killed; and many others, beating some and killing some. Therefore still having one son, his beloved, he also sent him to them last, saying, 'They will respect my son.' But those vinedressers said among themselves, 'This is the heir. Come, let us kill him, and the inheritance will be ours.' So they took him and killed *him* and cast *him* out of the vineyard."

a. **He leased it to vinedressers and went into a far country**: This sort of tenant farming relationship was a common practice in Jesus' day, especially in the region of Galilee. Archaeologists have discovered records of this same sort of dispute between landowners and tenant farmers.

   i. "In a day when title was sometimes uncertain, anyone who had had the use of land for three years was presumed to own it in the absence of an alternative claim." (Morris)

b. **That he might receive some of the fruit of the vineyard from the vinedressers**: Because Jesus spoke to a Jewish audience, they were aware that the vineyard was used in the Old Testament as a picture of Israel (Isaiah 5:1-7). Therefore, the **vinedressers** represented the rulers of Israel and the vineyard represented the people of God as a whole.

c. **And they took him and beat him and sent him away empty-handed**: The vinedressers didn't buy the vineyard, and they did not build it. A generous owner allowed them to work in his vineyard, yet they turned against the owner and one day had to answer for it.

> i. **Again he sent them another servant... And again he sent another... and many others**: The owner was very patient. He sent messenger after messenger, even though they were all abused and mistreated. Because the owner of the vineyard was not present at the time, the vinedressers doubted and mocked his authority. They soon found out that even though they couldn't see the owner, his authority was still real.

> ii. **This is the heir. Come, let us kill him, and the inheritance will be ours**: The vinedressers were very foolish. They apparently thought that if they killed the owner's son, the owner would then just give up and let them have the vineyard.

d. **So they took him and killed him and cast him out of the vineyard**: This parable tells us that Jesus knew He was the Son - the Son of God - and that He knew that He would soon be killed.

> i. The Son was the final messenger. There would be no other. Either they would accept the message of the Son or face certain judgment. "If you do not hear the wellbeloved Son of God, you have refused your last hope. *He is God's ultimatum.* Nothing remains when Christ is refused. No one else can be sent; heaven itself contains no further messenger. If Christ be rejected, hope is rejected." (Spurgeon)

2. (9-12) Jesus applies the parable.

"Therefore what will the owner of the vineyard do? He will come and destroy the vinedressers, and give the vineyard to others. Have you not even read this Scripture:

'The stone which the builders rejected
Has become the chief cornerstone.
This was the LORD's doing,
And it is marvelous in our eyes'?"

And they sought to lay hands on Him, but feared the multitude, for they knew He had spoken the parable against them. So they left Him and went away.

a. **Therefore what will the owner of the vineyard do?** The vinedressers were foolish enough to think that if they only killed the owner's son, the vineyard would be theirs. Jesus drew the correct point - they rejected messenger after messenger, finally rejecting the Son, so their day of reckoning would come (**He will come and destroy the vinedressers**).

b. **Have you not even read this Scripture**: Jesus instructed them from the "Hosanna Psalm" (Psalm 118:22-28), because the Messiah was officially presented to Israel. The hostility of the Jewish leaders showed that He was rejected, even if He was initially greeted with hosannas quoting from Psalm 118.

c. **The stone which the builders rejected has become the chief cornerstone**: Jesus is often likened unto a stone or a rock in the Bible. He is the rock of provision that followed Israel in the desert (1 Corinthians 10:4). He is the stone of stumbling (1 Peter 2:8). He is the stone cut without hands that crushes the kingdoms of this world (Daniel 2:45).

d. **They knew He had spoken the parable against them**: They were cut to the heart and convicted by the Holy Spirit. They reacted to the conviction of the Holy Spirit by *rejecting*, not by *receiving*. They plotted to murder Jesus instead of repenting before Him.

B. God and Caesar.

1. (13-15a) The Pharisees try to trap Jesus with a question about taxes.

Then they sent to Him some of the Pharisees and the Herodians, to catch Him in *His* words. When they had come, they said to Him, "Teacher, we know that You are true, and care about no one; for You do not regard the person of men, but teach the way of God in truth. Is it lawful to pay taxes to Caesar, or not? Shall we pay, or shall we not pay?"

a. **They sent to Him some of the Pharisees and the Herodians, to catch Him in His words**: Public opinion kept them from laying hold of Jesus, so they tried to turn the tide of public opinion against Him. Using a clever question, they wanted to make Jesus seem to agree with the Roman government against the Jews.

i. We again see **the Pharisees and the Herodians** working together (last time was in Mark 3:6). Former enemies came together because of Jesus, but it was because they both *opposed* Jesus and wanted to destroy Him.

b. **Teacher, we know that You are true, and care about no one; for You do not regard the person of men, but teach the way of God in truth**: Jesus knew enough to not regard this flattery from His enemies. Sometimes our enemies flatter us because they want to hurt us. Sometimes our friends flatter us because they want to be kind and helpful. Either way, it is a mistake to put too much stock in what others say about us, either good or bad.

i. Charles Spurgeon said to pastors, "It is always best not to know, nor wish to know, what is being said about you, either by friends or foes. Those who praise us are probably as much mistaken as those who abuse us."

ii. "Here is a fair glove drawn upon a foul hand... There are those who will smile in your face, and at the same time cut your throat." (Trapp)

c. **Is it lawful to pay taxes to Caesar, or not?** Since the year 6 A.D. the Jews were forced to pay taxes directly into the emperor's treasury. Some Jewish patriots (like the Zealots) refused to pay this tax because they did not want to recognize Roman rule as legitimate. Most people grudgingly paid it, but everybody hated it. It wasn't just the *money*, but also the *principle* of paying the Roman oppressor.

i. Three taxes were imposed by the Romans on Judea. The first was the *ground tax*, which was 10% of all grain and 20% of all wine and fruit. The second was the *income tax*, which amounted to 1% of a man's income. The third was the poll tax, paid by men aged 12 to 65 and women 14 to 65. This was one denarius a year, about a day's wage for a laborer.

d. **Shall we pay, or shall we not pay?** They seemed to put Jesus in a trap. If He agreed the tax should be paid, Jesus then seemed to deny the sovereignty of God over Israel, and He would lose popular support. If Jesus agreed that the tax should not be paid, He would openly declare Himself an enemy of Rome and be treated like a revolutionary.

i. We can almost see the smug, self-satisfied smiles of the Pharisees and the Herodians as they skillfully threw this question on Jesus. They thought He was in a trap He could not get out of, but you can't put Jesus in a trap.

2. (15b-17) Jesus answers the question about taxes.

But He, knowing their hypocrisy, said to them, "Why do you test Me? Bring Me a denarius that I may see *it*." So they brought *it*. And He said to them, "Whose image and inscription *is* this?" They said to Him, "Caesar's." And Jesus answered and said to them, "Render to Caesar the things that are Caesar's, and to God the things that are God's." And they marveled at Him.

a. **Why do you test Me?** We should never say that Jesus taunted His adversaries in an ungodly way, but He did let them know that they could never win against Him.

b. **Bring Me a denarius that I may see it**: On the denarius they showed to Jesus, there was a head of Tiberius, the reigning Roman Emperor. Around his head was written the abbreviation for "Tiberius Caesar, the Divine

Augustus." On the back was the title "Pontifex Maximus," declaring that Caesar was the high priest of the Roman Empire.

> i. As Jesus held the coin, He knew the government of Caesar would soon pierce His hand and crucify Him. Yet He still said, "pay your taxes to the Roman government."

c. **Whose image and inscription is this?** Essentially Jesus said, "You recognize Caesar's civil authority when you use his coins; therefore, you are obliged to pay him the taxes he asks for."

d. **Render to Caesar the things that are Caesar's**: If we take advantage of the benefits of governmental rule, we are obliged to submit to government, as long as it does not infringe on our service to God. Simply said, Jesus told us to pay our taxes. The Apostle Paul repeated the same idea in Romans 13:6-7.

> i. "Jesus is saying that we are citizens of heaven and earth at the same time." (Morris)

> ii. Given the promises of blessing and cursing under the Old Covenant, had the Jews rendered God His due, they would have never had to render Caesar anything. The fact that they were under Roman domination was due to their own departure from the Lord.

e. **And to God the things that are God's**: Just as it is important to **render to Caesar**, we must also render **to God the things that are God's**. The coin belonged to Caesar because his image was stamped on it. We should give our *self* to God because His image is stamped on us.

> i. Give the coin to Caesar but give your life to God. It may be fitting for you to die for your country, but only God is worth living for.

> ii. Jesus' answer tells us that Caesar does not have all authority; there are some things that should be rendered to God alone. When the State asks something of us that belongs to God alone, we are duty bound to obey God before the State.

> iii. "This answer is full of consummate wisdom. It establishes the *limits*, regulates the *rights*, and distinguishes the *jurisdiction* of the two *empires* of *heaven* and *earth*." (Clarke)

f. **And they marveled at Him**: They marveled, but they did not change. In fact, they twisted this wise answer of Jesus into a lying accusation against Him. In Luke 23:2, they accused Jesus of *forbidding to pay taxes to Caesar* - when He actually said just the opposite!

> i. Sometimes it doesn't matter how good an answer you give; some people will still twist your good words. They did this to Jesus, yet

God's truth prevailed. In the answer of Jesus, God was *glorified*, Caesar was *satisfied*, the people were *edified*, and His critics were *stupefied*.

C. A question about the resurrection.

1. (18-23) The Sadducees ask Jesus a ridiculous question.

Then *some* Sadducees, who say there is no resurrection, came to Him; and they asked Him, saying: "Teacher, Moses wrote to us that if a man's brother dies, and leaves *his* wife behind, and leaves no children, his brother should take his wife and raise up offspring for his brother. Now there were seven brothers. The first took a wife; and dying, he left no offspring. And the second took her, and he died; nor did he leave any offspring. And the third likewise. So the seven had her and left no offspring. Last of all the woman died also. Therefore, in the resurrection, when they rise, whose wife will she be? For all seven had her as wife."

a. **In the resurrection, when they rise, whose wife will she be?** The **Sadducees** were well educated, sophisticated, influential and wealthy. They did not believe in immortality, spirits, or angels. The purpose of their question was to make the idea of resurrection seem absurd.

i. Morris on the Sadducees: "The conservative, aristocratic, high-priestly party, worldly minded and very ready to cooperate with the Romans, which, of course, enabled them to maintain their privileged position."

ii. The Law of Moses (in Deuteronomy 25:5-6) established something that came to be called *levirate marriage*, from the Latin word *levir*, meaning "brother-in-law." Essentially, the practice made sure that if a married man died childless, his brother had to take the widow as a wife so a son and heir could be provided for the deceased man, and his family name and inheritance would not perish.

b. **Now there were seven brothers**: Their question was absurd. It was similar to asking, "how many angels can dance on the head of a pin?" or "did Adam have a belly-button?" An absurd question isn't less absurd because we direct the question to God.

i. The Sadducees believed that when the body died, the soul died. The Bible not only tells us that the soul lives when the body dies, but also that the soul will have a new body, a body fit for eternity - a resurrection body.

2. (24-25) Jesus corrects their misunderstanding about resurrection life.

Jesus answered and said to them, "Are you not therefore mistaken, because you do not know the Scriptures nor the power of God? For

when they rise from the dead, they neither marry nor are given in marriage, but are like angels in heaven."

a. **Are you not therefore mistaken**: The Sadducees thought that if there was a resurrection, it was just this same life lived forever. With the principle **when they rise from the dead, they neither marry nor are given in marriage**, Jesus showed that in the age to come our lives will be lived on a completely different principle and in a dimension that we can't imagine.

i. Many people make the same mistake as the Sadducees when it comes to their ideas about heaven. They think of heaven as just a glorious version of earth. So the Native American thought of heaven as the happy hunting ground. The ancient Viking thought of heaven as Valhalla, where they fought as warriors all day and at the end of the day all the dead and wounded rose whole again, and celebrated all night at a banquet, drinking wine from the skulls of their enemies. All these ideas mistake heaven for simply a better earth. Heaven's life is of a different order all together.

b. **Are you not therefore mistaken, because you do not know the Scriptures nor the power of God?** Jesus explained *why* the Sadducees had wrong ideas about resurrection. Their wrong thinking came from *ignorance* (**you do not know**) of both **the Scriptures** and **the power of God**.

i. When we don't know **the Scriptures**, we don't have an anchor for truth and belief. When we don't know **the power of God**, we doubt God's ability to actually do what He has promised in the Scriptures.

ii. "The Sadducees posed as men of superior intelligence and knowledge in opposition to the traditionalists among the Pharisees... and yet on this very point they were ignorant of the Scriptures." (Robertson) Many today who are regarded as intelligent become dull when it comes to Jesus.

c. **They neither marry nor are given in marriage, but are like angels in heaven**: We can't take our present relationships and just figure they will be the same in heaven. On earth, human relationships are largely a matter of time and place - a man can be a son, then an adult, then a husband, then a father, and so on. In heaven, all of that changes.

i. From everything we know, angels don't have babies. Angels are made directly by God. In the resurrection, we won't have babies any more. In that respect, we will be just like the angels. "Marriage ceases to have any sexual significance in heaven." (Cole)

ii. We know it won't be the same as what we know on earth, but we can't say for sure what it will be like in heaven - other than to know that we won't be disappointed.

iii. Knowing that the resurrection of the dead is true doesn't answer all of our questions. There are mysteries that remain, but they don't take away from the basic truth of the resurrection.

3. (26-27) Jesus proves the resurrection from the Scriptures.

"But concerning the dead, that they rise, have you not read in the book of Moses, in the *burning* bush *passage,* how God spoke to him, saying, 'I *am* the God of Abraham, the God of Isaac, and the God of Jacob'? He is not the God of the dead, but the God of the living. You are therefore greatly mistaken."

a. **Concerning the dead, that they rise, have you not read**: Jesus assured the skeptical Sadducees that there was indeed a resurrection of the dead, that they do rise, and that this was demonstrated by the Scriptures.

i. "He has already explained what He meant by their ignorance of God's power; now He will explain what He meant by their ignorance of the Scripture." (Cole)

ii. The Sadducees said they believed in the Bible, but said the true Bible only contained the first five books of the Old Testament. That was one reason why Jesus proved the resurrection from Exodus 3, one of the books of the Bible the Sadducees said was genuine.

b. **I am the God of Abraham, the God of Isaac, and the God of Jacob**: If Abraham, Isaac and Jacob did not *continue* to live, God would not say that He *is* their God, speaking in the present tense. He would have said that He *was* their God. Therefore, the Scriptures proved there is a resurrection of the dead.

4. (28-34) Which is the greatest commandment?

Then one of the scribes came, and having heard them reasoning together, perceiving that He had answered them well, asked Him, "Which is the first commandment of all?" Jesus answered him, "The first of all the commandments *is:* 'Hear, O Israel, the LORD our God, the LORD is one. And you shall love the LORD your God with all your heart, with all your soul, with all your mind, and with all your strength.' This *is* the first commandment. And the second, like *it, is* this: 'You shall love your neighbor as yourself.' There is no other commandment greater than these." So the scribe said to Him, "Well *said,* Teacher. You have spoken the truth, for there is one God, and there is no other but He. And to love Him with all the heart, with all the understanding, with all the soul, and

with all the strength, and to love one's neighbor as oneself, is more than all the whole burnt offerings and sacrifices." Now when Jesus saw that he answered wisely, He said to him, "You are not far from the kingdom of God." But after that no one dared question Him.

a. **Which is the first commandment of all?** With this question, they tested Jesus to see if He would show disregard or neglect for some area of the Law of Moses. Instead of promoting one command over another, Jesus defined the law in its essence: love God with everything you have and love your neighbor as yourself.

b. **Love the LORD your God... love your neighbor as yourself**: In this we see that what God really wants from man is **love**. We can obey God without loving Him, but if we do love Him obedience will follow.

i. Jesus said this was the **first of all the commandments**.

- It is the first commandment in regard to age. Before Adam and Eve had any other command, they were commanded to love the Lord their God who created them.

- It is the first commandment in regard to priority. Every other act of obedience is empty if we do not love God first.

c. **To love Him with all... and to love one's neighbor as oneself, is more than all the whole burnt offerings and sacrifices**: The scribe's response to Jesus was right on the mark. It is easy to think that religious ceremony and devotion are more important than love for God and our neighbor, but this isn't the case. A thousand empty burnt offerings do not mean more to God than a single act of love done in His name.

D. Jesus questions, warns, and commends.

1. (35-37) Jesus asks a question: how can the Messiah be both the *Son of David* and the *Lord* of David?

Then Jesus answered and said, while He taught in the temple, "How *is it* that the scribes say that the Christ is the Son of David? For David himself said by the Holy Spirit:

'The LORD said to my Lord,
"Sit at My right hand,
Till I make Your enemies Your footstool."'

Therefore David himself calls Him 'Lord'; how is He *then* his Son?" And the common people heard Him gladly.

a. **How is it that the scribes say that the Christ is the Son of David?** Since Jesus is the Christ, He spoke of Himself here. With the questions of the scribes, Pharisees, and Sadducees to Jesus, they tried to trap Him. Jesus did not do the same in His questions to them; instead He got to the heart of the matter: "Do you really know who I am?"

i. These religious leaders thought they knew just about everything there was to know about the Messiah. Jesus challenged this thought, and He asked them to consider that they may have something to learn.

b. **David himself calls Him 'Lord'; how is He then his Son?** Jesus is not only the *Son of David* but also the **Lord** of David. As Revelation 22:16 says, He is b*oth the root and offspring of David.* With this question Jesus challenged the religious leaders, asking them "do you understand this truth about the Messiah?"

2. (38-40) Jesus warns about the hypocrisy of the scribes.

Then He said to them in His teaching, "Beware of the scribes, who desire to go around in long robes, *love* greetings in the marketplaces, the best seats in the synagogues, and the best places at feasts, who devour widows' houses, and for a pretense make long prayers. These will receive greater condemnation."

a. **Beware of the scribes**: The **scribes** were the "Bible Scholars" of Jesus' day. They were entrusted with preserving, learning, and teaching the Word of God to the world. These were the men that the people of God should have been able to trust, but Jesus said instead they should **beware of the scribes**. The scribes represented a complete contrast to the picture of how a disciple should be - as a servant, as a child, as one carrying a cross. Jesus said that we should notice what they *do* as well as what they *say*.

i. **Beware of the scribes**, because they liked to wear their **long robes**. The scribes were men of leisure, who watched while others worked.

ii. **Beware of the scribes**, because they **love greetings**. They demanded recognition from others in their walk with God, and they loved the image of a holy man.

iii. **Beware of the scribes**, because they loved **the best seats in the synagogue** and at **feasts**, showing they demanded the perks of status and privilege.

iv. **Beware of the scribes**, because they **devour widows' houses**. They sinned against the weak and vulnerable but excused it because they thought they were so spiritual. In that day, a Jewish teacher could not be *paid* for teaching - but he could receive gifts. Apparently, many scribes used flattery and manipulation to wrangle big gifts from those who could least afford to give them - such as widows. The Jews of Jesus' day taught that teachers were to be respected almost as much as God; they said that they deserved more honor and respect than any other people in life. They taught that the greatest act someone could do was to give money to a teacher. Of course, it was the teachers themselves who taught this.

v. **Beware of the scribes**, because they **for a pretense make long prayers**. Their relationship with God was far more show than substance. The scribes thought they were more spiritual because of their long prayers. But G. Campbell Morgan wrote that when a man is away from his wife and the journey is short, the letters are short. The farther he is from his wife, the longer the letters become. Morgan said that some people must be a long way from God because their prayers are so long.

b. **These will receive a greater condemnation**: As in Mark 6:11, Jesus presented the idea of a **greater condemnation** - that some will receive a worse judgment and a worse condemnation than others.

3. (41-42) Jesus observes the widow's giving.

Now Jesus sat opposite the treasury and saw how the people put money into the treasury. And many *who were* rich put in much. Then one poor widow came and threw in two mites, which make a quadrans.

a. **Jesus sat opposite the treasury and saw how the people put money into the treasury**: The sight of this poor widow must have been a welcome sight to a weary Jesus, after enduring a storm of questions from His enemies.

i. The line at the offering box and the pride shown by the rich men in their giving shows us that it isn't necessarily more spiritual to have an offering box instead of passing offering bags. It isn't a matter of right and wrong, but a matter of which is an easier way for people to give in a way that doesn't call attention to their gifts.

b. **Saw how the people put money into the treasury**: Jesus looks at us when we give and He notices how we give. As Jesus looks, He is more interested in **how** we give than in *how much* we give. In seeing **how** the people gave, Jesus wasn't studying technique. He looks more at motive and heart.

c. **Many who were rich put in much. Then one poor widow came in and threw in two mites**: Jesus noticed a long line of rich people who put in a lot of money, perhaps making some kind of display to call attention to their gifts. The **one poor widow** was different and offered **two mites**.

i. Mark tells us that **two mites** make one **quadrans**. Matthew Poole says that we can calculate the value of a mite based on the value of a denarius, which was the going rate of one day's labor for a working man. According to Poole's calculations, a denarius equals six meahs;

one meah equals two pondions; one pondion equals two issarines; one issarine equals eight mites. When you figure it all out, two mites are 1% of a denarius. A mite was pretty small - perhaps our equivalent of putting $1 in the collection plate.

ii. A **quadrans** was a Roman coin. Mark helped his Roman readers to understand how much a mite was worth. It wasn't worth much.

iii. The ancient Greek word *lepton* literally means "a tiny thing," and so in the Old English was translated *mite*, which comes from the word for a "crumb" or "very small morsel."

d. **Two mites**: The wonderful thing about this widow's giving was that she had **two mites** and gave them *both*. She might have kept one coin for herself, and no one would blame her if she did. Instead, she gave with staggering generosity.

4. (43-44) Jesus assesses the widow's gift.

So He called His disciples to *Himself* and said to them, "Assuredly, I say to you that this poor widow has put in more than all those who have given to the treasury; for they all put in out of their abundance, but she out of her poverty put in all that she had, her whole livelihood."

a. **This poor widow has put in more than all those who have given**: Jesus did not say that she put in more than *any one* of them; He said that she put in more than **all** of them - all of them put together.

b. **They all put in out of their abundance, but she out of her poverty put in all that she had**: This explains how Jesus could say that the widow **put in more than all**. It was because all the others gave out of **their abundance** but she gave sacrificially.

i. Jesus' principle here shows us that before God, the *spirit* of giving determines the value of the gift more than the amount. God doesn't want grudgingly given money or guilt money. God loves the cheerful giver.

ii. The widow's gift and Jesus' comment on it also shows us that the value of a gift is determined by what it *costs* the giver. This is what made the widow's gift so valuable. David refused to give God *that which cost me nothing* (2 Samuel 24:24).

iii. Jesus' principle here shows us that God does not *need* our money. If God needed our money, then *how much* we give would be more important than our *heart* in giving. Instead, it is *our* privilege to give to Him, and we need to give because it is good for us, not because it is good for God.

c. **Out of her poverty**: The woman was poor because she was a widow and had no husband to help support her. It also may be significant that Jesus had just criticized the scribes as those *who devour widow's houses.* Then a lone widow made a spectacular contribution. Perhaps a scribe devoured her house.

    i. The widow challenged the mindset that says, "I'll give when I have more." The widow had virtually nothing yet was a giver. This means that we can all please God with our giving just as much as the richest man can please God with his giving. Whatever we give sacrificially to God, He sees it and is pleased.

Mark 13 - The Olivet Discourse

A. The destruction of the temple and its implications.

1. (1-2) Jesus predicts the destruction of the temple.

Then as He went out of the temple, one of His disciples said to Him, "Teacher, see what manner of stones and what buildings *are here!*" And Jesus answered and said to him, "Do you see these great buildings? Not *one* stone shall be left upon another, that shall not be thrown down."

a. **Teacher, see what manner of stones and what buildings are here!** The disciples seemed like tourists amazed at the sites of the city of Jerusalem. They had good reason to be amazed, because the temple compound, as remodeled by Herod the Great, was one of the magnificent structures of the ancient world. The Jewish people were justifiably proud of this great building.

i. This temple was originally rebuilt by Zerubbabel and Ezra (Ezra 6:15) but greatly expanded and improved by Herod. It was the center of Jewish life for almost 1,000 years - so much so, that it was customary to swear by the temple (Matthew 23:16) and speaking against the temple could be considered blasphemy (Acts 6:13).

ii. After Herod's work, the temple was huge - nearly 500 yards long and 400 yards wide. Herod's rebuilding started in 19 B.C., and was not completed until A.D. 63, taking more than 80 years. The magnificent temple compound was finished only seven years before it was destroyed.

iii. The beauty of the ancient temple is well documented. The Jewish historian Josephus says that the temple was covered on the outside with gold plates that were so brilliant that when the sun shone it was blinding. Where there wasn't gold, there were blocks of marble of such a pure white that from a distance, strangers thought there was snow on the temple.

iv. The comment of the disciples - **see what manner of stones and what buildings are here** - is especially appropriate given the massive stones Herod used in building the temple. Today, tourists can see some of these massive stones, at least the ones used to build merely *the retaining wall* for the temple compound. These cut, quarried blocks of limestone are so big - some 50 feet wide, 25 feet high, and 15 feet deep - that most *modern* construction cranes could not lift them.

v. As great as the temple was, Jesus never hesitated to claim that He was greater than the temple (Matthew 12:5). For many Jews of that day, the temple had become an idol - it subtly began to mean more to the people than God Himself meant. The temple was a good thing, but good things can become the worst idols. Sometimes God sours even good things if we allow them to become our idols.

b. **Not one stone shall be left upon another, that shall not be thrown down**: Some 40 years after Jesus said this there was a widespread Jewish revolution against the Romans in Palestine, and the rebels enjoyed many early successes. But ultimately, Rome crushed the Jews of that day. Jerusalem was leveled, including the temple - just as Jesus said.

i. It is said that at the fall of Jerusalem, the last surviving Jews of the city fled to the temple because it was the strongest and most secure building remaining. Roman soldiers surrounded it, and one drunken soldier started a fire that soon engulfed the whole building. Ornate gold detail work in the roof melted down in the cracks between the stone walls of the temple. To retrieve the gold, the Roman commander ordered that the temple be dismantled stone by stone. The destruction was so complete that today researchers have some difficulty learning exactly where the temple was.

ii. "Now, as soon as the army had no more people to kill or plunder... Caesar gave orders that they should now demolish the entire city and temple... this was the end which Jerusalem came to." (Josephus, *Wars of the Jews*, 7.1.1) Interestingly, Josephus tells us that the Romans never *intended* to destroy the temple but were driven to it by the fierceness of Jewish opposition and by accident. (*Wars of the Jews*, 6.4)

iii. The literal fulfillment of this prophecy establishes the tone for the rest of the prophecies in the chapter. We should expect a literal fulfillment for these other prophecies also.

2. (3-4) Jesus' prediction brings up two questions in the minds of His disciples.

Now as He sat on the Mount of Olives opposite the temple, Peter, James, John, and Andrew asked Him privately, "Tell us, when will these things be? And what *will be* the sign when all these things will be fulfilled?"

a. **As He sat on the Mount of Olives**: The **Mount of Olives** is a hill that rises above the temple mount. Between the temple mount and the **Mount of Olives** lies a small valley, the Kidron Valley. From the **Mount of Olives** is a dramatic view of the temple mount.

b. **Tell us, when will these things be?** As Jesus sat with His disciples on the Mount of Olives, they could see the majestic structure of the temple. With this view, the first question in the mind of the disciples was about the destruction of the temple. Jesus said it would be destroyed, and they wanted to know when. Mark does not record Jesus' answer to this first question, but Luke does in Luke 21:8-23.

c. **What will be the sign when all these things will be fulfilled?** The second question is answered in the remainder of Mark 13.

i. This question was asked perhaps as they remembered the events surrounding the last temple's destruction: the temple was destroyed in the context of national judgment and exile. If the temple will be destroyed, then what will become of Israel and the Jews?

B. The flow of history until Jesus' return.

1. (5-8) Jesus describes general world conditions during the period between His Ascension and the time immediately preceding His Second Coming.

And Jesus, answering them, began to say: "Take heed that no one deceives you. For many will come in My name, saying, 'I am *He,*' and will deceive many. But when you hear of wars and rumors of wars, do not be troubled; for *such things* must happen, but the end *is* not yet. For nation will rise against nation, and kingdom against kingdom. And there will be earthquakes in various places, and there will be famines and troubles. These *are* the beginnings of sorrows."

a. **Take heed that no one deceives you**: Jesus warns of the danger of false messiahs who come in His **name**. They will pretend to be Jesus or representatives of Jesus, but they will not be true representatives of Jesus.

b. **Wars and rumors of wars**: Jesus reminded us that before He returned there would be many wars and threats of war on the earth. In troubled times, many people assume that the end of the age is near, but Jesus said that **wars and rumors of wars** are not signs of the end.

i. "Our Lord's outlook upon this age was not that of one in which there should be a gradual cessation of strife between the nations, by the victory of the preaching of His Gospel, until the whole earth should be reduced by that preaching to a condition of peace." (Morgan)

c. **Such things must happen, but the end is not yet**: Things such as false messiahs, **wars**, **famines** and **earthquakes** have certainly marked man's history since the time of Jesus' Ascension. In effect, Jesus said, "Catastrophes will happen, but these do not signal the end."

i. Man has often thought that such things would signal the end, but Jesus would point to a more specific sign to watch for.

d. **These are the beginning of sorrows**: Jesus said these calamites were not *specific* signs of the end, but were **the beginning of sorrows**, which is literally *the beginning of labor pains*. The idea is both of giving birth to a new age, and perhaps implying an increase of intensity and frequency in these calamities.

2. (9-13) Jesus describes what His disciples must expect during the time between His Ascension and Second Coming.

"But watch out for yourselves, for they will deliver you up to councils, and you will be beaten in the synagogues. You will be brought before rulers and kings for My sake, for a testimony to them. And the gospel must first be preached to all the nations. But when they arrest *you* and deliver you up, do not worry beforehand, or premeditate what you will speak. But whatever is given you in that hour, speak that; for it is not you who speak, but the Holy Spirit. Now brother will betray brother to death, and a father *his* child; and children will rise up against parents and cause them to be put to death. And you will be hated by all for My name's sake. But he who endures to the end shall be saved."

a. **Watch out for yourselves, for they will deliver you up to councils**: Jesus told His disciples to be prepared for the persecution that would come against them before the end. This persecution was not the sign of the end, but simply should be expected.

b. **The gospel must first be preached to all the nations**: Jesus also promised that before the end the gospel must go out to the whole world. The presence of persecution does not relieve the Church of this responsibility.

c. **When they arrest you and deliver you up, do not worry beforehand, or premeditate what you will speak**: Jesus told His followers to not worry about what to say when they had to give an answer for being a follower of Jesus. At that moment, the Holy Spirit would give them words to say.

i. A powerful example of this principle is found in Acts 4:1-22, where Peter and the other disciples made a dramatic proclamation of Jesus before the hostile Sanhedrin.

ii. Here Jesus spoke of the inspiration that comes at a moment of persecution, not of teaching in the church. "There is no excuse for the lazy preacher who fails to prepare his sermon out of the mistaken reliance upon the Holy Spirit." (Robertson)

d. **Brother will betray brother to death**: The followers of Jesus should expect the most painful kinds of rejection and betrayal as they sought to stand strong for Jesus.

i. It is easy for us to underestimate how difficult a time of persecution can be. While few Christians in the Western world face persecution, Christians in other parts of the world often face these trials.

- If I came from an orthodox Jewish family, they might consider me a blasphemer and account me as dead for choosing Jesus.

- If I came from a strict Muslim family, I might be rejected by my family and be literally killed for choosing Jesus.

- If I came from a Hindu family in India, I could be rejected and martyred for choosing Jesus.

- In China, I would be allowed to practice Christianity only in the state-sponsored church - or be persecuted. My church might be one of the 1,500 destroyed or shut down since November of 2000.

- In Sudan, I might be killed or literally enslaved by a Muslim army.

- In Indonesia, I might be given a choice by Muslims: convert to Islam or die, or I might have my church bombed during a worship service.

- In Pakistan, I might be jailed by Muslim government officials.

ii. According to David B. Barrett in his book *Today's Martyrs*, some 165,000 Christians died for their faith in the year 2000. Researchers estimate that since the Day of Pentecost, more than 43 million Christians have been killed for their faith. A persecution index provided by Open Doors with Brother Andrew listed 28 countries with strong or massive persecution. In another 23 countries, Christians suffer discrimination and, in some regions, severe harassment.

e. **He who endures to the end shall be saved**: **Endures** is translated from the ancient Greek word *hupomeno*, which literally means to "remain under." When trials and persecution swirl about, we can't be so desperate for an escape that we will compromise. Instead, we must *remain under*.

C. The sign of His coming and the end of the age.

1. (14a) The sign: The abomination of desolation, spoken of by Daniel.

"So when you see the 'abomination of desolation,' spoken of by Daniel the prophet, standing where it ought not" (let the reader understand),

a. **When you see the 'abomination of desolation'**: This mention of the **abomination of desolation** is taken from Daniel 11:31: *They shall defile the sanctuary fortress; then they shall take away the daily sacrifices, and place there the abomination of desolation.* This described a complete desecration of the temple, prefigured by Antiochus Epiphanies in the time between the Old and New Testaments.

i. This Antiochus desecrated the temple in Jerusalem in a horrible way. "He desecrated the Temple by offering swine's flesh on the great altar and by setting up public brothels in the sacred courts. Before the very Holy Place itself he set up a great statue of the Olympian Zeus and ordered the Jews to worship it." (Barclay) As bad is this was, it did not fulfill the **abomination of desolation**, because Jesus said these words long *after* Antiochus did this.

ii. The Hebrew word translated **abomination** in Daniel 11:31 is *shikkoots*. It appears in the Old Testament 29 times, and it has the idea of a filthy, disgusting idol. However, this is more than just an idol. First, it is an idol set in the holy place of the temple in Jerusalem - **standing where it ought not**, and as Matthew puts it, *standing in the holy place* (Matthew 24:15). Second, this is a filthy, disgusting idol that brings **desolation** - the complete and devastating judgment of God.

iii. It is important to point out that this is not merely an idol set up in the Jewish temple. Passages like Jeremiah 7:30, Jeremiah 32:34, and Ezekiel 5:11 describe abominable idols in the temple - but they were not the **abomination** that brings **desolation**.

iv. Something nearly like this happened in 40 A.D. when Caligula was the Emperor of Rome. He was a madman and decided to set up a statute of himself in the holy place of the temple in Jerusalem. He sent the statue by ship on its way down to Jerusalem, but he died before it arrived, and they never set it up.

b. **When you see the 'abomination of desolation'**: Essentially, the **abomination of desolation** speaks of the ultimate desecration of a Jewish temple, an idolatrous image in the holy place itself, which will inevitably result in the judgment of God. It is the **abomination** that brings **desolation**.

i. The **abomination of desolation** is "the object of religious nausea and loathing who has to do with desolation." (Wuest) "The Semitic expression used in Daniel describes an abomination so detestable it causes the Temple to be abandoned by the people of God and provokes desolation. . . Jesus' use of this distinctive expression, however, indicates that the prophecy was not ultimately fulfilled by the events of the Maccabean period." (Lane)

ii. Paul elaborated on the future fulfillment of this in 2 Thessalonians 2:3-4: *That day will not come unless the falling away comes first, and the man of sin is revealed, the son of perdition, who opposes and exalts himself above all that is called God or that is worshipped, so that he sits as God in the temple of God, showing himself that he is God.*

iii. Daniel 12:11 gives additional insight: *And from the time that the daily sacrifice is taken away, and the abomination of desolation is set up, there shall be 1,290 days* (until the end). When this sign is set up, the end can be determined - almost three and one-half years to go before the triumphant return of Jesus to this earth.

iv. This is not a new understanding of the **abomination of desolation**. An early Christian writer named Irenaeus wrote this in the late second century: "But when this Antichrist shall have devastated all things in this world, he will reign for three years and six months, and sit in the temple at Jerusalem; and then the Lord will come from heaven in the clouds, in the glory of the Father, sending this man and those who follow him into the lake of fire; but bringing in for the righteous the times of the kingdom."

c. **When you see the 'abomination of desolation'**: When Jesus described the **abomination of desolation**, there was the presupposition of an operating temple in Jerusalem. You can't have the **abomination of desolation** without a temple.

i. For centuries, there was only a small Jewish presence in Judea and Jerusalem. Their presence in the region was definite and continuous, but small. It was unthinkable that this weak Jewish presence could rebuild a temple. Therefore, the fulfillment of this prophecy was highly unlikely until Israel was gathered as a nation again in 1948. The restoration of a nation that the world had not seen for more than 2,000 years was a remarkable event in the fulfillment and future fulfillment of prophecy.

ii. One of the more fascinating developments in recent history is the focus of Jewish and Arab conflict over the temple mount, where a rebuilt temple must stand. There is a small but dedicated group of Jews who are passionately committed to rebuilding the temple. Today you can visit the Temple Institute in the Jewish Quarter of the old city in

Jerusalem. There, a group of Jews absolutely dedicated to rebuilding the temple attempt to educate the public and raise awareness for a new temple. They are trying to replicate everything they can for a new temple, down to the specific pots and pans used for sacrifice.

iii. It is important to understand that most Jews – religious or secular – do not care one bit about building a temple. And if one were rebuilt, sacrifice would be difficult in a day of aggressive animal rights activists! Yet, there is a small, strong, highly dedicated group who live to see a rebuilt temple – a temple that will fulfill prophecy.

iv. Rightly, Christians get excited when they see efforts to rebuild the temple. At the same time, we should understand that the basic impulse behind rebuilding the temple is not of God at all – the desire to have a place to sacrifice for sin. Christians believe that all sacrifice for sin was finished at the cross, and any further sacrifice for sin is an offense to God, because it denies the finished work of Jesus on the cross.

d. **Spoken of by Daniel the prophet**: In a sense, Jesus told us nothing new here. He simply called us back to what was prophesied in Daniel. The comment **let the reader understand** could have been said by Jesus Himself and not written by Mark.

e. **Let the reader understand**: Some say that **the abomination of desolation** was fulfilled in A.D. 70 when Jerusalem was destroyed, and that this ties in with the destruction of the temple promised in Mark 13:2. This interpretation must spiritualize Mark 13:19-27, which says that Jesus would return in glory soon after the **abomination of desolation**.

i. F.F. Bruce rightly notes: "While Josephus mentions the sacrifices offered by the victorious Romans to their legionary standards in the Temple court, he does not describe this action as an abomination, whatever he may have thought privately." (*New Testament History*, page 383)

2. (14b-18) Jesus warns of what to do when the abomination of desolation appears.

"Then let those who are in Judea flee to the mountains. Let him who is on the housetop not go down into the house, nor enter to take anything out of his house. And let him who is in the field not go back to get his clothes. But woe to those who are pregnant and to those who are nursing babies in those days! And pray that your flight may not be in winter."

a. **Let those who are in Judea flee to the mountains**: Jesus directed this warning to the Jewish people. This is evident in His specific mention of **Judea** and of **the housetop** (a common feature of architecture in both ancient and modern Judea). To the citizens of Judea, Jesus said: "When you see the abomination of desolation established, flee because trouble is coming."

i. These words of Jesus have led some to believe that everything Jesus spoke of here was fulfilled in the first century, in the Roman destruction of Jerusalem. It is true that this exhortation by Jesus was taken literally by Christians in A.D. 66 when Roman armies first came to Jerusalem. At that time, Christians fled to the mountains and were spared the great destruction of A.D. 70 However, Jesus also said that these events would bring in the Great Tribulation (Mark 13:19) and that those days would culminate in the triumphant return of Jesus (Mark 13:26-27). Since we're still here 2,000 years later, we know that the abomination of desolation wasn't fulfilled in the first century.

ii. These words of Jesus have led some to believe that all Christians - the church as a whole - will go through this time known as the Great Tribulation, and that this warning must be for us. However, Jesus promised to catch His people up from the earth and meet them in the air (1 Thessalonians 4:16-18). He also told us to pray that we would be counted worthy to escape this time (Luke 21:36) and promised to keep His faithful from the time of judgment that would come upon the earth (Revelation 3:10). Jesus gave this warning primarily as a specific, amazing prophecy of events thousands of years before they happened so that the Jewish people during the days of the abomination of desolation would have a unique witness to Jesus and His Word.

b. **Let him who is in the field not go back to get his clothes**: This shows the *urgency* of the warning. This is consistent with other passages of Scripture that promise great persecution against the Jewish people during the Great Tribulation (Revelation 12:13-17).

3. (19-23) Coming after the abomination of desolation: great **tribulation**.

"For *in* those days there will be tribulation, such as has not been since the beginning of the creation which God created until this time, nor ever shall be. And unless the Lord had shortened those days, no flesh would be saved; but for the elect's sake, whom He chose, He shortened the days. Then if anyone says to you, 'Look, here *is* the Christ!' or, 'Look, He *is* there!' do not believe it. For false christs and false prophets will rise and show signs and wonders to deceive, if possible, even the elect. But take heed; see, I have told you all things beforehand."

a. **Tribulation, such as has not been since the beginning of the creation... nor ever shall be**: Jesus said that this will be the most awful time in all of human history. When we consider the massive calamities humanity has suffered through the centuries, this is a terribly sobering statement. The Book of Revelation describes this terrible time when God pours out His wrath on a God-rejecting world.

i. In 1343 bubonic plague started to sweep across Europe. Over eight years, two-thirds of the population of Europe was afflicted with the plague, and half of those afflicted died - an incredible total of 25 million people. This coming time of **tribulation** will be worse.

ii. Zbigniew Brzezinski in his book *Out of Control: Global Turmoil on the Eve of the Twenty-first Century* (1993) sets the number of "Lives deliberately extinguished by politically motivated carnage" at between 167 million and 175 million. Most other statisticians have roughly the same estimates. Yet, Jesus said that this time of **tribulation** will be worse.

b. **Unless the Lord had shortened those days**: If the terrors of the great tribulation were to continue indefinitely, mankind could not survive. Therefore, **for the elect's sake**, the days will be limited.

c. **Then if anyone says to you, "Look, here is the Christ!" or, "Look, He is there!" do not believe it**: No one should be deceived about the nature of Jesus' coming. It will not be secret or private, and it won't be a "different" Jesus. In the midst of such tribulation, men will be tempted to follow after false messiahs.

d. **But take heed; see, I have told you all things beforehand**: Jesus told this to His followers as a warning so that they would **take heed**. It wasn't just for those who come to faith in Jesus during the Great Tribulation. It wasn't just for those who live at the end of the age. It is for everyone to **take heed**.

i. We live in a cynical age when people are naturally distrustful and pessimistic when it comes to promises. Among Christians in the 1970's, there was great emphasis on the return of Jesus and being ready for His return. It is easy in our cynical age to think, "I've been waiting for 30 years and Jesus still hasn't come. I don't need to be so ready and so worked up over something that might not happen for another 30 or 300 years."

ii. It is easy to sympathize with that way of thinking - but Jesus told us **take heed; see, I have told you all things beforehand**. He has reasons why He wants you to **take heed**, anticipating and being ready for His soon return:

- It has a purifying effect in our lives.
- It gives us a sense of urgency.

- It makes us bold in speaking to the lost.
- It helps us keep a light touch on the things of this world.

iii. Think of it this way: if a person woke every morning and said, "Jesus is coming soon and I have to live like He is coming soon," would it make their life better or worse?

iv. We should also remember that God has a reason for the time He has established. If Jesus had caught up His church in 1978, how many would have missed the rapture? If He returned in glory seven years later in 1985, how many of us would have gone through the Great Tribulation? We can all see the time is close; any extended time is pure grace to allow more people to come in before the horrific events Jesus described in the Great Tribulation.

4. (24-27) On the heels of great tribulation: the return of Jesus Christ.

"But in those days, after that tribulation, the sun will be darkened, and the moon will not give its light; the stars of heaven will fall, and the powers in the heavens will be shaken. Then they will see the Son of Man coming in the clouds with great power and glory. And then He will send His angels, and gather together His elect from the four winds, from the farthest part of earth to the farthest part of heaven."

a. **In those days, after that tribulation**: Jesus said that the cosmic catastrophes He described here would happen **in those days**, the days connected with **that tribulation**.

b. **The sun will be darkened, and the moon will not give its light; the stars of heaven will fall**: Immediately before the return of Jesus, before His **coming in the clouds with great power and glory**, the world will be wracked by cosmic catastrophes. In a sense, this will be the groaning of all creation (Romans 8:22) and it will come to one last crescendo before the return of Jesus.

i. This kind of cosmic calamity is described in many Old Testament passages such as Isaiah 13:9-11, Ezekiel 32:7-9, Joel 2:30-31, Amos 8:9-10, and Zephaniah 1:14-15.

c. **He will send His angels, and gather together His elect**: When Jesus returns to this earth **after that tribulation**, He will come *with* the saints in heaven and to **gather** those who have come to Jesus during the **tribulation** and have survived.

5. (28-31) Jesus speaks more regarding the timing of these events.

"Now learn this parable from the fig tree: When its branch has already become tender, and puts forth leaves, you know that summer is near. So

you also, when you see these things happening, know that it is near; at the doors! Assuredly, I say to you, this generation will by no means pass away till all these things take place. Heaven and earth will pass away, but My words will by no means pass away."

a. **Now learn this parable from the fig tree**: The **fig tree** has a regular pattern - the leaves appear and then summer follows. When you see the leaves, you know **summer is near**. In the same way, when these signs - particularly the abomination of desolation - appear, the world can know that the triumphant return of Jesus is **near; at the doors**.

i. This is just as Daniel prophesied in Daniel 12:11: the end *will come* 1,290 days after the abomination of desolation. In this, Jesus assured that the agonies of the great tribulation would not continue indefinitely; they will have an end. Song of Solomon 2:11-13 also mentions the idea that the blossoming of the fig tree shows winter is past and summer is near.

ii. "In contrast to most of the trees of Palestine... the fig loses its leaves in the winter, and in contrast to the almond, which blossoms very early in the spring, the fig tree shows signs of life only later." (Lane)

iii. This was the perfect illustration at this time and place. Jesus taught this on the Mount of Olives, and "The Mount of Olives was famous for its fig trees, which sometimes attained a height of 20 or 30 feet." (Lane) It was also the perfect time, because Jesus taught this right before Passover, when fig trees were in the condition described in the parable - branches tender, leaves sprouting.

b. **This generation will be no means pass away till all these things take place**: What **generation** did Jesus refer to? It cannot be the **generation** of the disciples because they did not see the triumphant return of Jesus. It is undoubtedly the **generation** that will see these signs - especially the abomination of desolation. These events and Jesus' return won't be on some 1,000-year timetable but will happen in succession.

i. It is also possible that the word **generation** can be understood as a *race* or *people*. This may be a promise that the Jewish race will not perish before history comes to a conclusion.

c. **Heaven and earth will pass away, but My words will by no means pass away**: Jesus made the amazing claim of uttering eternal words. This is certainly enough to establish His claim to deity.

6. (32-37) The emphasis: be ready; watch.

"But of that day and hour no one knows, not even the angels in heaven, nor the Son, but only the Father. Take heed, watch and pray; for you

do not know when the time is. *It is* like a man going to a far country, who left his house and gave authority to his servants, and to each his work, and commanded the doorkeeper to watch. Watch therefore, for you do not know when the master of the house is coming; in the evening, at midnight, at the crowing of the rooster, or in the morning; lest, coming suddenly, he find you sleeping. And what I say to you, I say to all: Watch!"

a. **That day and hour no one knows**: This means that we must **take heed**, because we face the danger of being unprepared.

i. **Nor the Son, but only the Father**: How could Jesus *not* know that day and hour? Did not He, as God, know all things? Jesus did not know this, but it was not because He gave up His omniscience - He is the unchanging God. It was because He voluntarily, in submission to God the Father, restricted His knowledge of this event.

b. **Take heed, watch**: We must **watch**. Anyone who watches is not caught by surprise. People are not ready because they fail to **watch**. The emphasis couldn't be clearer:

- **Of that day and hour no one knows** (Mark 13:32).
- **You do not know when the time is** (Mark 13:33).
- **You do not know when the master of the house is coming** (Mark 13:35).

i. Some people have the idea, "We don't know when Jesus is coming, so it doesn't really matter." Others have the idea, "We don't know when Jesus is coming, so we have to find out and set a date." The right response is, "I don't know when Jesus is coming so I have to be alert, eager, and ready for His coming."

c. **Take heed... pray**: We must **pray**, that we may be found worthy to *escape all these things that will come to pass* (Luke 21:36). The good news in Jesus is that we don't have to go through this calamity that will come. He will take from the earth as many as are ready to go before this calamity begins.

i. When Jerusalem was destroyed in 70 A.D., those who listened to and obeyed Jesus escaped the horrible destruction that came upon the city. When it comes to the far greater destruction that will come upon the whole earth, those who listen to and obey Jesus can escape the horrible destruction that will come.

d. **It is like a man going to a far country**: Jesus now spoke to His followers about how they should live *until* He comes. Jesus is like the **man going**

to a far country, who left three things to his servants: **his house**, his **authority**, and **his work**. The traveling man also appoints a **doorkeeper** to keep watch. He may return at any time, and does not want to find his servants sleeping. The point of it all: **Watch!**

i. "The Parable of the Fig Tree cautions Tribulation saints to watch and know the 'signs of the times.' But the Parable of the Householder warns *all of us today*." (Wiersbe)

ii. Think of what Jesus has left you:

- **His house**: The church belongs to Jesus, but He entrusts it to each one of us.

- His **authority**: We are to live and serve in the **authority** of Jesus, and *responsibility* is always coupled with **authority**.

- **His work**: Each servant has **his work** to do. We aren't responsible for someone else's work, but we certainly are responsible for ours.

Mark 14 - Jesus' Betrayal, Arrest, and Trial

A. Preparations for death.

1. (1-2) The rulers resolve to kill Jesus.

After two days it was the Passover and *the Feast* of Unleavened Bread. And the chief priests and the scribes sought how they might take Him by trickery and put *Him* to death. But they said, "Not during the feast, lest there be an uproar of the people."

a. **After two days it was the Passover**: The *time* is significant, because there was at **Passover** not only a great expectation of the Messiah, but Jerusalem was also crowded with these Messiah-expecting multitudes. Since Passover remembered the time when God raised up a great deliverer and freed Israel from foreign oppression, it was a time of great patriotic and messianic anticipation. The Romans were on guard and ready for any hint of revolt.

i. Every possible preparation was made for the Passover. For a month ahead of time, the meaning of Passover was explained in each synagogue and Jewish school so that no one was unprepared. As pilgrims streamed into Jerusalem, they noticed that every tomb near a road was painted with fresh whitewash, to prevent them from defiling themselves accidentally by brushing against a tomb.

ii. Every male Jew who lived within 15 miles of Jerusalem *had* to come to Jerusalem for Passover. Many more came from great distances - including Galilee. Many people who heard and saw Jesus in the region of Galilee were here, with great respect and great expectation regarding Jesus.

iii. The feasts of **Passover and the Feast of Unleavened Bread** were held one after the other. "In popular usage the two festivals were merged and treated for practical purposes as the seven-day 'feast of the Passover.'" (Lane)

b. **How they might take Him by trickery**: As the **chief priests and the scribes** plotted the murder of an innocent man, it showed that they did not fear God. Nevertheless, they feared the people (**lest there be an uproar of the people**). These religious leaders were not afraid to murder the Son of God; they just believed they had to do it in a politically smart way.

c. **Not during the feast**: The religious leaders did not *want* to kill Jesus during the Passover feast, but they ended up doing it during that time anyway. This clearly shows that Jesus was in command and though the leaders acted according to the evil inclination of their hearts, their actions fulfilled prophecy and the plan of Jesus.

> i. From John 11:57 it seems that the religious leaders originally intended to seize Jesus during the feast. When they saw the popularity of Jesus at the triumphal entry and His authority on the temple mount, they changed their minds and decided to do it *after* the feast. Their plan changed again when Judas volunteered to arrange a private, quiet arrest.

2. (3) What the woman did: Jesus is anointed with perfume.

And being in Bethany at the house of Simon the leper, as He sat at the table, a woman came having an alabaster flask of very costly oil of spikenard. Then she broke the flask and poured *it* on His head.

a. **A woman came**: John's account of this incident (John 12:1-8) tells us that this was Mary of Bethany, the sister of Lazarus and Martha.

> i. This isn't the same event as when a sinful woman brought the alabaster box with ointment, broke it and anointed Jesus' feet. That occasion was precious, but it was different in that the woman was overwhelmed with her own sense of sinfulness and adoration to her pardoning Lord. Mary seems focused on Jesus alone, not even on her own forgiven sin. It is a great thing to love Jesus for all He has done for us; it can be greater still to love Him simply for who He is in all His wonder and majesty.

b. **Having an alabaster flask of very costly oil**: This was an extravagant display of devotion to Jesus. Often spices and ointments were used as investments because they were small, portable, and could be easily sold.

> i. "Early in the first century Pliny the Elder remarked that 'the best ointment is preserved in alabaster.' The value of the perfume, and its identification as nard, suggests that it was a family heirloom that was passed on from one generation to another, from mother to daughter." (Lane)

c. She broke the flask and poured it on His head: The **flask** was a small bottle with a thin neck and breaking the neck of the bottle opened it. Mark's wording indicates that she poured the entire contents of the bottle on the head of Jesus.

i. When a guest arrived for a meal, it was customary to anoint the guest's head with a dab of oil. Here, this **woman** went much farther than the customary greeting. She **poured** the entire contents of an **alabaster flask of very costly oil** on the head of Jesus.

ii. This was a wonderful, perceptive act of Mary. Jesus just rode into Jerusalem as a King - and shouldn't kings be anointed? Mary understood this, but the disciples didn't.

iii. Mary did this without a word. We gather that her sister Martha was quite the talker, but Mary was a doer. She didn't announce what she was going to do, and she didn't describe it as she did it. Nor did she explain it after she did it. She simply did it.

iv. "If we could all *do* more and *talk* less it might be a blessing to ourselves at least, perhaps to others. Let us labor in our service for the Lord to be more and more hidden; as much as the proud desire to catch the eye of man, let us endeavor to avoid it." (Spurgeon)

v. When Mary was finished, she didn't look to the disciples and ask their opinion of what she did. "You should rise above such idle dependence upon man's opinion; what matters it to you what your fellow-servant thinks? To your own Master you stand or fall. If you have done a good thing do it again. You know the story of the man who comes riding up to the captain, and says, 'Sir, we have taken a gun from the enemy.' 'Go and take another,' said the matter-of-fact officer. That is the best advice which I can render to a friend who is elated with his own success. So much remains to be accomplished that we have no time to consider what has been done." (Spurgeon)

3. (4-9) The reaction to what the woman did.

But there were some who were indignant among themselves, and said, "Why was this fragrant oil wasted? For it might have been sold for more than three hundred denarii and given to the poor." And they criticized her sharply. But Jesus said, "Let her alone. Why do you trouble her? She has done a good work for Me. For you have the poor with you always, and whenever you wish you may do them good; but Me you do not have always. She has done what she could. She has come beforehand to anoint My body for burial. Assuredly, I say to you, wherever this gospel

is preached in the whole world, what this woman has done will also be told as a memorial to her."

a. **Some who were indignant**: John 12:1-8 tells us that it was specifically Judas who was indignant about the expense. His indignation was entirely self-serving. John 12:6 says, *this he said, not that he cared for the poor, but because he was a thief, and had the money box; and he used to take what was put in it.*

i. **They criticized her sharply**: It's easy to criticize those who show more love to Jesus than we do. We sometimes want to define a fanatic as someone who is more devoted to Jesus than we are.

ii. Judas may have started the criticism, but he wasn't alone for long. Mark made it clear that *they* **criticized her sharply**. Each one looked at the oil on Jesus' head and considered it **wasted**. Mary probably started to wonder if she did something wrong.

iii. "It is interesting that the word translated 'waste' in Mark 14:4 is translated 'perdition' in John 17:12 *and applied to Judas!* Judas criticized Mary for 'wasting money,' but he wasted his entire life!" (Wiersbe)

b. **It might have been sold for more than three hundred denarii**: This particular alabaster flask seems to have been worth more than a year's wages for a laborer. "I shall always feel obliged to Judas for figuring up the price of that box of costly nard. He did it to blame her, but we will let his figures stand, and think the more of her the more he put down to the account of waste. I should never have known what it cost, nor would you either, if Judas had not marked down in his pocket-book." (Spurgeon)

c. **Let her alone. Why do you trouble her? She has done a good work for Me**: The disciples thought that this extravagant anointing with oil was a waste, but Jesus received it as a **good work**. With her simple love and devotion to Jesus, Mary understood what the disciples did not - that Jesus was about to die, and she intended this gift as a preparation for his **burial**.

i. **She has done a good work**: "In the Greek there are two words for *good*. There is *agathos* which describes a thing which is morally good; and there is *kalos* which describes a thing which is not only good but *lovely*. A thing might be *agathos*, and yet be hard, stern, austere, unattractive. But a thing which is *kalos* is winsome and lovely, with a certain bloom of charm upon it." (Barclay)

ii. Jesus gave her the highest compliment: **she has done what she could**. God expects no *more* from us than what we can do; but beware of setting your sights so low that you believe that doing *nothing* is doing what you *can*. "There can be no higher commendation than this.

All cannot do great things for Christ, but it is well if each one does what he can as unto the Lord Himself." (Ironside)

d. **She has come beforehand to anoint My body for burial**: Mary's act was all the more precious because it was *planned* (**she has come beforehand**). This wasn't a spontaneous, seized by the moment kind of action. It was carefully planned **beforehand**.

> i. Apparently, Mary listened and believed the teaching of Jesus in a way that the other disciples simply didn't. When He said that He would be delivered into the hands of wicked men and mocked and scourged and crucified, she believed it. She said, "If my precious Jesus will be mocked and tortured like this, then allow me to give Him some special honor."

> ii. It seems that the disciples did not want to think about the death of Jesus. When Peter heard of it, he tried to talk Jesus out of it. Mary had a different devotion, and instead of debating or denying His death, she turned it into an occasion of deep devotion.

> iii. "Nothing puts life into men like a dying Savior. Get you close to Christ, and carry the remembrance of him about you from day to day, and you will do right royal deeds. Come, let us slay sin, for Christ was slain. Come, let us bury all our pride, for Christ was buried. Come, let us rise to newness of life, for Christ has risen. Let us be united with our crucified Lord in his one great object - let us live and die with him, and then every action of our lives will be very beautiful." (Spurgeon)

e. **Wherever this gospel is preached in the whole world**: Jesus knew He was going to die, but He did not waver in confidence one bit. He also knew He would rise from the dead that **this gospel** would be **preached in the whole world**.

f. **As a memorial to her**: The disciples longed for fame and influence, but this woman found an enduring memorial. She found it not by longing for a position, but simply by loving Jesus and serving Him.

> i. There is a tendency within us all to look at this story and to say, "I love Jesus also. Tell me what I should do to show it." But part of the woman's great love was displayed in the fact that *she* came up with the idea to express her love for Jesus in this way. If there was a command to do this, it would never be this precious. "'Oh,' cries a brother, 'tell me what I could do for Jesus!' Nay, but, brother, I must not tell you. The better part of the whole matter will lie in the hallowed ingenuity of your spirit in inventing something for him out of your own fervent soul." (Spurgeon)

4. (10-11) Judas agrees to betray Jesus, changing the plans of the Jewish rulers.

Then Judas Iscariot, one of the twelve, went to the chief priests to betray Him to them. And when they heard *it,* they were glad, and promised to give him money. So he sought how he might conveniently betray Him.

a. **Judas Iscariot, one of the twelve**: Many speculate on the motive of Judas. Perhaps his feelings were hurt when Jesus rebuked him after Mary poured the ointment over Jesus' feet. Perhaps it was plain greed. Some speculate that Judas wanted to force Jesus into an open display of Messianic glory.

i. Matthew 26:15 makes it clear that Judas *bargained* with the religious leaders for the life of Jesus. He asked them, *"What are you willing to give me if I deliver Him to you?"* Certainly, part of his motivation was pure greed.

ii. Whatever Judas' motive was, it was *his* motive. God used the wicked work of a *willing* Satan, who used a *willing* Judas. God ordained that these things happen, but He did not *prompt* Judas to sin.

b. **When they heard it, they were glad**: The religious leaders had wanted to destroy Jesus for a long time (Mark 3:6). Now they had a precious ally - a disciple willing to **betray Him**.

B. Jesus' final Passover with His disciples.

1. (12-16) Preparation for Passover; the feast remembering Israel's redemption.

Now on the first day of Unleavened Bread, when they killed the Passover *lamb,* His disciples said to Him, "Where do You want us to go and prepare, that You may eat the Passover?" And He sent out two of His disciples and said to them, "Go into the city, and a man will meet you carrying a pitcher of water; follow him. Wherever he goes in, say to the master of the house, 'The Teacher says, "Where is the guest room in which I may eat the Passover with My disciples?"' Then he will show you a large upper room, furnished *and* prepared; there make ready for us." So His disciples went out, and came into the city, and found it just as He had said to them; and they prepared the Passover.

a. **A man... carrying a pitcher**: This was an unusual sight. Women usually carried liquids in pitchers, and men normally carried liquids in animal skin containers. Therefore, **a man... carrying a pitcher** was a distinctive sign to the disciples.

b. **The Teacher says, "Where is the guest room"**: The scene here implies secrecy, and Jesus had good reason to quietly make arrangements for Passover. Jesus didn't want Judas to betray Him before He could give a final important talk to the disciples.

i. "The Lord must have had many unknown disciples, upon whom He could rely at such moments to render unquestioning service." (Cole)

c. **And they prepared the Passover**: There seems to be a difference between the synoptic gospels (Matthew, Mark, Luke) and John about the Passover. The implication in the synoptic gospels is that Jesus was crucified *on the day after* Passover and that this meal was the day before. John seems to say that Jesus was crucified *on the day of Passover* itself, as a Passover lamb (John 18:28 and 19:14).

i. "Possibly the best explanation is that there were different calendars in use. Jesus died as the Passover victims were being slain according to the official calendar; but he had held the Passover with his followers the previous evening, according to an unofficial calendar." (Morris)

ii. None of the synoptic gospels mention a *lamb* at the Passover meal. Some believe that this is because they could not obtain one before the "official" day of Passover. Jesus may have wanted it this way in order to emphasize the idea that *He* was the Passover sacrifice.

2. (17-21) Jesus gives Judas a chance to repent.

In the evening He came with the twelve. Now as they sat and ate, Jesus said, "Assuredly, I say to you, one of you who eats with Me will betray Me." And they began to be sorrowful, and to say to Him one by one, "Is it I?" And another *said, "Is it I?"* He answered and said to them, "It is one of the twelve, who dips with Me in the dish. The Son of Man indeed goes just as it is written of Him, but woe to that man by whom the Son of Man is betrayed! It would have been good for that man if he had never been born."

a. **He sat down with the twelve**: At the first Passover, God commanded them to eat the meal standing and ready to leave Egypt (Exodus 12:11). Since Israel came into the Promised Land, they believed that they could eat the Passover sitting or reclining, because now they were at rest in the land God gave them.

b. **One of you who eats with Me will betray Me**: The disciples heard many surprising things from Jesus, but certainly this was one of the most surprising things they ever heard. Not one of them suspected Judas, and the idea that one of them would seek to **betray** and kill Jesus must have seemed absurd.

c. **It is one of the twelve, who dips with Me**: In saying **who dips with Me**, Jesus did not single out Judas (though Judas, sitting in the place of honor, would have been given the special portion). All the disciples dipped with Him, so this phrase identified the betrayer as a *friend*.

i. In Middle Eastern culture, betraying a friend after eating a meal with him *was* and *is* regarded as the worst kind of treachery.

d. **Woe to that man by whom the Son of Man is betrayed!** Judas is rightly regarded as one of the most notorious sinners of all time. Even though his actions fulfilled prophecy (**the Son of Man indeed goes just as it is written of Him**), his own wicked motive condemned him. Judas will never be able to justify himself before God on the Day of Judgment by claiming, "I was fulfilling prophecy."

i. In the warning of Jesus we see a profound love for Judas. This was his last, fleeting opportunity to turn back from his evil plot. A remarkable thing to remember is that Jesus loved both Mary and Judas. We almost want to think that He loved Mary and hated Judas, but that isn't the case. If we miss His love towards Judas - rejected love, to be sure - if we miss that love, we miss the whole story.

3. (22-25) The Last Supper.

And as they were eating, Jesus took bread, blessed and broke *it,* **and gave** *it* **to them and said, "Take, eat; this is My body." Then He took the cup, and when He had given thanks He gave** *it* **to them, and they all drank from it. And He said to them, "This is My blood of the new covenant, which is shed for many. Assuredly, I say to you, I will no longer drink of the fruit of the vine until that day when I drink it new in the kingdom of God."**

a. **Jesus took bread, blessed and broke it**: When the bread was lifted up at Passover, the head of the meal would say: "This is the bread of affliction which our fathers ate in the land of Egypt. Let everyone who hungers come and eat; let everyone who is needy come and eat the Passover meal."

i. Everything eaten at the Passover meal had a symbolic meaning. The bitter herbs recalled the bitterness of slavery; the salt water remembered the tears shed under Egypt's oppression. The main course of the meal - a lamb freshly sacrificed for that particular household - did not symbolize anything connected to the agonies of Egypt. It was the sin-bearing sacrifice that allowed the judgment of God to pass over the household that believed.

b. **Take, eat; this is My body... This is My blood of the new covenant**: Jesus didn't give the normal explanation of the meaning of each of the foods. He reinterpreted them in Himself, and the focus was no longer on the suffering of Israel in Egypt, but on the sin-bearing suffering of Jesus on their behalf.

c. **This is My body**: Christians have debated for centuries about the true nature of the **bread** and the **cup** at this supper.

i. The Roman Catholic Church holds the idea of *transubstantiation*, which teaches that the bread and the wine *actually* become the body and blood of Jesus.

ii. Martin Luther held the idea of *consubstantiation*, which teaches the bread remains bread and the wine remains wine, but by faith they are the same as Jesus' actual body. Luther did not believe in the Roman Catholic doctrine of transubstantiation, but he did not go far from it.

iii. John Calvin taught that Jesus' presence in the bread and wine was real, but only *spiritual*, not physical. Zwingli taught that the bread and wine are *symbols* that represent the body and blood of Jesus.

iv. According to Scripture, we can understand that the **bread** and the **cup** are not *mere* symbols, but they are powerful pictures to partake of - to enter into - as we see the Lord's Table as the new Passover.

d. **Take, eat**: We can't get so caught up in discovering what the **bread** and the **cup** mean that we forget to do what Jesus said to do *with them*. We must **take** and **eat**.

i. **Take** means that it won't be *forced* upon you. You have to receive it. **Eat** means that this is absolutely vital for you. Without food and drink, we perish. Without Jesus, we perish. It also means that you must take Jesus into your innermost being.

e. **This is My blood of the new covenant, which is shed for many**: Beyond all the controversy about what the elements of this supper really are and what they really mean, the announcement that Jesus brings a **new covenant** stands out.

i. No mere man could ever institute a **new covenant** between God and man, but Jesus is the God-man. He has the authority to establish a **new covenant**, sealed with blood, even as the old covenant was sealed with blood (Exodus 24:8).

ii. This covenant is focused on an inner transformation that cleanses us from all sin: *For I will forgive their iniquity, and their sin I will remember no more* (Jeremiah 31:34). This transformation puts God's Word and will in us: *I will put My law in their minds, and write it on their hearts* (Jeremiah 31:33). This covenant is all about a new, close relationship with God: *I will be their God, and they shall be My people* (Jeremiah 31:33).

f. Until that day when I drink it new in the kingdom of God: Jesus has not yet celebrated a Passover in heaven. He still waits for all His people to be gathered to Him and then there will be a great supper - *the marriage supper of the Lamb* (Revelation 19:9). This is the fulfillment **in the kingdom of God** Jesus longed for.

4. (26-31) Jesus predicts the desertion of the disciples and Peter's denial.

And when they had sung a hymn, they went out to the Mount of Olives. Then Jesus said to them, "All of you will be made to stumble because of Me this night, for it is written:

'I will strike the Shepherd,
And the sheep will be scattered.'

But after I have been raised, I will go before you to Galilee." Peter said to Him, "Even if all are made to stumble, yet I *will* not *be*." Jesus said to him, "Assuredly, I say to you that today, *even* this night, before the rooster crows twice, you will deny Me three times." But he spoke more vehemently, "If I have to die with You, I will not deny You!" And they all said likewise.

a. **When they had sung a hymn**: We don't often think of Jesus singing, but He did. He lifted His voice in adoration and worship to God the Father. We can endlessly wonder what His voice sounded like, but we know for certain that He sang with more than His voice, and He lifted His whole heart up in praise. This reminds us that God *wants* to be praised with singing.

i. It is remarkable that Jesus could sing on this night before His crucifixion. Could you sing in such circumstances? Will you let Jesus be your worship leader? "What! A Christian silent when others are praising his Master? No; he must join in the song. Satan tries to make God's people dumb, but he cannot, for the Lord has not a tongue-tied child in all his family. They can all speak, and they can all cry, even if they cannot all sing, and *I* think there are times when they can all sing; yea, they must, for you know the promise, 'Then shall the tongue of the dumb sing.' Surely, when Jesus leads the tune, if there should be any silent ones in the Lord's family, they must begin to praise the name of the Lord." (Spurgeon)

ii. This means we should sing to God our Father - *just as Jesus did* - because this is something that pleases Him, and when we love someone we want to do the things that please *them*. It really doesn't matter if it does or doesn't please *us*.

iii. "What is singing but emotional expression? Oh! The value and the power of emotion. Evil emotion slays the Lord of life and glory! Pure emotion makes possible the saving of the slayers." (Morgan)

b. **Sung a hymn**: It is wonderful that Jesus sang, but *what* did He sing? A Passover meal always ended with singing three Psalms known as the *Hallel*, Psalms 116-118. Surely the words of these Psalms ministered to Jesus as He sang them on the night before His crucifixion.

i. "When Jesus arose to go to Gethsemane, Psalm 118 was upon his lips. It provided an appropriate description of how God would guide his Messiah through distress and suffering to glory." (Lane)

c. **They went to the Mount of Olives**: "Jesus tarried with them in the Upper Room for the wonderful discourse and prayer in John 14 to 17. They may have gone out to the street after John 14:31." (Robertson)

i. "Our Lord knew that his time was now come when he must be actually delivered into the hands of his enemies. That he might not therefore cause any disturbance either to the master of the family wherein he was, or to the city, though it was now midnight, he goeth out of the city." (Ironside)

d. **All of you will be made to stumble**: Jesus said this not to condemn His disciples, but to show them that He really was in command of the situation, and to demonstrate that the Scriptures regarding the suffering of the Messiah *must* be fulfilled.

i. This was not the first time Jesus warned Peter and the other disciples that they would forsake Him. From a careful reconstruction of the Gospels, we find that Jesus first warned them about this in the upper room, now again in the Garden of Gethsemane.

e. **After I have been raised**: This shows that Jesus was already looking beyond the cross. He had His eyes fixed on *the joy set before Him* (Hebrews 12:2).

f. **Even if all are made to stumble, yet I will not be**: We wonder how Peter could ever say such a thing. Tragically, Peter was unaware of both the spiritual *reality* and the spiritual *battle* that Jesus clearly saw. Peter only looked to how he felt at the moment, and at the moment he felt pretty brave.

i. "It is sometimes easier to bear a great load for Christ than a small one. Some of us could be martyrs at the stake more easily that confessors among sneering neighbors." (Maclaren)

g. **Assuredly, I say to you that today, even this night, before the rooster crows twice, you will deny Me three times**: Peter, despite his bold proclamation that he would never be made to stumble, would fail in what he thought was his strong area - courage and boldness. Through this solemn warning Jesus gave Peter an opportunity to take heed and consider his own weakness.

i. Sadly, it was an opportunity that Peter did not take: **he spoke more vehemently, "If I have to die with You, I will not deny You!"** Jesus knew Peter far better than Peter did, and in overestimating himself, Peter was set up for a fall.

ii. **He spoke more vehemently**: "This strong compound adverb [is found] only in Mark and probably preserves Peter's own statement of the remark." (Robertson)

iii. The rest of the disciples also overestimated their strength and did not rely on the Lord in the critical hour: **And they all said likewise**. The Apostle Paul warned us against falling where we think we are strong: *therefore let him who thinks he stands take heed lest he fall* (1 Corinthians 10:12). When we think we are beyond the reach of some sins, we are ready for a fall.

C. Jesus' prayer and arrest in Gethsemane.

1. (32-36) Jesus' prayer of distress.

Then they came to a place which was named Gethsemane; and He said to His disciples, "Sit here while I pray." And He took Peter, James, and John with Him, and He began to be troubled and deeply distressed. Then He said to them, "My soul is exceedingly sorrowful, *even* to death. Stay here and watch." He went a little farther, and fell on the ground, and prayed that if it were possible, the hour might pass from Him. And He said, "Abba, Father, all things *are* possible for You. Take this cup away from Me; nevertheless, not what I will, but what You *will*."

a. **Gethsemane**: This was a place just east of the temple mount area in Jerusalem, across the ravine of the Brook Kidron, and on the lower slopes of the Mount of Olives. Surrounded by ancient olive trees, **Gethsemane** means "olive press." It was a place where olives from the neighborhood were crushed for their oil. So too, the Son of God would be crushed here.

b. **He began to be troubled and deeply distressed... My soul is exceedingly sorrowful, even to death**: Jesus knew what the Father's will was; yet He still endured this agony. It was because Jesus was to be a sacrifice for sins, and He wasn't an unknowing sacrificial animal. Nor was He a victim of circumstances. He resolved willingly to lay down His life.

i. It was not so much the horror of physical torture that affected Jesus so, but it was the spiritual horror of the cross - of *being made sin* (2 Corinthians 5:21). This is what made Jesus **troubled and deeply distressed**.

ii. Hebrews 5:7-8 describes Jesus' agony in the Gethsemane: *Who, in the days of His flesh, when He had offered up prayers and supplications, with vehement cries and tears to Him who was able to save Him from death, and was heard because of His godly fear, though He was a Son, yet He learned obedience by the things which He suffered.*

iii. "His holy soul shrank from the awfulness of being made sin upon the tree. It was not death, but the divine anger against sin, the imputation to Him of all our iniquities that filled His soul with horror. There was no conflict of wills." (Ironside)

c. **Abba, Father**: In this moment of deep distress, Jesus didn't feel *far* from God the Father. He felt so close to the Father that He used the name **Abba**, a child's familiar name for daddy.

d. **Take this cup away from Me**: In response to Jesus' deeply moved prayers, the Father did not take the cup from Jesus. Instead He strengthened Jesus to be able to take and drink the cup.

i. Repeatedly in the Old Testament, the **cup** is a powerful picture of the wrath and judgment of God (Psalm 75:8, Isaiah 51:17, Jeremiah 25:15). Jesus became, as it were, an enemy of God, who was judged and forced to drink the cup of the Father's fury so that we would not have to drink from that cup - *this* was the source of Jesus' agony.

ii. Matthew 20:22-23 speaks of a cup that the followers of Jesus must also drink. "In any case, our cup can never be as deep or as bitter as was his, and there were in his cup some ingredients that never will be found in ours. The bitterness of sin was there, but he has taken that away for all who believe in him. His Father's wrath was there, but he drank that all up, and left not a single dreg for any one of his people." (Spurgeon)

e. **Nevertheless, not what I will, but what You will**: Jesus came to a point of decision in Gethsemane. It wasn't that He had not decided nor consented before, but now He came upon a unique point of decision. He drank the cup at Calvary, but He *decided* once for all to drink it at Gethsemane. The struggle of the cross was won at the Garden of Gethsemane.

i. This struggle at Gethsemane - the place of crushing - has an important place in fulfilling God's plan of redemption. If Jesus failed here, He would have failed at the cross. His success here made the victory at the cross possible.

f. **If it were possible**: Jesus wasn't asking for permission to let humanity perish in hell; He was asking the Father, "If there is any other possible way to save humanity other than the agony which awaits Me at the cross - let it be." Yet there was no other way, so Jesus went to the cross.

i. This prayer of Jesus eliminates any other way of salvation. If there is another way, His death was not *necessary*, and His prayer was not answered.

g. **Not what I will, but what You will**: Some criticize this kind of prayer in the mouth of a Christian, saying it is a prayer that lacks faith. But to pray **not what I will, but what You will** *is* a prayer of great faith and trust in God. If such a prayer insults God, then Jesus insulted His Father at this crucial moment in the Garden of Gethsemane.

2. (37-42) The sleeping disciples.

Then He came and found them sleeping, and said to Peter, "Simon, are you sleeping? Could you not watch one hour? Watch and pray, lest you enter into temptation. The spirit indeed *is* willing, but the flesh *is* weak." Again He went away and prayed, and spoke the same words. And when He returned, He found them asleep again, for their eyes were heavy; and they did not know what to answer Him. Then He came the third time and said to them, "Are you still sleeping and resting? It is enough! The hour has come; behold, the Son of Man is being betrayed into the hands of sinners. Rise, let us be going. See, My betrayer is at hand."

a. **He came and found them sleeping**: At this moment of great agony, Jesus was alone. His disciples gave Him no support at all. Though this was not to their credit - they failed Jesus - it was the way it had to be - Jesus had to face the terror of the cross all alone.

b. **Simon, are you sleeping?** It is not necessary to see Jesus as irritated at His disciples. He said this in love, and in compassionate understanding. He knew them better than they knew themselves.

i. Peter must have been a bit startled to hear Jesus call him **Simon**. This was the old sleeping **Simon**, not the new man **Peter**. Peter was ready to resist any attack, except the attack of the *Sandman*.

c. **Watch and pray, let you enter into temptation**: Jesus knew Peter would fail; yet He encouraged him to victory knowing that the resources are found in *watching* and *praying*. If Peter woke up (both physically and spiritually), and drew close in dependence on God, he could have kept from denying Jesus at the critical hour.

> i. Jesus found victory at the cross by succeeding in the struggle in Gethsemane. Peter - just like us - failed in later **temptation** because he failed to **watch and pray**. The spiritual battle is often won or lost *before* the crisis comes.

d. He went away and prayed, and spoke the same words: Jesus repeated the prayer outlined in Mark 14:34-36. Some say it is unspiritual, or reflects a lack of faith, to repeat prayers, yet we could never accuse Jesus of being unspiritual or of lacking faith.

e. When He returned, He found them asleep again... Then He came a third time and said to them, "Are you still sleeping and resting?" Three times Jesus prayed; three times Jesus checked to see if His disciples would stand by Him in prayer and pray for their own strength in the coming trial. They were asleep each time.

> i. It was bad enough that the disciples didn't **watch and pray** for *themselves*, but they should have been willing to **watch and pray** simply for the sake of Jesus. Through prayer and companionship, we must stand beside others in their time of need.

> ii. "He told them to 'Sleep on now'; and they slept; and He watched them while they slept... He said in effect: Go and have your sleep out; I can watch; and He watched them while they slept." (Morgan)

f. It is enough! We should not think that Jesus was angry or irritated because His disciples did not help Him. He wanted the disciples to help Him and stand in prayer, not for His own sake, but for their own benefit. Jesus *could* stand alone against the trial of the cross, but *they*, being without prayer, would not.

3. (43-52) The arrest of Jesus of Nazareth in the Garden of Gethsemane.

And immediately, while He was still speaking, Judas, one of the twelve, with a great multitude with swords and clubs, came from the chief priests and the scribes and the elders. Now His betrayer had given them a signal, saying, "Whomever I kiss, He is the One; seize Him and lead *Him* away safely." As soon as He had come, immediately he went up to Him and said to Him, "Rabbi, Rabbi!" and kissed Him. Then they laid their hands on Him and took Him. And one of those who stood by drew his sword and struck the servant of the high priest, and cut off his ear. Then Jesus answered and said to them, "Have you come out, as against a robber, with swords and clubs to take Me? I was daily with you in the temple teaching, and you did not seize Me. But the Scriptures must be

fulfilled." Then they all forsook Him and fled. Now a certain young man followed Him, having a linen cloth thrown around *his* naked *body*. And the young men laid hold of him, and he left the linen cloth and fled from them naked.

a. **Whomever I kiss**: Apparently, Jesus was normal enough in appearance that it was necessary for Judas to identify Him. He chose to identify Jesus by greeting Him with a kiss. This was a cruel pretence of affection, especially adding **"Rabbi, Rabbi!"** to the greeting.

b. **One of those who stood by drew his sword and struck the servant of the high priest**: John 18:10 identified this unnamed swordsman as Peter. Here Peter was a great example of someone who, wielding the power of this world in his hands, could only cut off ears. When he wielded the Word of God, Peter pierced hearts for God's glory (Acts 2:37).

i. "When the Church takes sword in hand, it usually shows that it does not know how to wield it, and as often as not has struck the wrong man." (Maclaren)

ii. Luke tells us that Jesus healed the damage done by Peter (Luke 22:51). It isn't the last time Jesus has had to leave behind a mess left by one of His followers. "Had Jesus not healed Malchus, Peter would have been arrested as well; and there might have been four crosses at Calvary." (Barclay)

c. **But the Scriptures must be fulfilled**: Jesus marveled that they sent a small army to arrest Him. Yet, He was in command; with a word He could destroy all those who came to arrest Him. But Jesus went along in order to fulfill Scripture.

d. **They all forsook Him and fled**: At this point, all the disciples scattered and ran for their own safety. A few (Peter and John at least) followed back to see what would happen at a distance. None of them stood beside Jesus and said, "I have given my life to this Man. What you accuse Him of, you may accuse me of also." Instead, it was fulfilled what Jesus said: *All of you will be made to stumble because of Me* (Mark 14:27).

e. **Now a certain young man followed Him... and he left the linen cloth and fled from them naked**: Jesus was forsaken even by a young follower, who in the confusion fled naked. Since the earliest days of the church, commentators have supposed this young man to be Mark himself. It was his humble way of saying, "I was there."

i. Many people suppose that the upper room where Jesus held the last supper just a few hours earlier was at a home owned by Mark's family. Acts 12:12 says that the disciples used to meet at the home of Mark's mother. It may be that the arresting army led by Judas first came to Mark's home, because that is where Judas last left Jesus. When Judas and the group came and found them gone, it would have been easy for Judas to suppose that they went to Gethsemane, because Jesus was accustomed to going there (Luke 22:39). When Judas and the group started out for Gethsemane, we can imagine that young Mark hurriedly dressed in a simple **linen cloth** and set out to beat Judas and his gang to Gethsemane so that he could warn Jesus.

ii. "It is usually supposed that Mark himself, son of Mary (Acts 12:12) in whose house they probably had observed the Passover meal, had followed Jesus and the apostles to the Garden." (Robertson)

iii. "The modest spirit of Mark seemed to say, 'Friend Peter, while the Holy Ghost moves me to, tell thy fault, and let it stand on record, he also constrains me to write my own as a sort of preface to it, for I, too, in my mad, hare-brained folly, would have run, unclothed as I was, upon the guard to rescue my Lord and Master; yet, at the first sight, of the rough legionaries, at the first gleam of their swords, away I fled, timid, faint-hearted, and afraid that I should be too roughly handled.'" (Spurgeon)

D. The trial before the Sanhedrin.

1. Mark did not record the preliminary trial before Annas, who was the real power behind the high priest's office (recorded in John 18:12-13 and 19-23), nor did he record the second trial of Jesus before the Sanhedrin, the "official" daylight trial recorded in Luke 22:66-71.

a. There are similarities between the trials because the same people were involved. There were actually three phases of Jesus' trial before the Jewish authorities and three phases of His trial before the Roman authorities, and they should not be confused.

b. Upon His arrest, Jesus was first taken to Annas, then to an illegal night court of the Sanhedrin (which Mark will describe next), then to an official daylight trial of the Sanhedrin, then to Pilate, who sent Jesus to Herod, who sent Jesus back to Pilate, where He then went to the cross.

2. (53-59) Jesus is accused before the Sanhedrin.

And they led Jesus away to the high priest; and with him were assembled all the chief priests, the elders, and the scribes. But Peter followed Him at a distance, right into the courtyard of the high priest. And he sat with the servants and warmed himself at the fire. Now the chief priests and all the council sought testimony against Jesus to put Him to death, but found none. For many bore false witness against Him, but their

testimonies did not agree. Then some rose up and bore false witness
against Him, saying, "We heard Him say, 'I will destroy this temple
made with hands, and within three days I will build another made
without hands.'" But not even then did their testimony agree.

a. **They led Jesus away to the high priest**: This trial of Jesus was terribly
illegal according to Jewish law. There was much in the Jewish legal process
to protect the rights of the accused, and all of this was ignored and
deliberately broken by those who were determined to put Jesus to death.

b. **Heard Him say, "I will destroy this temple"**: Jesus, as recorded in
John 2:19, spoke clearly of the temple of His body. Jesus never said the
words reported by His false accusers - "**this temple made with hands**."
Essentially, they accused Jesus of being a terrorist who wanted to destroy
the temple.

i. "The accusation was utterly serious, for throughout the Graeco-
Roman world the destruction or desecration of places of worship was
regarded as a capital offense." (Lane)

ii. Morgan on their accusation: "This is the most diabolical form of
untruth, because it is an untruth in which there is an element of truth.
We remember Tennyson's words: 'A lie that is all a lie, may be met and
fought outright; But a lie that is partly the truth, is a harder matter to
fight.'"

c. **But not even then did their testimony agree**: Though it was a false case,
the accusers of Jesus could not put together a good case. The false witnesses
kept disagreeing with one another.

i. "It was harder to agree on a consistent lie than to tell the simple
truth." (Cole)

3. (60-62) Jesus testifies at His own trial.

**And the high priest stood up in the midst and asked Jesus, saying, "Do
You answer nothing? What *is it* these men testify against You?" But
He kept silent and answered nothing. Again the high priest asked Him,
saying to Him, "Are You the Christ, the Son of the Blessed?" Jesus said,
"I am. And you will see the Son of Man sitting at the right hand of the
Power, and coming with the clouds of heaven."**

a. **And the high priest stood up in the midst and asked Jesus**: "For greater
solemnity he arose to make up by bluster the lack of evidence." (Robinson)

i. "Suggesting that the high priest arose from his seat and advanced
into the semi-circle of the council towards Jesus - the action of an
irritated, baffled man." (Bruce)

ii. "It was a tacit confession that Christ had been proved innocent up till then. The high priest would not have needed to draw something out of the accused one if there had been sufficient material against him elsewhere. The trial had been a dead failure up to that point, and he knew it, and was red with rage. Now he attempts to bully the prisoner that he may extract some declaration from him which may save all further trouble of witnesses, and end the matter." (Spurgeon)

b. **He kept silent and answered nothing**: Jesus *could* have mounted a magnificent defense here, calling forth all the various witnesses to His deity, power and character. The people He taught, the people He healed, the dead risen, the blind who see, even the demons themselves testified to His deity. But Jesus *opened not His mouth; He was led as a lamb to the slaughter, and as a sheep before its shearers is silent, so He opened not His mouth* (Isaiah 53:7).

c. **I am. And you will see the Son of Man sitting at the right hand of the Power**: Jesus, when asked under formal oath to incriminate Himself, essentially said, "You now stand in judgment of Me, but I will be the ultimate judge." These words would have given any wise judge pause but did not slow down His accusers.

i. Here we see that Jesus was on trial - He seemed to lose, but He really won. His conduct at His trial showed His innocence and was all part of the plan of redemption - which we must receive as God's gift.

ii. In a real sense, it wasn't Jesus on trial at all - it was more accurate to say that the religious leaders were on trial. They seemed to win, but they really lost. In fact, we all are on trial before Jesus and will be held to account for what we do with Him.

4. (63-65) The Sanhedrin condemns Jesus to death.

Then the high priest tore his clothes and said, "What further need do we have of witnesses? You have heard the blasphemy! What do you think?" And they all condemned Him to be deserving of death. Then some began to spit on Him, and to blindfold Him, and to beat Him, and to say to Him, "Prophesy!" And the officers struck Him with the palms of their hands.

a. **The high priest tore his clothes... You have heard the blasphemy!**: First they reacted with self-righteous, melodramatic horror, then with abuse and brutality (**some began to spit on Him... and to beat Him**).

b. **And the officers struck Him with the palms of their hands**: As terrible as the judgment of the religious leaders against Jesus was, at least it had a *reason* - envy and fear of Jesus. These **officers**, taking a bizarre pleasure in torturing Jesus, didn't even have a *reason*. They did it only because of what others (the religious leaders) said about Jesus.

> i. "Be astonished, O heavens, and be horribly afraid. His face is the light of the universe, his person is the glory of heaven, and they 'began to spit on him.' Alas, my God, that man should be so base!" (Spurgeon)

c. **Then some began to spit on Him, and to blindfold Him, and to beat Him**: Understanding that Jesus endured such pain and humiliation should cause us to respond in three ways.

> i. *We should bravely bear pain and humiliation for the sake of Jesus ourselves.* "How ready should we be to hear slander and ridicule for Jesus' sake. Do not get into a huff, and think it a strange thing that people should mock you. Who are you, dear sir? Who are you? What can you be if compared with Christ? If they spat upon him, why should they not spit upon you? If they buffeted him, why should they not buffet you? Shall your Master have all the rough of it? Shall he have all the bitter, and you all the sweet? A pretty soldier you, to demand better fare than your Captain!" (Spurgeon)

> ii. *We should be more diligent to praise Jesus.* "How earnestly, next, ought we to honor our dear Lord. If men were so eager to put him to shame, let us be ten times more earnest to bring him glory. Is there anything we can do today by which he may be honored? Let us set about it. Can we make any sacrifice? Can we perform any difficult task which would glorify him? Let us not deliberate, but at once do it with our might. Let us be inventive in modes of glorifying him, even as his adversaries were ingenious in the methods of his shame." (Spurgeon)

> iii. *We should have more assurance and confidence in receiving the finished work of Jesus for our redemption.* "Surely I know that he who suffered this, since he was verily the Son of the Blessed, must have ability to save us. Such griefs must be a full atonement for our transgressions. Glory be to God, that spittle on his countenance means a clear, bright face for me. Those false accusations on his character mean no condemnation for me." (Spurgeon)

5. (66-75) Peter's denial.

Now as Peter was below in the courtyard, one of the servant girls of the high priest came. And when she saw Peter warming himself, she looked at him and said, "You also were with Jesus of Nazareth." But he denied it, saying, "I neither know nor understand what you are saying." And he went out on the porch, and a rooster crowed. And the servant girl saw him again, and began to say to those who stood by, "This is one of

them." But he denied it again. And a little later those who stood by said to Peter again, "Surely you are *one* of them; for you are a Galilean, and your speech shows *it.*" Then he began to curse and swear, "I do not know this Man of whom you speak!" A second time *the* rooster crowed. Then Peter called to mind the word that Jesus had said to him, "Before the rooster crows twice, you will deny Me three times." And when he thought about it, he wept.

a. **Now as Peter was below in the courtyard**: As Mark concludes the story of Peter's denial in Mark 14:66-72, he does it as a flashback. This didn't happen as Jesus was beaten, but as He was on trial.

   i. Peter's first problem was that he *followed Him at a distance* (Mark 14:54). When we distance ourselves from Jesus, it is hard to make a proper stand for Him at the critical time.

   ii. Next, Peter *sat with the servants and warmed himself at the fire* (Mark 14:54). Peter found fellowship and warmth in the company of the ungodly, having forsaken the fellowship of the fleeing disciples. Peter wanted to seem just one of this crowd, not a follower of Jesus.

   iii. The *officers* of Mark 14:65 who struck Jesus are the same people as the *servants* of Mark 14:54, because the same ancient Greek word is used of both groups. Peter sat and associated himself with the same men who beat Jesus, and they beat Him just because someone else told them that Jesus was a wicked man.

b. **I neither know nor understand what you are saying**: A hostile man of authority interrogated Jesus. Peter did not face this kind of interrogation, only **one of the servant girls**. But she was enough to make Peter deny Jesus. "A silly wench daunteth and dispiriteth this stout champion." (Trapp)

   i. **I neither know nor understand**: "Peter denied the charge, using the form common in rabbinical law for a formal, legal denial." (Lane)

   ii. "Yet all this evil sprung from the *fear of man.* How many denials of Christ and his truth have sprung since, from the same cause!" (Clarke)

   iii. Thinking it might help distance himself from association with Jesus, Peter **began to curse and swear**. When we hear that kind of language, we assume the person is not a follower of Jesus Christ.

c. **And when he thought about it, he wept**: Peter finally **called to mind the word that Jesus had said to him**, but he remembered it too late - it was *after* he had sinned. Then all Peter could do was to weep bitterly - but he will be restored.

i. "It was not the crowing of the cock that convicted Peter; it was the remembering of Christ's words." (Wiersbe)

ii. There is a significant contrast between Judas and Peter. Both of them denied Jesus in one way or another, but one was restored and the other was not. Restoring Peter was important to Jesus; after His resurrection, Jesus had a private meeting with Peter (Luke 24:34) and a public restoration with Peter (John 21). Judas ended up as an apostate, and Peter was a backslider who suffered spiritual decline from an experience he once enjoyed.

Mark 15 - The Crucifixion of Jesus

A. The trial before Pilate.

1. (1-5) The first audience with Pilate.

Immediately, in the morning, the chief priests held a consultation with the elders and scribes and the whole council; and they bound Jesus, led *Him* away, and delivered *Him* to Pilate. Then Pilate asked Him, "Are You the King of the Jews?" He answered and said to him, "*It is as* you say." And the chief priests accused Him of many things, but He answered nothing. Then Pilate asked Him again, saying, "Do You answer nothing? See how many things they testify against You!" But Jesus still answered nothing, so that Pilate marveled.

    a. **Held a consultation with the elders and scribes and the whole counsel**: This was the official daylight trial of Jesus before the Sanhedrin described in Luke 22:66-71.

        i. This trial was held **immediately, in the morning** for good reason. "The detail that Jesus was delivered to Pilate's forum early in the morning is a significant index of the historical accuracy of the tradition. It was necessary for the Sanhedrin to bring its business to Pilate as soon after dawn as possible because the working day of a Roman official began at the earliest hour of daylight. Legal trials in the Roman forum were customarily held shortly after sunrise." (Lane)

    b. **Delivered Him to Pilate**: The Jewish leaders took Jesus to Pilate because they did not have the legal right to execute their own criminals.

        i. There were times when the Jews disregarded this prohibition of the Romans and executed those they considered criminals, such as at the stoning of Stephen (Acts 7:57-60). Yet they did not take things into their own hands regarding Jesus because they knew the multitudes had a favorable opinion of Jesus and if Pilate executed Him, they could distance themselves from the political fallout.

c. **Delivered Him to Pilate**: The Jewish leaders had reason to expect a favorable result when they sent Jesus to Pilate. Secular history shows us he was a cruel, ruthless man, and completely insensitive to the moral feelings of others - surely, they thought, **Pilate** will put this Jesus to death.

i. There was something working *against* this expectation. History tells us that Pilate simply didn't like the Jews, and that he believed they were a stubborn and rebellious people. Since he was constantly suspicious of the Jews, when *they* brought him a prisoner for execution he immediately suspected there was a hidden agenda at work.

ii. Nevertheless, before Pilate could make a decision, he had to follow the normal procedures for a trial. Just like everything the Romans did, there was an established procedure for a criminal trial - trials that were public by principle.

- The plaintiff brought an indictment against the accused.
- The magistrate - the judge - examined both the accusation and the accused.
- The two main sources of evidence were the statements of the accused and evidence brought by witnesses, either for or against the accused.
- When all the evidence was received, a court official declared that all the evidence was in.
- The magistrate was then free to consult with advisors, and then announce his verdict from the judgment seat. The sentence was executed immediately.

iii. Mark picked up the trial of Jesus at the second step - the charges were brought to Pilate ("This man is guilty of treason because He claims to be the king of the Jews in opposition to Caesar"). Therefore, Pilate examined the accused: **Are You the king of the Jews?**

d. **Are You the King of the Jews?** The Jewish rulers knew that if they brought Jesus before Pilate on the charge of claiming to be God, Pilate would merely yawn. He would say, "We Romans have hundreds of gods. What is the harm with one more?" Yet, if they brought Jesus before Pilate as **the King of the Jews**, Pilate would have to take Jesus seriously as a potential *political* threat, because there could be no king except Caesar, and Pilate was Caesar's representative.

i. Ironically, Jesus stood accused of doing exactly what He refused to do: taking a political stand against Rome.

ii. Jesus was indeed the king of the Jews, but not in a political or military sense. This is why He said "yes" to Pilate's question, but "yes" with a reservation (**It is as you say**), and why He said nothing to the further accusations against Him (**the chief priests accused Him of many things, but He answered nothing**). If Jesus answered a plain "yes" to Pilate's question, Pilate would have immediately declared Jesus guilty of treason against Rome. Because Jesus gave a qualified "yes," it merited further examination.

iii. Luke 23:2 tells us what these accusations were. They said Jesus incited the people to riot, that He told them not to pay their taxes, and that He fancied Himself a king in political opposition to Rome. Pilate was unconvinced, so the accusers repeated and strengthened their third charge: *He stirs up the people, teaching throughout all Judea, beginning in Galilee to this place* (Luke 23:5).

e. **The chief priests accused Him of many things**: "The Sanhedrists must have seen from Pilate's manner, a smile on his face perhaps, that he did not take the confession seriously." (Bruce)

f. **Pilate marveled**: No doubt, Pilate had seen many men grovel for their lives before him. He also stood in judgment of many men as the governor of a Roman province. Yet there was something different about Jesus that Pilate marveled at.

i. "Such silence was wholly unusual in the forum, and demonstrated a presence and a dignity which puzzled the prefect." (Lane)

ii. Without a defense from the accused, the law was on the side of the accusers. Roman magistrates didn't like to find an undefended man guilty, but they often felt they had to.

2. (6-15) The second audience with Pilate.

Now at the feast he was accustomed to releasing one prisoner to them, whomever they requested. And there was one named Barabbas, *who was* chained with his fellow rebels; they had committed murder in the rebellion. Then the multitude, crying aloud, began to ask *him to do* just as he had always done for them. But Pilate answered them, saying, "Do you want me to release to you the King of the Jews?" For he knew that the chief priests had handed Him over because of envy. But the chief priests stirred up the crowd, so that he should rather release Barabbas to them. Pilate answered and said to them again, "What then do you want me to do *with Him* whom you call the King of the Jews?" So they

cried out again, "Crucify Him!" Then Pilate said to them, "Why, what evil has He done?" But they cried out all the more, "Crucify Him!" So Pilate, wanting to gratify the crowd, released Barabbas to them; and he delivered Jesus, after he had scourged *Him*, to be crucified.

a. **He was accustomed to releasing one prisoner to them**: Pilate knew Jesus was an innocent man (Luke 23:14 records him as saying, *I have found no fault in this Man*). Yet Pilate had a politically explosive situation on his hands. He had the choice between doing what was right (free an innocent man) or what was politically expedient (execute a man brought before him by the Jews for treason).

i. In addition, Pilate was no friend of the Jews. He could see through their manipulation, and **he knew that the chief priests had handed Him over because of envy**. This made Pilate want to find a way to free Jesus even more.

b. **Then the multitude, crying aloud, began to ask**: This Jewish **multitude** - mostly Jews from Jerusalem, because most of the visiting pilgrims stayed out in *the country* (Mark 15:21) and were not in the city this early - didn't like or trust Pilate at all. When he suggested the release of one of two prisoners, they immediately chose the *other* one, as much as anything just to be "against" the Roman magistrate. As far as the crowd was concerned, it was simple. *Their* Sanhedrin said Jesus should die, but said nothing about Barabbas. *Rome's* magistrate said Jesus should be set free and Barabbas executed. They would always side with *their* Sanhedrin against *Rome's* magistrate.

i. "If one wonders why the crowd was fickle, he may recall that this was not yet the same people who followed him in triumphal entry and in the temple. That was the plan of Judas to get the thing over before those Galilean sympathizers waked up." (Robertson)

c. **Do you want me to release to you the King of the Jews?** In the midst of this, Pilate believed he found a way to do what was right, yet not pay a price for it. Pilate thought Jesus could escape death if He were released according to the custom of releasing a prisoner every Passover season.

i. Pilate figured, "If this man claimed to be king, and was even the slightest bit hostile to Rome, then the crowd will love him. These Jewish leaders don't want Jesus to go free, but the crowd will sympathize with Him."

ii. It was a strange scene: a cruel, ruthless Roman governor trying to win the life of a miracle-working Jew against the strenuous efforts of both the Jewish leaders and the crowd.

d. **They cried out again, "Crucify Him"**: Pilate was convinced the crowd would release Jesus, but instead they chose **Barabbas, who was chained with his fellow insurrectionists**. The word **"insurrectionists"** basically amounts to "terrorists." Barabbas was a *real* political enemy of Rome, not a falsely accused political enemy, as Jesus was.

   i. **What then do you want me to do with Him whom you call the King of the Jews?** Pilate probably hoped that the crowd would be satisfied with a lesser punishment - that Jesus could be beaten and then let go. Pilate was probably surprised and horrified that they **cried out more exceedingly, "Crucify Him!"**

   ii. As the crowd rejected Jesus, they embraced Barabbas - whose name means "son of the father," and who was a terrorist and a murderer. They accepted a false son of the father.

   iii. Yet if anyone was able to say, "Jesus died for me," it was **Barabbas**. He knew what it was to have Jesus die on his behalf, the innocent in the place of the guilty.

e. **They cried out more exceedingly, "Crucify Him"**: Pilate was now in a dangerous place. The crowd was almost becoming a riot. If there was one thing that would get him in trouble with his Roman superiors, it was a riot. With both the people and the Jewish rulers demanding the death of Jesus, Pilate was unwilling to oppose them both, and he began the process of execution by having Jesus **scourged**.

   i. Even before Jesus was to be **scourged**, His physical condition was weak. We can assume that Jesus was in good physical condition up until the night of His arrest. "The rigors of Jesus' ministry (that is, traveling by foot throughout Palestine) would have precluded any major physical illness or a weak general constitution." (Dr. William Edwards [with others] in the *Journal of the American Medical Association*, March 21, 1986)

   ii. Add to Jesus' condition the horror of being **scourged**. The goal of the scourging was to weaken the victim to a state just short of collapse and death. "As the Roman soldiers repeatedly struck the victim's back with full force, the iron balls would cause deep contusions, and the leather thongs and sheep bones would cut into the skin and subcutaneous tissues. Then, as the flogging continued, the lacerations would tear into the underlying skeletal muscles and produce quivering ribbons of bleeding flesh. Pain and blood loss generally set the stage for circulatory shock. The extent of blood loss may well have determined how long the victim would survive the cross." (Edwards)

iii. "The severe scourging, with its intense pain and appreciable blood loss, most probably left Jesus in a pre-shock state. Moreover, hematidrosis had rendered his skin particularly tender. The physical and mental abuse meted out by the Jews and the Romans, as well as the lack of food, water, and sleep, also contributed to his generally weakened state. Therefore, even before the actual crucifixion, Jesus' physical condition was at least serious and possibly critical." (Edwards)

f. **To be crucified**: In pronouncing the sentence, "The mode of death had to be specified under Roman law, and it may be assumed that Pilate used the conventional form, 'You shall mount the cross' (*ibis in crucem*) or 'I consign you to the cross' (*abi in crucem*)." (Lane)

B. The humiliation and death of Jesus.

1. (16-20) Jesus is beaten and mocked.

Then the soldiers led Him away into the hall called Praetorium, and they called together the whole garrison. And they clothed Him with purple; and they twisted a crown of thorns, put it on His *head*, and began to salute Him, "Hail, King of the Jews!" Then they struck Him on the head with a reed and spat on Him; and bowing the knee, they worshiped Him. And when they had mocked Him, they took the purple off Him, put His own clothes on Him, and led Him out to crucify Him.

a. **Clothed Him with purple... twisted a crown of thorns**: A king of that day often wore a purple robe and a gilded wreath of leaves. The rag of purple and crown of thorns mocked this common practice.

i. "It was probably a scarlet military cloak, 'a cast-off and faded rag, but with color enough left in it to suggest the royal purple." (Wessel)

b. **And began to salute Him, "Hail, King of the Jews!"** It was common to greet the Roman emperor with the cry, "Hail, Caesar!" (*Ave Caesar!*) These mockers twisted this into **Hail, King of the Jews!**

c. **Then they struck Him**: From Matthew 27:29, it seems that the soldiers first gave Jesus the **reed** - a stick - to hold as if it were a royal scepter. Then they grabbed it from His hand and hit Him in the head with it, adding great insult to all their injury against Jesus.

i. We should expect that the Roman soldiers were tense during the Passover season, because it was a time of messianic expectation among the Jews and riots were likely. Mocking and beating a bruised, bleeding, exhausted man provided a few moments of stress-relieving entertainment.

ii. **Bowing the knee** was a standard act of respect to any king. Instead of giving the normal kiss of warm respect, they **spat on Him**. **Spat on Him** is better translated *kept spitting on Him*.

iii. "See that scarlet robe; it is a contemptuous imitation of the imperial purple that a king wears... See, above all, that crown upon his head. It has rubies in it, but the rubies are composed of his own blood, forced from his blessed temples by the cruel thorns. See, they pay him homage; but the homage is their own filthy spittle which runs down his cheeks. They bow the knee before him, but it is only in mockery. They salute him with the cry, 'Hail, King of the Jews!' but it is done in scorn. Was there ever grief like his?" (Spurgeon)

d. **Led Him out to crucify Him**: After a scourging, a man to be crucified was forced to march in a parade, led by a centurion on horseback and a herald who shouted the crime of the condemned. This was Rome's way of advertising a crucifixion, and to make the people afraid of offending Rome.

i. This procession is the very thing Jesus was referring to when He asked people to *take up your cross and follow Me* (Mark 8:34).

2. (21-23) Jesus is led to Golgotha (in Latin, *Calvary*).

Then they compelled a certain man, Simon a Cyrenian, the father of Alexander and Rufus, as he was coming out of the country and passing by, to bear His cross. And they brought Him to the place Golgotha, which is translated, Place of a Skull. Then they gave Him wine mingled with myrrh to drink, but He did not take *it*.

a. **To bear His cross**: As Jesus was led away for crucifixion, He was - like every victim of crucifixion - forced to carry the beam of wood He would hang upon.

i. The weight of the entire cross was typically 300 pounds. Typically, the victim carried only the crossbar, which weighed anywhere from 75 to 125 pounds. When the victim carried the crossbar, he was usually stripped naked and his hands were often tied to the wood.

ii. The upright beams were often permanently fixed in a visible place outside the city walls, next to a major road. Many times, before this day Jesus probably passed by the very upright He would hang upon.

b. **They compelled a certain man**: It was the custom of the Romans to make the condemned criminal bear the cross, but in this case, Jesus was simply too weak to carry it. They preferred to keep the victim alive until he was crucified, because a public crucifixion was good advertisement for Rome. When Jesus fell under the weight of the cross, no Roman would help Him carry it. The centurion had the right to compel a local Jew to help carry it, but such an outrage might lead to uproar or riot. The best solution was to make a stranger carry the cross, so they found a foreigner (**Simon** from Cyrene in North Africa) to help Him.

i. Simon probably visited Jerusalem as a Passover pilgrim from his native land (some 800 miles away, on the other side of the Mediterranean Sea). He knew little if anything of Jesus and had no desire to be associated with this Man who was condemned to die as a criminal.

ii. Yet the Romans were the law and Simon did not have a choice - **they** *compelled* **him to bear His cross**. We are often blessed by the things we are **compelled** to do. Simon did not want to carry this cross and probably resented it terribly when he was asked. Nevertheless, it probably became the most special and memorable moment of his life.

iii. **Father of Rufus**: Apparently Rufus was known in the early church and was himself a Christian. If this **Rufus** is the same one mentioned in Romans 16:13, we can surmise that Simon came to know what it really meant to take up one's cross and follow Jesus. Perhaps his sons became leaders among the early Christians.

iv. "His name was Simon: and where was that other Simon? What a silent, but strong rebuke this would he to him. Simon Peter, Simon son of Jonas, where wast thou? Another Simon has taken thy place. Sometimes the Lord's servants are backward where they are expected to be forward, and he finds other servitors for the time. If this has ever happened to us it ought gently to rebuke us as long as we live. Brothers and sisters, keep your places, and let not another Simon occupy your room." (Spurgeon)

c. **They brought Him**: Mark 15:20 says they *led Him out to crucify Him*. By Mark 15:22 the situation changed: **they brought Him to the place Golgotha**. Jesus could walk when He left His trial before Pilate, but before He reached Golgotha He could hardly walk - they had to *bring* Him.

i. "It would appear that Jesus was so weak through the strain of the last few days, and the scourging, that he was unable to walk, not to speak of carrying His cross. He had to be borne and the sick were borne to Him (Mark 1:32)." (Bruce)

ii. "These two words are just a little window on the supreme physical exhaustion of the Saviour in this the greatest hour of His agony. You see, when He left the Praetorium they were leading Him; when they came to Golgotha they were bearing Him." (Morrison)

d. **To the place Golgotha**: There was a specific place right outside the city walls of Jerusalem where people were crucified - and where Jesus died for our sins, where our salvation was accomplished. It was the **Place of a Skull**; it was the place where criminals were crucified.

i. There is some controversy about the exact historical location of **Golgotha**. We know that it was outside the city walls and that it was associated with a place of the skull. The present Church of the Holy Sepulcher was built upon the place believed to be Calvary in the fourth century, but some researchers favor the site known as Gordon's Calvary, which sits atop a hill that looks remarkably like a skull, and is near ancient garden tombs. Most scholars consider the Church of the Holy Sepulcher as more accurate, but many people say that Gordon's Calvary feels more like the real spot.

ii. **Place of a Skull**: Some people think it was called Golgotha because it was littered with the skulls of men previously executed. Some think it was called Golgotha because it was on a hill that looked like a skull, with the shadows of a skull's face in the hillside. Some think it was called Golgotha because the hill was barren, smooth and round like the top of a skull.

e. **He did not take it**: Jesus refused any drug to numb His pain. He chose to face the agony of the cross with a clear mind and without medication.

i. "According to an old tradition, respected women of Jerusalem provided a narcotic drink to those condemned to death in order to decrease their sensitivity to the excruciating pain... This human practice was begun in response to the biblical injunction of Proverbs 31:6-7: 'Give strong drink to him who is perishing, and wine to those in bitter distress; let them drink and forget their poverty, and remember their misery no more.'" (Lane)

ii. "The local sour wine was 'laced' with myrrh; this would give it a bitter taste, but a soporific effect. Thus is explained the reference to 'gall'... He would not take any anaesthetic; all His faculties must be unclouded for what lay before Him." (Cole)

iii. "Was it out of any love to suffering that he thus refused the wine-cup? Ah, no; Christ had no love of suffering. He had a love of souls, but like us he turned away from suffering, he never loved it... Why, then, did he suffer? For two reasons: because this suffering to the utmost was necessary to the completion of the atonement, which saves to the utmost; and because this suffering to the utmost was necessary to perfect his character as 'a merciful High Priest' who has to compassionate souls that have gone to the utmost of miseries themselves; that he might know how to succor them that are tempted." (Spurgeon)

3. (24-26) The crucifixion of Jesus Christ.

And when they crucified Him, they divided His garments, casting lots for them to determine what every man should take. Now it was the third hour, and they crucified Him. And the inscription of His accusation was written above: THE KING OF THE JEWS.

a. **They divided His garments**: This was in fulfillment of the prophecy in Psalm 22: *They divide My garments among them, and for My clothing they cast lots* (Psalm 22:18).

i. "Men were ordinarily crucified naked (Artemidorus II. 61). Jewish sensitivities, however, dictated that men ought not to be publicly executed completely naked, and men condemned to stoning were permitted a loin-cloth (M. *Sanhedrin* VI. 3). Whether the Romans were considerate of Jewish feelings in this matter is unknown." (Lane)

b. **And they crucified Him**: In the days the New Testament was first written, the practice of crucifixion needed no explanation. Centuries later, we do well to appreciate just what happened when someone was **crucified**.

i. "Although the Romans did not invent crucifixion, they perfected it as a form of torture and capital punishment that was designed to produce a slow death with maximum pain and suffering." (Edwards)

ii. The victim's back was first torn open by the scourging, then the clotting blood was ripped open again when the clothes were torn off the victim. When he was thrown to the ground to fix his hands to the crossbeam, the wounds were torn open again and contaminated with dirt. Then, as he hung on the cross each breath made the painful wounds on the back scrape against the rough wood of the upright beam.

iii. When the nail was driven through the wrists, it severed the large median nerve going to the hand. This stimulated nerve produced excruciating bolts of fiery pain in both arms, and could result in a claw-like grip in the victim's hands.

iv. Beyond the excruciating pain, the posture of crucifixion made it painful to simply breathe. The weight of the body pulling down on the arms and shoulders made it feel like you could breathe in but not out. The lack of oxygen led to severe muscle cramps, which made it even harder to breathe. To get a good breath, one had to push against the feet and flex the elbows, pulling from the shoulders. Putting the weight of the body on the nail-pierced feet produced searing pain, and flexing the elbows twisted the hands hanging on the nails. Lifting the body for a breath also scraped the open wounds on the back against the rough wooden post. Each effort to get a proper breath was agonizing, exhausting, and led to a quicker death.

v. "Not uncommonly, insects would light upon or burrow into the open wounds or the eyes, ears, and nose of the dying and helpless victim, and birds of prey would tear at these sites. Moreover, it was customary to leave the corpse on the cross to be devoured by predatory animals." (Edwards)

vi. Death from crucifixion could come many different ways:

- Acute shock from blood loss.
- Suffocation from being too exhausted to breathe.
- Dehydration.
- Heart attack, induced by stress.
- Heart rupture from congestive heart failure.

However, if the victim did not die quickly enough, his legs were broken, and he was soon unable to breathe.

vii. How bad was crucifixion? We get our English word *excruciating* from the Roman word "out of the cross." "Consider how heinous sin must be in the sight of God, when it requires such a sacrifice!" (Clarke)

c. **They crucified Him**: In Jesus' own day, crucifixion was known to be a horrible practice, yet the Romans used to execute many criminals who were not Roman citizens. No Roman citizen could be crucified except by direct order of Caesar; it was reserved for the worst criminals and lowest classes.

i. The Roman statesman Cicero said: "It is a crime to bind a Roman citizen; to scourge him is an act of wickedness; to execute him is almost murder: What shall I say of crucifying him? An act so abominable it is impossible to find any word adequately to express." The Roman historian Tacitus described crucifixion as "a torture fit only for slaves."

d. **Now it was the third hour**: This is a problem, because John 19:14 says that it was at the *sixth hour* (about noon) that Pilate pronounced his verdict. Some think John and Mark counted time differently; some think the difference is due to copyist error; others think it is a *gloss* (a well-intentioned addition by an early copyist).

e. **And the inscription of His accusation was written above: THE KING OF THE JEWS**: "The wording was designed to convey a subtle insult to Jewish pretensions and to mock all attempts to assert the sovereignty of a subject territory." (Lane)

i. "It may be that the message of this sign first aroused the hopes of the repentant thief. He may have reasoned: 'If His name is Jesus, then He is a Saviour. If He is from Nazareth, then He would identify with rejected people. If He has a kingdom, then perhaps there is room for me!" (Wiersbe)

4. (27-32) Jesus is mocked on the cross.

With Him they also crucified two robbers, one on His right and the other on His left. So the Scripture was fulfilled which says, "And He was numbered with the transgressors." And those who passed by blasphemed Him, wagging their heads and saying, "Aha! *You* who destroy the temple and build *it* in three days, save Yourself, and come down from the cross!" Likewise the chief priests also, mocking among themselves with the scribes, said, "He saved others; Himself He cannot save. Let the Christ, the King of Israel, descend now from the cross, that we may see and believe." Even those who were crucified with Him reviled Him.

a. **Even those who were crucified with Him reviled Him**: Jesus was mocked by those crucified with Him, yet one of the mocking criminals came to a saving faith in Jesus (Luke 23:39-43).

b. **Those who passed by blasphemed Him**: Jesus not only endured mocking and humiliation at the hands of the pagan Roman soldiers, but also from the religious leaders. They **blasphemed Him, wagging their heads... they mocked and said among themselves, "He saved others, Himself He cannot save."**

i. Greek scholar A.T. Robinson says **mocking** in Mark 15:31 describes "Acting like silly children who love to mock one another." It was bad enough that the Son of God came to earth and man murdered Him in the most tortured way possible. Worst of all, sinful men *enjoyed* doing it.

ii. **Let the Christ... descend now from the cross, that we may see and believe**: It is precisely because He would *not* come down that we believe in Him. Jesus did something greater than come down from the cross - He rose from the dead. Yet they did not believe even then. But many of the priests *did* eventually believe: *A great many of the priests were obedient to the faith.* (Acts 6:7)

c. **He saved others**: "That was a fact which even they could not deny. Everywhere, in Jerusalem, in all the towns and villages and hamlets through the countryside, were those whom He had saved." (Morgan)

5. (33-37) The last words of Jesus from the cross.

Now when the sixth hour had come, there was darkness over the whole land until the ninth hour. And at the ninth hour Jesus cried out with a loud voice, saying, "Eloi, Eloi, lama sabachthani?" which is translated, "My God, My God, why have You forsaken Me?" Some of those who stood by, when they heard *that*, said, "Look, He is calling for Elijah!" Then someone ran and filled a sponge full of sour wine, put *it* on a reed, and offered *it* to Him to drink, saying, "Let Him alone; let us see if Elijah will come to take Him down." And Jesus cried out with a loud voice, and breathed His last.

a. **There was darkness over the whole land**: The remarkable darkness showed the agony of creation itself in the Creator's suffering. "Origen (*Contra Celsus*, ii, 33) and Eusebius (*Chron.*) quote the writing of Phlegon (a Roman historian) in which he makes mention of an extraordinary solar eclipse as well as of an earthquake about the time of the crucifixion." (Geldenhuys)

i. Luke tells us that *the sun was darkened* (Luke 23:45), but Mark makes it clear that it stayed dark for three hours (**there was darkness over the whole land until the ninth hour**).

ii. Phlegon, Roman historian: "In the fourth year of the 202nd Olympiad, there was an extraordinary eclipse of the sun: at the sixth hour, the day turned into dark night, so that the stars in heaven were seen; and there was an earthquake." (cited in Clarke)

iii. This is especially remarkable because during a full moon - which Passover was always held at - a natural eclipse of the sun is impossible. This was an extraordinary miracle in the heavens.

b. **My God, My God**: By quoting Psalm 22, Jesus declared that He fulfilled that passage, in both its agony and its victory.

c. **My God, My God, why have You forsaken Me?** Jesus knew great pain and suffering (both physical and emotional) in His life but never knew separation from His Father. Now He knew it. There was a significant sense in which Jesus rightly felt **forsaken** by God the Father at this moment.

i. This happened in the sense that *God made Him who knew no sin to be sin for us, that we might become the righteousness of God in Him* (2 Corinthians 5:21). Jesus not only endured the *withdrawal* of the Father's fellowship, but also the actual outpouring of the Father's *wrath* upon Him as a substitute for sinful humanity.

ii. Horrible as this was, it fulfilled God's good and loving plan of redemption. Therefore, Isaiah could say *Yet it pleased the Lord to bruise Him* (Isaiah 53:10).

iii. At the same time, we cannot say that the separation between the Father and the Son at the cross was complete, because as 2 Corinthians 5:19 says, *God was in Christ reconciling the world to Himself* at the cross.

iv. From *Throned Upon the Awful Tree* (John Ellerton, 1875)

Throned upon the awful tree,
King of grief, I watch with Thee.
Darkness veils Thine anguished face:
None its lines of woe can trace:
None can tell what pangs unknown
Hold Thee silent and alone

Silent through those three dread hours,
Wrestling with the evil powers,
Left alone with human sin,
Gloom around Thee and within,
Till the appointed time is nigh,
Till the Lamb of God may die.

d. **A sponge full of sour wine**: "The *vinegar* was the sour wine not only of the soldier's ration, but of everyday use... This is apparently quite a different occasion from the official offering of the drugged wine in verse 23." (Cole)

i. "A sour wine vinegar is mentioned in the OT as a refreshing drink (Numbers 6:3; Ruth 2:14), and in Greek and Roman literature as well it is a common beverage appreciated by laborers and soldiers because it relieved thirst more effectively than water and was inexpensive." (Lane)

e. **Let us see if Elijah will come**: Sadly, Jesus was misunderstood and mocked until the bitter end. These spectators at the cross knew just enough of the Bible to get it really wrong, and they speculated wildly, thinking that **Elijah** might come and rescue Jesus.

i. As Jesus hung on the cross, His listeners misunderstood Him by taking the part for the whole. He said, "**Eloi, Eloi, lama sabachthani?**" Not only did they get wrong what they heard (Jesus said, "**Eloi**" not "**Elijah**"), but they also only heard *one word* of what He said. This will not do for the true follower of Jesus; we hear not only *one word* from Jesus, but every word that proceeds from the mouth of God.

ii. One of the first things we know about Jesus was that He was misunderstood. When Joseph and Mary left Him behind at Jerusalem, they didn't understand that He had to be about His Father's business. Now at the end of His earthly ministry, He was also misunderstood on the cross.

f. **Jesus cried with a loud voice and breathed His last**: Most victims of crucifixion spent their last hours in complete exhaustion or unconsciousness before death. Jesus was not like this; though tremendously tortured and weakened, He was conscious and able to speak right up to the moment of His death.

i. John 19:30 tells us what He said when He **cried with a loud voice**: *it is finished*, which is one word in the ancient Greek language, the word *tetelestai*. This ancient word *tetelestai* means, "Paid in Full." This is the cry of a winner because Jesus *paid in full* the debt of sin we owed and had finished the eternal purpose of the cross.

ii. At some point before He died, before the veil was torn in two, before He cried out *it is finished*, an awesome spiritual transaction took place. God the Father set upon Jesus all the guilt and wrath our sin deserved, and Jesus bore it in Himself perfectly, totally satisfying the wrath of God toward us.

iii. As horrible as the physical suffering of Jesus was, this spiritual suffering, this act of being judged for sin in our place, was what Jesus really dreaded about the cross. This was the *cup* - the cup of God's righteous wrath - that Jesus trembled at drinking (Luke 22:39-46, Psalm 75:8, Isaiah 51:17, and Jeremiah 25:15). On the cross Jesus became, as it were, an *enemy* of God who was judged and forced to drink the cup of the Father's fury. He did it so that we would *not* have to drink that cup.

iv. "Reader! *one drop* of this cup would bear down thy soul to endless ruin; and these agonies would annihilate the universe. He suffered *alone*: for the people there was none with him; because his sufferings were to make an atonement for the sins of the world: and in the work of redemption he had no helper." (Clarke)

v. The death of Jesus on the cross was and is the ultimate demonstration of God's love towards all mankind (Romans 5:8). It is the power of God unto salvation, though it seems foolish to those who reject it (1 Corinthians 1:18). At the cross, Jesus wiped out our record of sin and rebellion against God, nailing it to the cross (Colossians 2:14). If Jesus had not endured the cross, it might be said that there is a limit to God's love, that there was something God could have done but was unwilling to do in order to demonstrate His love for man.

6. (38-41) The visible, immediate results of the death of Jesus.

Then the veil of the temple was torn in two from top to bottom. So when the centurion, who stood opposite Him, saw that He cried out

like this and breathed His last, he said, "Truly this Man was the Son of God!" There were also women looking on from afar, among whom were Mary Magdalene, Mary the mother of James the Less and of Joses, and Salome, who also followed Him and ministered to Him when He was in Galilee, and many other women who came up with Him to Jerusalem.

a. **The veil of the temple was torn in two from top to bottom**: The tearing of the temple veil signified that now man had free access to the throne of grace by the cross and that no one should ever think again that God dwells in temples made with hands.

i. Significantly, as the wall of separation between God and man was removed, the veil was torn **from top to bottom**. God tore it from heaven instead of man tearing it from earth.

b. **Truly this man was the Son of God!** The centurion saw Jesus for who He was and is a picture of all who come to Jesus through the cross. At the cross, people saw that Jesus **was the Son of God** and this fulfilled Jesus' promise *if I am lifted up from the earth, I will draw all peoples to Myself* (John 12:32).

i. This centurion saw many people crucified before, yet there was something so remarkable about Jesus that he said something he could not say about anyone else.

c. **There were also women looking on from afar**: Finally, the most faithful disciples of Jesus are revealed. They were His female followers: **Mary Magdalene**, **Mary the mother of James**, **Salome** and **many other women**.

7. (42-47) The burial of Jesus.

Now when evening had come, because it was the Preparation Day, that is, the day before the Sabbath, Joseph of Arimathea, a prominent council member, who was himself waiting for the kingdom of God, coming and taking courage, went in to Pilate and asked for the body of Jesus. Pilate marveled that He was already dead; and summoning the centurion, he asked him if He had been dead for some time. So when he found out from the centurion, he granted the body to Joseph. Then he bought fine linen, took Him down, and wrapped Him in the linen. And he laid Him in a tomb which had been hewn out of the rock, and rolled a stone against the door of the tomb. And Mary Magdalene and Mary *the mother* of Joses observed where He was laid.

a. **Joseph of Arimathea was a prominent council member**: This Joseph was apparently silent when the council sentenced Jesus to death (Mark

15:1). He shrunk back then but was not ashamed to identify with Jesus in His death.

> i. "In the hours of crisis it is often the Peters who have sworn loyalty to Jesus with big gestures and fullness of self-confidence, that disappoint, and it is the secret and quiet followers of the Master (like Joseph, Nicodemus and the women) that do not hesitate to serve Him in love - at whatever the cost." (Geldenhuys)

> ii. Joseph did *not* serve Jesus in many ways, but he did serve Him in ways no one else did or could. It was not possible for Peter, James, John, or even the many women who served Jesus to provide a tomb, but Joseph could and did. We must serve God in whatever way we can.

b. **Went in to Pilate and asked for the body of Jesus**: Customarily, the bodies of crucified criminals were left on their crosses to rot or be eaten by wild animals. However, the Jews wanted no such horror displayed at the Passover season, and Romans were known to grant friends or relatives a corpse for proper burial.

> i. "In antiquity the execution of a condemned man did not mark the final moment of his humiliation. Roman law dictated the loss of all honors in death, and even the right of burial was determined by magisterial decree... It was not at all uncommon for a body to be left upon a cross either to rot or to be eaten by predatory birds or animals." (Lane) It wasn't unusual to grant the body to a friend or relative for burial, but the point is that they had to *request* this of the Roman magistrate. The fate of even the executed corpse was in his hands.

> ii. Of course, Joseph took a risk with this request. He risked Pilate's animosity or scorn, but it mattered little to Joseph. "Is there no holy chivalry in you? Can it be so, that, because God has dealt so well with you, and trusted you so generously, you will repay him by denying his Son, violating your conscience, and turning your back on truth; and all for the sake of being in the fashion? I know it may seem hard to receive the cold shoulder in society, or to have the finger of scorn pointed at you; but to bow before this selfish dread is scarcely worthy of a man, and utterly disgraceful to a Christian man." (Spurgeon)

c. **Pilate marveled that He was already dead**: Typically, crucifixion was a long, agonizing death - yet Jesus died in a matter of hours. However, we can be sure that He was dead because the death was confirmed by careful examination of eyewitnesses (John 19:31-36).

> i. **When he found out from the centurion**: Pilate personally investigated the matter of Jesus' death and found reliable eyewitness

testimony from **the centurion**, who had witnessed perhaps hundreds of crucifixions and knew if a man was dead or not. "A Roman sergeant had seen too many deaths to be in any uncertainty about such a fact." (Cole)

d. **Wrapped Him in the linen**: Because of the coming Sabbath, they were unable to properly prepare the body of Jesus for burial. So, with hurried preparation, Jesus' body was placed in a borrowed tomb.

e. **Laid Him in a tomb**: Tombs such as this were very expensive, and it was quite a sacrifice for Joseph of Arimathea to give his up. But Jesus needed the tomb for only a few days.

Mark 16 - Jesus Is Risen

A. The testimony to the resurrection.

1. (1-5) The women discover an empty tomb and a special messenger.

Now when the Sabbath was past, Mary Magdalene, Mary *the mother* of James, and Salome bought spices, that they might come and anoint Him. Very early in the morning, on the first *day* of the week, they came to the tomb when the sun had risen. And they said among themselves, "Who will roll away the stone from the door of the tomb for us?" But when they looked up, they saw that the stone had been rolled away; for it was very large. And entering the tomb, they saw a young man clothed in a long white robe sitting on the right side; and they were alarmed. But he said to them, "Do not be alarmed. You seek Jesus of Nazareth, who was crucified. He is risen! He is not here. See the place where they laid Him."

a. **When the Sabbath was past**: The earliest the women could go to the tomb and properly embalm the body of Jesus was on Sunday morning. Sabbath was over at the start of Saturday evening, but it wasn't light enough until Sunday morning to do the work. The time from sundown on Friday to sunrise on Sunday must have been dark, empty, desperate days for the disciples.

b. **Mary Magdalene, Mary the mother of James, and Salome**: These women proved themselves to be the most devoted followers of Jesus, and they were the first to proclaim His resurrection.

i. **Brought spices**: "Spices were not used for mummification, which was not a Jewish custom, but to offset the odors from decomposition." (Lane)

c. **Who will roll away the stone from the door of the tomb for us?** The women were not expecting to find an empty tomb. They came wondering how the stone door would be opened. This shows that the resurrection accounts cannot be the product of wishful thinking. The disciples of Jesus did not expect it to happen.

i. Matthew 27:65-66 reminds us that there was a guard set round the tomb. All this shows that the stone could not have been rolled away by the women (they were not strong enough) or by the disciples (even if they were brave enough, they could not overcome the armed guards). We also understand that no one else *wanted* to roll away the stone. Matthew 28:2 tells us that it was an angel who rolled it away.

ii. The stone was not rolled away to let Jesus out. John 20:19 tells us that Jesus, in His resurrection body, could pass through material barriers. It was rolled away so that others could see into the tomb and be persuaded that Jesus Christ was risen from the dead.

d. **A young man clothed in a long white robe sitting**: The women saw an angel in human form, who told them of the resurrected Jesus and showed them the empty tomb.

e. **Who was crucified. He is risen!** The angel painted the contrast between what Jesus **was** and what He **is**. He **was crucified**, beyond all doubt - that means He was dead. Now, **He is risen** - not only *resuscitated*, but *resurrected*.

i. There are several examples in the Bible of people being *resuscitated* before this, such as the widow's son in the days of Elijah (1 Kings 17:17-24) and Lazarus (John 11:38-44). Each of these was resuscitated from death, but none of them were *resurrected*. Each of them was raised in the same body they died in and raised from the dead to eventually die again. Resurrection isn't just living again; it is living again in a new body, based on our old body, perfectly suited for life in eternity. Jesus was not the first one brought back from the dead, but He was the first one *resurrected*.

ii. We should also say that Jesus *still* **is risen**. He ascended into heaven and continues to reign as resurrected man, still fully man and fully God.

iii. **Jesus of Nazareth... who was crucified**: These were not exalted titles for Jesus. **Nazareth** was not a place to be proud of and **crucified** was a title of shame, not honor. Yet Jesus was not ashamed to be called "**of Nazareth**" and "**crucified**." "This description of his shame has become his crown of glory, for Paul and all who look to the Crucified and Risen Christ as Saviour and Lord." (Robertson)

f. **See the place where they laid Him**: The actual *event* of Jesus' resurrection is nowhere described, but the discovery of it is recorded in some detail. Here, the women who intended to give Jesus' body a more proper preparation for burial discovered that the stone was rolled away from the tomb and that the body of Jesus was not inside the tomb.

i. Those women were later grateful that the angel told them to **see the place where they laid Him**. It would have - it should have - been enough to merely hear the testimony of the angel. Nevertheless, when they *saw* it, it gave them ground to stand on even more solid than the testimony of an angel. "One eye-witness is better than twenty ear-witnesses; men will believe what you have seen if they do not believe what you have heard." (Spurgeon)

- When we **see the place where they laid Him** is now empty, we see that the Father did not forsake Jesus.

- When we **see the place where they laid Him** is now empty, we see that death is conquered.

- When we **see the place where they laid Him** is now empty, we see that we have a living friend in Jesus.

g. **He is risen!** The *fact* of Jesus' resurrection is a matter of history. What it *means* can only be understood by what the Bible tells us. Therefore, it is important to consider what the empty tomb of Jesus and His resurrection means.

i. The resurrection means that Jesus was *declared to be the Son of God with power, according to the Spirit of holiness, by the resurrection from the dead* (Romans 1:4).

ii. The resurrection means that we have assurance of our own resurrection: *For if we believe that Jesus died and rose again, even so God will bring with Him those who sleep in Jesus* (1 Thessalonians 4:14).

iii. The resurrection means that God has an eternal plan for these bodies of ours. "There was nothing in the teaching of Jesus approaching the Gnostic heresy that declared that the flesh is inherently evil. Plato could only get rid of sin by getting rid of the body. Jesus retains the body; and declares that God feeds the body as well as the soul, that the body is as sacred thing as the soul, since the soul makes it its sanctuary." (Morgan)

iv. The resurrection means that Jesus has a continuing ministry: *He is also able to save to the uttermost those who come to God through Him, since He ever lives to make intercession for them* (Hebrews 7:25).

v. The resurrection means that Christianity and its God are unique and completely different and unique among world religions.

vi. The resurrection proves that though it looked like Jesus died on the cross like a common criminal He actually died as a sinless man, out of love and self-sacrifice to bear the guilt of our sin. The death of Jesus on the cross was the payment, but the resurrection was the receipt, showing that the payment was perfect in the sight of God the Father.

2. (7-8) The angel gives the women a message to relay.

"But go, tell His disciples; and Peter; that He is going before you into Galilee; there you will see Him, as He said to you." So they went out quickly and fled from the tomb, for they trembled and were amazed. And they said nothing to anyone, for they were afraid.

a. **Go and tell**: Through the angel, the women received a message from Jesus they had to deliver. We might think of this message as an *invitation*, because through this message the disciples were invited to meet with Jesus.

i. This shows that the *invitations of Jesus are filled with grace*. The disciples had completely failed Jesus. He had every right to be done with them, but in grace He extended this kind invitation to them.

ii. This shows us that the *invitations of Jesus are always fulfilled on His part*. He said that He would meet them in Galilee and indeed He did (John 21:1 is one example).

iii. This shows us that *when Jesus invites us He wants to reveal Himself to us*. "**He is going before you into Galilee, there you shall see Him**" was the message. The main object was to **see Him**, for Jesus to reveal Himself to His people.

iv. This shows us that *when Jesus invites us He always remembers His promises*. "**As He said to you**," the angel added to the invitation. What Jesus says, He will do, and He can never fail in any promise.

b. **His disciples; and Peter**: We are amazed that Jesus wanted to meet with these men who failed Him so deeply, yet He made special notice of **Peter**. Some say He distinguished **Peter** because he was *separate* from the rest of the disciples in the sense that he was no longer among them. This was probably not the case. Instead, Jesus distinguished **Peter** because He had special hope, special forgiveness, special restoration for the one who denied Him the worst.

i. "If any of you have behaved worse to your Master than others, you are peculiarly called to come to him now. You have grieved him, and you have been grieving because you have grieved him. You have been brought to repentance after having slidden away from him, and now he seals your pardon by inviting you to himself." (Spurgeon)

c. **For they trembled and were amazed**: "These women left the tomb, and fled. Seized with trembling, and astonishment; - the actual Greek word there is 'ecstasy,' - seized with trembling and ecstasy, filled with fear; so they fled." (Morgan)

d. **And they said nothing to anyone**: This does not mean that they made no report of the resurrection because we plainly know that they did (Mark 16:11 and Luke 24:9). It means that as they left the scene of the empty tomb, they did not discuss it among themselves. They didn't try to figure it out or match their stories. They simply went to make a report to the disciples as the angel invited them to do.

B. Preface to Mark 16:9-20: Do these verses belong in our Bible?

1. In many Bibles, this last portion of the Gospel of Mark is footnoted in some way, indicating that it did not exist in the earliest Greek manuscripts of the gospel of Mark. This troubles some Christians regarding the reliability of God's Word. They wonder if this passage belongs in our Bible.

2. The argument *against* including Mark 16:9-20 in our Bibles.

a. The two oldest existing Greek manuscripts (dated from 325 and 340 A.D.) do not contain this section and neither do about 100 other ancient manuscripts translated into other languages. A few ancient manuscripts put asterisks next to Mark 16:9-20 to indicate that it is an addition to the original text.

b. According to their writings, almost all the Greek manuscripts known to Eusebius (who died in 339) and Jerome (who died in 419) did not have these verses.

c. In a few other manuscripts there are two other endings - one shorter, one with some additions.

d. About one-third of the vocabulary is totally different from the rest of the Gospel of Mark and there is a very awkward grammatical transition between Mark 16:8 and 16:9.

e. Most contemporary scholars reject these verses as original.

3. The argument *for* including Mark 16:9-20 in our Bibles.

a. Many very early Christian writers refer to this passage in their writings. This shows that the early Christians knew about this passage in the Gospel of Mark and accepted it as genuine.

• Papias refers to Mark 16:18. He wrote around A.D. 100.

- Justin Martyr's first *Apology* quoted Mark 16:20 (A.D. 151).

- Irenaus in *Against Heresies* quoted Mark 16:13 and remarked on it (A.D. 180).

- Hippolytus in *Peri Charismaton* quoted Mark 16:18 and 19. In his homily on the heresy of Noetus, he refers to Mark 16:19. He wrote while he was Bishop of Portus (A.D. 190-227).

- Vicentius, Bishop of Thibari, quoted from 2 of the verses in the 7th Council of Carthage held under Cyprian (A.D. 256). Augustine, a century and a half later, in his reply, recited the words again.

- The apocryphal *Acts of Pilate* contains Mark 16:15-18 (thought to be written in the somewhere around A.D. 200).

- The *Apostolic Constitutions* clearly allude to 16:15 in two places and quote Mark 16:16 outright (thought to be written somewhere in the late third century or the early fourth century).

b. The overwhelming majority of ancient manuscripts *do* include this passage.

4. Thoughts on the problem of including or not including this passage.

a. It is highly unlikely that the Gospel of Mark ended so abruptly at Mark 16:8, with the women simply being afraid but seeing no concrete evidence of the resurrected Jesus, only of an empty tomb. However, it is possible that the original ending of Mark's gospel was lost rather early.

i. Noted Greek scholar A.T. Robertson wrote, "It is difficult to believe that Mark ended his Gospel with verse 8 unless he was interrupted. A leaf or column may have been torn off at the end of the papyrus roll."

b. But importantly, the *earliest* testimony we presently have, from writers like Irenaeus and others, argues that the *earliest* Christians accepted Mark 16:9-20 as genuine.

C. Appearances of a risen Lord.

1. (9-11) The appearance to Mary Magdalene.

Now when *He* rose early on the first *day* of the week, He appeared first to Mary Magdalene, out of whom He had cast seven demons. She went and told those who had been with Him, as they mourned and wept. And when they heard that He was alive and had been seen by her, they did not believe.

a. **He appeared first to Mary Magdalene**: Mary's dramatic meeting with Jesus (whom she first supposed to be the gardener) is described more fully in John 20:11-18.

b. **When they heard that He was alive**: Jesus sent her to tell the other disciples that He was risen from the dead. In that day, her testimony would not be considered reliable because she was a woman. Yet Jesus trusted her, even though the disciples did not (**they did not believe**).

2. (12-13) The appearance to the two disciples on the road to Emmaus.

After that, He appeared in another form to two of them as they walked and went into the country. And they went and told *it* to the rest, *but* they did not believe them either.

a. **He appeared in another form to two of them as they walked**: This remarkable encounter with the risen Jesus is described more fully in Luke 24:13-27.

b. **They did not believe them either**: The disciples did not receive the testimony of the women, but they did not receive the testimony of these two men either. They were equal opportunity unbelievers.

3. (14-18) The commission of the eleven, and all the followers of Jesus.

Later He appeared to the eleven as they sat at the table; and He rebuked their unbelief and hardness of heart, because they did not believe those who had seen Him after He had risen. And He said to them, "Go into all the world and preach the gospel to every creature. He who believes and is baptized will be saved; but he who does not believe will be condemned. And these signs will follow those who believe: In My name they will cast out demons; they will speak with new tongues; they will take up serpents; and if they drink anything deadly, it will by no means hurt them; they will lay hands on the sick, and they will recover."

a. **He rebuked their unbelief and hardness of heart**: They could have done better. They did not understand, but they could not escape responsibility.

i. "Unbelief is a bloody sin, Hebrews 10:26; a heavy sin, John 3:19; a most ungrateful, inexcusable sin, such as shuts a man up as a close prisoner in the dark dungeon of the law, unto unavoidable destruction, Galatians 3:23." (Trapp)

b. **Go into all the world and preach the gospel to every creature**. This was a *command*, not a suggestion. "Interest in missions is not an elective in God's university of grace. It is something in which every disciple is expected to major." (Ironside)

i. The idea of a faith that should **go into all the world** wasn't a part of the Jewish thinking in the days of Jesus. It wasn't part of the pagan thinking either. It was a revolutionary idea in its time.

ii. This command was not obeyed immediately; for many years, the disciples stayed at Jerusalem, and it was only until the church was persecuted that it began to spread out to the world. But it did spread and continues to.

iii. "An army chaplain once said to the Duke of Wellington, 'Do you think that it is of any use our taking the gospel to the hill tribes in India? Will they ever receive it?' The duke replied, 'What are your marching orders?' That was the only answer he gave. Stern disciplinarian as that great soldier was, he only wanted marching orders, and he obeyed; and he meant that every soldier of the cross must obey the marching orders of Christ, his great Commander." (Spurgeon)

c. **He who believes and is baptized will be saved, but he who does not believe will be condemned**: This was a combined promise of salvation and a warning. Jesus did not say that *condemnation* belonged to the one who was not **baptized**, only to the one **who does not believe**.

i. "A superficial reading of Mark 16:15-16 would suggest that sinners must be baptized to be saved, but this misinterpretation disappears when you note that the emphasis is on *believing*. If a person does not believe, he is condemned, even if he has been baptized." (Wiersbe)

ii. "The omission of *baptized* with 'disbelieveth' would seem to show that Jesus does not make baptism essential to salvation. Condemnation rests on disbelief, not on baptism. So salvation rests on belief. Baptism is merely the picture of the new life not the means of securing it." (Robertson)

iii. At the same time, it would be *terribly wrong* to regard baptism as "non-essential." It may not be essential to *salvation*, but it is absolutely essential to *obedience*. Jesus told the believer to be baptized, and they must do it. It becomes essential as soon as Jesus commands it.

d. **And these signs will follow those**: Jesus gave His disciples a promise of divine power and protection.

i. This promise is to be understood in the context of the dangers inherent in the worldwide spread of the gospel, as Paul was bitten by a snake and preserved on the island of Malta (Acts 28:1-6). Jesus never intended drinking poison or handling snakes to be a specific test or measure of faith.

4. (19-20) The ascending Jesus; the working disciples.

So then, after the Lord had spoken to them, He was received up into heaven, and sat down at the right hand of God. And they went out and

preached everywhere, the Lord working with *them* and confirming the word through the accompanying signs. Amen.

a. **He was received up into heaven**: It was important that Jesus leave this earth in His bodily presence, Jesus had to ascend - so that confidence would be put in the power and ministry of the Holy Spirit, not in the geographical presence of Jesus.

i. Jesus went ahead to *prepare a place for you* (John 14:3); to *make intercession for us* (Romans 8:34); and to *give gifts to men* (Ephesians 4:8).

b. **Sat down at the right hand of God**: "He is said to sit *on the right hand of God*, to distinguish him from angels, whose places are but places of ministration." (Poole)

c. **They went out and preached everywhere**: This means that they didn't remain together to bless each other, **they went out**. The followers of Jesus should come together, but they come together to properly equip them to go out and touch a needy world.

i. "I do want you all to feel that it is not the end, though it may be the beginning, of Christian life to come and hear sermons. Scatter as widely as ever you can the blessing which you get for yourself; the moment you find the light, and realize that the world is in the dark, run away with your match, and lend somebody else a light." (Spurgeon)

d. **The Lord working with them and confirm the word through the accompanying signs**: When we go out to do the work of God, Jesus will work with us. The disciples did what Jesus told them to do, and Jesus then did what only He could do - the **accompanying signs**.

i. This is an excellent pattern for ministry. The preaching came first and then the **signs** following. Signs are meant to follow believers, instead of believers following after signs.

ii. The final verse continues to this day. The followers of Jesus are still preaching everywhere, the Lord is still **working** with them, and He is still confirming His word through **accompanying signs**. Amen!

The Gospel of Mark - Bibliography

Barclay, William *The Gospel of Mark* (Philadelphia: Westiminster, 1975)

Bruce, Alexander Balmain "The Synoptic Gospels" *The Expositor's Greek Testament, Volume 1* (London: Hodder and Stoughton, ?)

Clarke, Adam *The New Testament, with A Commentary and Critical Notes Volume I* (New York: Eaton and Mains, ?)

Cole, R. Alan *The Gospel According to St. Mark* (Grand Rapids, Michigan: Eerdmans, 1988)

Lane, William L. T*he Gospel of Mark* (Grand Rapids, Michigan: Eerdmans, 1974)

Ironside, H. A. *Expository Notes on the Gospel of Mark* (Neptune, New Jersey: Loizeaux Brothers, 1979)

Maclaren, Alexander *Expostions of Holy Scripture, Volume 8* (Grand Rapids, Michigan: Baker Book House, 1984)

Meyer, F.B. *Our Daily Homily* (Westwood, New Jersey: Revell, 1966)

Meyer, F.B. David: *Shepherd, Psalmist, King* (Fort Washington, Pennsylvania: Christian Literature Crusade, 1977)

Morgan, G. Campbell *An Exposition of the Whole Bible* (Old Tappan, New Jersey: Revell, 1959)

Morgan, G. Campbell *Searchlights from the Word* (New York: Revell, 1926)

Morrison, George H. *Morrison on Mark* (Ridgefield, New Jersey: AMG Publishers, 1977)

Poole, Matthew *A Commentary on the Holy Bible, Volume III: Matthew-Revelation* (London: Banner of Truth Trust, 1969, first published in 1685)

Robertson, Archibald T. *Word Pictures in the New Testament, Volume I* (Nashville: Broadman Press, 1933)

Smith, Chuck *New Testament Study Guide* (Costa Mesa, California: The Word for Today, 1982)

Spurgeon, Charles Haddon *The New Park Street Pulpit, Volumes 1-6* and The *Metropolitan Tabernacle Pulpit, Volumes 7-63* (Pasadena, Texas: Pilgrim Publications, 1990)

Stedman, Ray *The Ruler Who Serves* (Waco, Texas: Word Books, 1976)

Stedman, Ray *The Servant Who Rules* (Waco, Texas: Word Books, 1976)

Trapp, John *A Commentary on the Old and New Testaments, Volume Five* (Eureka, California: Tanski Publications, 1997)

Vincent, Marvin R. *Vincent's Word Studies of the New Testament, Volume 1 Mark* (McLean, Virginia: MacDonald Publishing, ?)

Wessel, Walter W. "Mark" *The Expositor's Bible Commentary, Volume 8* (Grand Rapids, Michigan: Zondervan, 1984)

Wiersbe, Warren W. *The Bible Exposition Commentary, Volume 1* (Wheaton, Illinois: Victor Books, 1989)

Marrianne van de Vrede deserves double thanks, not only as the proofreader of this commentary, but also as a great teacher of effective writing. Her help with these books - this is now number three - helps me work on bad habits and become a little better as a writer. I hope that I my learning can be as good as her teaching. Thanks also to Jackie Jeanguenat, a student at our Bible College who helped reveiw the Scripture references before printing.

This book is dedicated to Tim and Martina Patrick, some of our longest and warmest friends in ministry. Inga-Lill and I wish we could better express how much their friendship has meant over the years. If you are blessed by any of the ministry that comes through us, you should thank God for the Patricks.

I am often amazed at the remarkable kindness of others, and thanks to all who give the gift of encouragement. With each year that passes, faithful friends and supporters become all the more precious. Through you all, God has been better to me than I have ever deserved.

David Guzik's Bible commentary is regularly used and trusted by many thousands who want to know the Bible better. Pastors, teachers, class leaders, and everyday Christians find his commentary helpful for their own understanding and explanation of the Bible. David and his wife Inga-Lill live in Santa Barbara, California.

You can email David at
david@enduringword.com

For more resources by David Guzik,
go to www.enduringword.com